D1707317

The Metaphysics of Capitalism

The Metaphysics of Capitalism

Andrea Micocci

LEXINGTON BOOKS
A division of
ROWMAN & LITTLEFIELD PUBLISHERS, INC.
Lanham • Boulder • New York • Toronto • Plymouth, UK

LEXINGTON BOOKS

A division of Rowman & Littlefield Publishers, Inc.
A wholly owned subsidiary of The Rowman & Littlefield Publishing Group, Inc.
4501 Forbes Boulevard, Suite 200
Lanham, MD 20706

Estover Road
Plymouth PL6 7PY
United Kingdom

British Library Cataloguing in Publication Information Available

Library of Congress Cataloging-in-Publication Data

Micocci, Andrea.
  The metaphysics of capitalism / Andrea Micocci.
      p. cm.
  Includes bibliographical references and index.
  ISBN-13: 978-0-7391-2837-4 (cloth : alk. paper)
  ISBN-10: 0-7391-2837-X (cloth : alk. paper)
  ISBN-13: 978-0-7391-3270-8 (electronic)
  ISBN-10: 0-7391-3270-9 (electronic)
  1. Capitalism. 2. Individuality. I. Title.
  HB501.M634 2009
  330.12'201—dc22   2008040469

Printed in the United States of America

Contents

Foreword

The bulk of the very first draft of the present volume was written quite a while ago. A long period of very painful struggling followed, which is far from over yet. My whole life, with each new day, seems to vindicate the arguments I have put forward in this work. This should be pleasing, if I could look at it from outside. But I am in it: it is tiring, and there is no end to it in sight.

As a consequence, before it is too late I should add a consideration to what is offered in the text. My interest in the kinds of problems dealt with in this volume is caused by a question I have been asking myself ever since I decided not to undertake literary studies. The question is: why, in the sad world that chance has destined to us, I can see no point in the writing of fresh literature in the known forms? That question has taken me to scientific-technical subjects first and to the social sciences after, and to practicing philosophy the ancient way. If what I say in this book makes sense, then this work itself is the type of literary work for our sad days I was struggling to identify. It is time for me to admit that much.

I hope, however, that someone proves that what I have argued is all wrong, freeing me from a burden that I have carried all alone for too long, and consigning me, at last, to normality and a decent job. Being wrong is a prerogative of the argument of a book: the various faults that can be found in the writing and the structure of this volume, and of which I am solely guilty, cannot work as a refutation of such argument.

Preface

Never has there been a time when the development of a "philosophy of economics" has been more urgent than now. It is from this imperious need that characterizes our time that we must start in order to profoundly rethink the fundamental problems and questions that the volume we are presenting here faces.

Ours is a time of "emergency." But there are at least two ways to conceptualize emergency. The first consists of looking at it as the "strong" and undeferrable occasion to seek sudden and ad hoc solutions for what is occurring. But such a way is inevitably tied to a contingent circumstance, however inevitable that might be.

The second way consists instead of seeing in the "emergency" what emerges from far away times which we cannot stop. This second approach observes in the event that has taken place what is simultaneously *originary and lasting*. It perceives in the event the presence of an originary foundation that was hidden and that, after having invisibly accompanied every evolution of the phenomena investigated, only now manifests itself in ultimate and simplified forms.

Only in this second case the approach to emergency is theoretically fertile and radical. This is precisely the approach that our present times require from us in at least three fundamental fields: the environment, technology and economics.

In the sudden appearing of the emergency we glimpse the crevice of catastrophe and the face of what is fundamental. It is only on the edge of the crevice, in fact, that we are able to truly think out what is radical and decisive. It is only in the time of exceptions that we are able to truly consider the identity and the necessity of rules. In this horizon, it is certainly true that our times require from us—from scientific thought, from theoretical thought, from ethical acting—a severe attention that rejects all *negligent* attitudes.

It is not by chance, therefore, that in the contemporary context the need emerges—emergency within emergency—of a new way to look at ethics and a new way to look at metaphysics. In the historical development of scientific and philosophical knowledge, in fact, we have progressively moved to think that ethics is simply a *duty of choice*, detached from theology, and that metaphysics is simply a *prospective option*. Later on, with the flowing of years, we have accommodated ourselves into thinking that ethics is a sort of simple *style* of thinking action, representative of a social model largely questionable, when not even ornamental. Also, the very metaphysical option has become, so to speak, an operation of pure intellectual gusto.

Before the numerous emergencies of our contemporary world ethics has become instead, suddenly, no longer a simple *duty*, no longer simply a *choice*, but an actual *necessity*. In the end this very bottom concept which an ethics—i.e. a metaphysics—should address us to has come back to be an essential question.

Let us reflect, for instance, on the environmental emergency: we cannot any longer choose between various possible types of ethics, if it is true (as it is true in fact) that if we want to avoid a catastrophe we must think about the world on the basis of some necessary behaviours; we are not allowed a choice, in the emergency of a complex knowledge, in between the various possible "metaphysics," if it is true (as it is true in fact), that we must think about the world and life on the basis of concepts and behaviours to be pursued lest the human world undergoes a catastrophe. On the basis of these same presuppositions we must consider the economic world, if it is true (as it is true in fact) that the sudden appearance of its crises reveals the non eludible need of looking at behaviours and rules that must be rethought and re-determined as necessary to avoid the catastrophe of our civilization. It even looks ironic, despite being only dramatically enlightening, that in our contemporary world the need has been suddenly rediscovered—as a foundation of what is economic—for an "ethics of economics," and even a "business ethics." A brief aside here is simply inevitable: was it not precisely the world of economics that accused, with a smirk, of "*moralism*" those who talk, in things to do with the economy, of the need for a morality? The time of catastrophe has had the miraculous merit of converting the *accusation of moralism into an appeal to morality*. That means, from the theoretical point of view, that even for the "anti-moralists" *ethics* has changed *face*. Ethics, that is, has been transformed from *distinct* region of acting and knowing into a *continent of foundation*. Ethics, from knowledge for taste or society gossip, has re-imposed itself as a radical and total civilization need. Deep theoretical thinking is the thinking that operates in the proximity of catastrophe.

All this leads us to a radical question about economic science. What are its fundamental concepts and presuppositions? What is its relationship with ethics? What is its relationship with law? What are its relationships with a philosophical knowledge that interrogates the foundations, once again and from the beginning?

Such a basic framework means to scrutinize again, one by one, all the epistemological pillars of economics, with the objective to critically probe their innocence and evaluate their actual orientations, which are hidden behind its presumed "objective" and "neutral" attitudes.

Such a critical tradition certainly has an illustrious birth, starting from the very founders of Classical political economy. It has then gone through a criticism of the very foundations of economics/political economy; but nowadays this critical tradition has conquered a new urgency before the events of the so-called "globalization," which present themselves at the planetary level, and in a radical fashion. All this must wake us up from our *dogmatic sleep of reason*, to keep us awake *to the reasons of the sleep itself*.

The signs of this new critical urgency are various and widespread in our world today. Surely an economist like Amartya Sen already indicates a path to illuminate some epistemological questions that are hidden at the bottom of economic science. He questions, as it is well known, the very ideas of "individual," of capability development and of "happiness." His reference to Aristotle is also as well known. But now we must go, along this road, well beyond that and much more radically.

In the globalized and super-fast world of the thousands of fractured and connected scientific specializations, then, it seems to this author that the need for a "philosophy of economics" is re-imposing itself, in the agenda of epochal urgencies, in a new form. It re-imposes itself to ask questions, in the rebirth to a second-degree power of critical thought, concerning some fundamental things, to be gotten after digging up quite a few strata.

Economics has acquired today a perfect centrality, comparable to that central architectural position that once upon a time seemed to belong to theology. The main point is that we must critically reflect on its epistemological pretences to "truth." In this sense, a strong philosophical reflection on the economic science is well worth a wide critical project with a radical breadth which, joining various competences and repositioning economic science as well as the phenomena it investigates in a context of complexity, outlines with neat precision some fundamental questions and connections. Nowadays the vast majority of the economic science is a science of the capitalist structure that is of the structure that, having been born and developed in modernity, is a historically determined formation. Economics is the science of this formation. It cannot avoid, as a consequence, all of the epistemological questions that concern both its own specific scientific credentials and the scientific credentials of any science as such. In this horizon, the economic science claims for itself a capacity to describe and explain. This opens up a train of questions. Does economic science, in fact, as the science that measures economic interests measuring their mingling together, only measure and describe? How much, and how "objective" and innocent" are the concepts which it uses to measure, admitting that they can ever be objective and innocent? Not only. Which idea of man, of his features and of his intrinsic goals, lies beneath those epistemological concepts? Not only. Is it not true that the economic science, in its role of a description and explanation of the world, does not only describe and explain, in that, being believed to be a science and being applied as a technique, *it penetrates the world*, becoming as a matter of fact an *objective* and *independent* production of its own thinking method? Not only. Is it not true that the epistemological concept of "Homo Oeconomicus" meant as a rational man who calculates his own individual interest separately from the other men and separately from the other interests and passions, must be critically regulated? Is it not true that other and different scenarios would derive if we assumed *another* concept of Homo Oeconomicus, with other interests and other goals? Is it not true that, if we go down to the level of the object that economic sciences investigate, i.e. if we situate ourselves at the level of the actual economic situations and relationships, it is necessary to radically interrogate ourselves about what are the *possibility boundaries* within which those economic activities are realizable, and what those possibility boundaries have become *today*? Is it not necessary in other words to wonder what the invisible and foundational conditions on top of which those economic activities are pursued are, and how much this discovery influences the theoretical configuration of the interests in those activities? Is it not true that beneath economic activities, and especially the activities of the capitalist economy, lies an invisible foundation which it would be unscientific for us not to look into, and whose discovery we cannot leave to what is visible at the moment of a catastrophe? What are the conditions for the existence of a "Homo Oeconomicus," and at which conditions can instead a more consciously complex man exist? The way to conceptualize the economic man, his interests, his development, his happiness, *is not* an epistemologically innocent act. Such a concept must be considered with a conscious and critical eye. The concepts of "individual," of "economic agent," of "money," of "market" not only describe. They are oriented epistemological notions, and they produce effects. They conceal an idea of man, of society, of its processes, of its objectives. At a closer look, the concept of "individual" is constructed in an epistemological way very conform to that of "money," i.e., with a logic of separation between elements, and of limitation of interests. These and other concepts thus reveal the hiding of metaphysics. This, in any case, does not necessarily mean refusing the idea of a metaphysics underlying it, nor does it mean, necessarily, to accept it. Yet it certainly means to critically investigate it, to ask whether this is the only possible one, and if it corresponds to truth. And if, by chance, it does not conceal its basic epistemological weakness behind the *methodical* denunciation of "unforeseeable events" and of "irrationalities."

It might look very strange to hear somebody talk of "metaphysics of capitalism." But at a second look, it would be much stranger to think that behind a human science and its concepts there is no metaphysics at all.

A philosophy of economics worth our new complex times must be able to investigate and discover the strong and unthinkable connections that act in the global anthropological world, for causes we can impute to the so-called Homo Oeconomicus and its science. Such a philosophical perspective must have radical intentions; must express a wide and thorough vision; must be able to catch strong and essential connections with simplicity, even when they appear to confusingly join far away events; must be able at the same time to evaluate with rigour which invisible metaphysics—mental, epistemological, of which values—influences such connections, knowing that a different metaphysics would lead to other epistemological models and to other effects in reality, not necessarily already known. Amartya Sen has been an important contemporary step in this direction.

The book we present here, produced by the scientific operosity of Andrea Micocci, is meant to be an intelligent act of awareness and a start towards this necessary critical undertaking, which we must all pursue for the sake of our future.

Giuseppe Limone
Professore Ordinario di Filosofia della Politica
presso la Seconda Università di Napoli
Naples, October 2008

Translated from Italian by Andrea Micocci

Acknowledgments

Acknowledging help and advice is always hard. One is afraid of missing somebody. I would like then to take this chance to thank all the very many who did anything for me, often rescuing my life and that of my family. What follows is just a restricted list of the most representative names.

First in such a list always comes those who helped me shape my academic work. Alex Callinicos and the late Professor Vito Saccomandi have been the most enduring influences. The late Professor Paolo Sylos Labini, with his consideration for me and his generous conversations on theoretical topics he considered of little momentum, has helped me at a crucial stage. Giuseppe Limone, Gian Maria Piccinelli, Mariella Eboli, and Luciano Vasapollo have been continuous in generously supporting me and helping me with my problems. Piccinelli, Limone, and everybody of the Jean Monnet faculty at SUN deserve special thanks for supporting the Italian translation of this volume, and for much else.

Franco Gallo, Massimiliano Biscuso, Mino Vianello, Carlo Scarfoglio, Michelguglielmo Torri, Wilma Salvatori Torri, Brunella Antomarini, Charles McCann, and Mark Mascal have been more than friends, and fundamental theoretical and practical references. They are not afraid to say that I am wrong, when I am. Franco and Mino have read the whole manuscript. Tony Lawson did more for this book and for me than he is willing to acknowledge. Dr. K. Puttaswamaiah has proved a consistent and patient presence.

Patrizia Pugliese, Nadine Valat, Antonio Grieco, Oscar Cetrangolo, and Liliana Casanovas have been courageously supporting me through my foolishness. Enzo Pesciarelli, Alessandro Sterlacchini, Paul Diesing, Guido Traversa, Giuseppe Tassone, Vittorangelo Orati, Michele Schwendtbauer, Francesco Pennacchi, and Paola Oliviero have helped me in various ways and moments.

I feel a great gratitude for Lexington, for reasons that are too long to explain. Patrick Dillon in particular has been able to make me feel well with each of his e-mails. Somehow, he always chooses words that please and encourage me. Jerome Krase did his best to improve my manuscript at a much too early stage.

A very, very special thanks goes to my present and past students of all subjects, levels, and universities. With their enthusiasm and interest they have rescued me several times from depression. I always enjoyed teaching to adults, but they made that already pleasant task intensely rewarding. I have tried with them some of my arguments and got a prompt, and I believe sincere, response. My wife Nino, and my sons Alessandro and David helped me with the index.

But all of the above would not mean anything, given that I would not be here writing this, if it were not for Nino Pardjanadze.

Rome, June 2008.

Chapter One

Outline of an Intellectual Monster

The tensions ensuing from the relationship between the individual and organized societies have been there ever since recorded history has been available. The shape, and above all the pervasivity, of the institutional arrangements determined their form and degree. The difference between the Greek polis and modern capitalism is abysmal in this respect.

In the Greek polis the citizen was a peculiar kind of man whose main duties were to his family and to the improvement of himself. Political commitments were a full part of his formal entitlements. He was surrounded by a majority of other men who had no such hereditary set of characterizations. These fellow men of his were simultaneously his inferior and his equal in their responsibilities to their own families and themselves.

Such differences were there to safeguard routines and meant little in everyday intercourses. It was possible, in other words, to set permeable limits to the rules of the game, which were kept formally only to be trespassed in some occasions and ignored in most others. Only wars, mob riots, and a few other events were the occasions for imposing and enforcing the differences: that is, the institutional setup itself.

Men could be, and could not be, citizens, and yet live in the polis and even make an eternal name for themselves, such as Aristotle in Athens. Or if citizens, they could be ostracized and chased away after years of eternally recognized work for their city, such as Themistocles.

Fundamentally, the game of social life and politics could be entered and exited (this latter case being the most interesting to our purposes): you could be kicked out, or you could simply want out and go. Similar possibilities were allowed in varying degrees in ancient Rome and even in the Middle Ages, and for some developing countries as far as the end of the nineteenth century (think of Muhammad Ali for Egypt or Garibaldi for Italy).

1

In all of these eras you could also, in the sanctuary of your own home or in faraway places, avoid accepting the power of shared and/or enforced beliefs, habits, and ideologies. The various Giordano Bruno, Baruch Spinoza, even Karl Marx himself at the dawn of capitalism, could move for a while or for good to regions of the known world where there was no objection to their not upholding the beliefs of their own religions, home countries, and home powers.

Escaping instead is precisely what is not possible with capitalism as we know it today. This is not so because of that jack-of-all-trades they call globalization, and the impossibility to avoid, for a powerful instance, the quasi-instantaneous transmission all over the world of your warrant for arrest.

The thesis of this book is that the theoretical equality of all men vis-à-vis state institutions, with the implicit supposed allegiance to such institutions everyone is automatically endowed with, cannot be shaken off. Whatever one does, one can only end up in two types of predicaments: in favor or against the present economic and institutional setup, but always from within it.

If you do not like capitalism you can only go along with it or fight it. Living in the Sahara or the heights of the Himalayas would only consign you to the realm of those in favor. The underdeveloped, in fact, are by definition a peculiarly primitive, yet rapidly progressing, form of capitalism.

If you refuse to conform you find yourself consigned to the realm of those against, like the hippies in Nepal or the South Cone of Latin America, or the al-Qaida madmen. But whatever you do, you cannot exit the game. Not only can you not want out: the system never lets you go, for it cannot provide for your departure.

From the economic point of view, the "market" has you whether you like it or not, despite all economists in fact agreeing that the market of the theory does not exist in reality. However, the "market forces" are supposed to be—indeed they are—active in practice. Once evoked, they come to stay, and thrive out of all actions, in favor as well as against them. The history of the twentieth century and the failure of anticapitalist movements have taught us that much, although I find the theoretical explanation I shall argue in this book the definitive one.

Thus, the individual-society tensions in capitalism acquire a peculiar role. In the preceding modes of production they were something you could get in doses of different intensity, and you could variate your degree of exposure to them. With capitalism you are completely submitted to them. The history of capitalism is the history of the absurdities ensuing from the thorough and inescapable enforcement of the physical and psychological constraints of the specific type of organized society capitalism itself claims each time to be.

This last point is basic: it is not the degree of development of capitalist institutions that matters. What counts is the idea that capitalism can claim, and is claimed to be, in action. The peculiar feature of capitalist time is that both its "sane" and "degenerated" forms are characteristically capillary in the way they involve those who find themselves in their net.

This peculiar character, well captured by Adorno, induces a frightening homogeneity in behaviors:

> The conception of unfettered activity, of uninterrupted procreation, of chubby insatiability, of freedom as frantic bustle, feeds on the bourgeois concept of nature that has always served solely to proclaim social violence as unchangeable, as a piece of healthy eternity. . . . It is . . . the collective as a blind fury of activity [to be feared]. (1989, 156)

This aspect of continuous motion is the most revelatory of the capillary penetration of capitalism, for it is found even in the opposers of capitalism.

Let me introduce the complexity of what I am talking about by means of a telling example. I usually avoid proceeding by examples, but as we are at the beginning I must make myself clear by all possible means.

Lessig (2005), in reviewing a book about open source softwares, mentions that there exists a large group of people (2 million contributions a year), linked by the Internet, who "volunteer" their time and labor to solve software problems for free. Their contribution to humanity falls under the rubric of "making Microsoft happy": they help run the software produced by Microsoft, and Microsoft itself helps them do so in various ways, except by supplying money.

This is, at a first level of analysis, truly bewildering. Microsoft has been charged, and found guilty, of anticompetitive practices. If these people were anticapitalist they should fight it rather than help it run its programs smoothly. If they were procapitalist they should do the same, in order to help the market run its "healthy" course. The phenomenon is not explicable at an economic, political, and social level, unless we hypothesize that these people feel that they are helping humankind by making Microsoft's software cause less headaches for users.

But there is another important question worth asking at a second level of analysis: why do they do this for softwares and through the Internet? Do forms of similar direct intervention on product development take place, say, in poultry farming or shirt making?

Instead of getting their hands dirty at actually raising broilers, some people in fact do "volunteer" in favor of poultry farming (another case of mono/oligopoly in many developed countries) by opposing the producers' disdain for quality, consumer's welfare, or the welfare of the chickens. They indirectly help corporations by alerting bureaucrats to impose quality standards for the final product and some production processes.

What is the reason why people devote their spare time to help their kind in the Internet and in computers, or by manipulating bureaucracy and administrations, and refuse to do so in those fields that are the normal realm of waged and salaried labor? Why do they even ignore the damage inflicted by the firm they are making happy on those very fellow human beings they are supposedly helping? Are they protecting their fellow human beings or helping the firm, and in general the system that lets firms become mono/oligopolistic?

At a third level, there is the question of why things as inefficient, illogically conceived, and arid as computers and bureaucracies raise so much interest in all types of persons, from sophisticated intellectuals to shepherds in rags. All these people bovinely refuse to get angry when the computer they are operating does what it was made for: alternate good performances with breakdowns, in the framework of a stupidly encumbering working logic. Even more unexplicably, the vast majority of them cannot go beyond using computers just as typewriters or diaries. They look at you with insulted expressions when you tell them so.

The answer to this question concerns all human activities under capitalism. If the system is capillary and you cannot escape it, if being against or in favor does not matter, if the consequences of all this are often violent and always tragic (these sedulous fools waste their lives in front of computer screens volunteering to contribute to "Microsoft's happiness"), it means that capitalism affects the whole life of the individuals who undergo it, alterating their natural drives.

The occasional outbursts of antisystem action that do happen witness to the fact that this affecting the whole life is not merely a psychological conditioning or a straightforward compulsion caused by rules and repression. There must be, indeed there is, a degree of participation, a mechanism that was only partially known, or partially enacted, in the preceding modes of production.

Such mechanism is not directly bodily and psychological. Thus, one has to look at the system's intellectual characteristics. Let us start from the economy, the "base." What astonished me since I undertook the study of economics (my first dab at what I would today call political philosophy) was that while it was clear that economics' explanations were stylizations and even straightforward proxies devised for the purposes of schematizing economic analysis, people (even teachers of economics!) act as if they were material component parts of reality. They cannot see the difference between the economic "abstract" (in economic technical parlance, theoretical entities) and the material. This approximation is tolerated almost always, and in all walks of life.

What all this points to, unequivocally, is that capitalism holds itself together in the actual not by virtue of its institutional organization and the perfection of its economic mechanisms. In the theory as well as in practice it works by means of a flawed intellectual mode of operation that mixes up the material with theoretical wishful thinking. This is what pushes the bourgeois to feed that "unfettered activity" and its cruel consequences that horrified Adorno.

This book shall explore, and demonstrate, this hypothesis, showing that the working structure of "capitalism" is an intellectual flawed logic. The whole thing is based on a mirroring logical structure between capitalism's intellectual (favorable and unfavorable) apprehension of itself and actual economic and political intercourses.

Capitalism amounts to a metaphysics in the sense of "beyond the physical." Its economic and political phenomena happen in that they are intellectually imposed by a dominant (flawed) logic that enforces homogenization and hence, socialization. These end up spreading themselves capillarily. Let us introduce this intellectual monster.

THE MATERIAL—THAT IS, NATURE

To pursue our analysis, it is imperative to set ourselves free from the dominant, capitalist metaphysics. We must recover our intellectual independence—that is., our capacity to directly see reality as such. We must reorganize our reasoning and our observations starting from the material itself (I shall use this term and the "concrete" interchangeably in the course of the book). Let us pose ourselves outside capitalism in order to see reality bare of invented links, connections, and prejudices.

The point is not to expect reality to be different from how we see it now, in fact. Rather, we need to see it in its silent concreteness. Our analysis must start from the concrete and finish with the concrete without drifting into metaphysics. We must learn to quit the habit that makes us wish for structural connections intellectually made up. These are not an endowment of nature, but rather mirror the intellectual poverty of our present mode of production.

I am proposing here a materialistic and naturalistic view of reality. This volume spells out the characteristics of the former term, while the latter, that needs some specific philosophical qualifications, cannot be dealt with here. Before delving into the actual subject matter I must explain, as a premise, the way I use the term intellectual, and the reason why I do not say rational instead.

The term rationality (see Micocci, 1999a, 1999b; Tassone, 1999) is usually meant as an extension of that peculiar way human beings have to articulate their perceptions and feelings by organizational means linked to language, or anyway to those communication devices that are socially shared at the moment of action. In philosophy and in many social sciences, rationality is used, however, in a very broad fashion, to indicate very generic forms of activity man pursues independently from the historical age in which he finds himself. We should not make the mistake of believing that that is the only, or even the main, "human" way to figure out the mechanisms of understanding.

The term intellectuality from now on will signify rational action according to the parameters set by the dominant culture. These last are different with the different modes of production and their rational setup.

In the case of capitalism, as I hinted in the preceding section and hope to demonstrate in the present book, intellectuality means a particularly poor and flawed set of maieutical devices that seem to lead to reassure the user of the hidden or evident harmony of whatever is being observed. I shall argue in what follows that in order to perform this role capitalist intellectuality refuses to directly observe and grasp the material. This is replaced by a metaphysical reasoning whose flawed logic keeps it suspended in between the abstract and the material.

If we recover the material and see it as it is, a whole set of traditional problems in philosophy will make a long overdue comeback. Just to quote a few of the most significant ones, there is the question of the reliability of the senses and the meaning in practice of the primacy that a materialistic and naturalistic attitude assigns to them. For another powerful and problematic instance, there is the question of the basic categories of logic (difference, otherness, the connections among things), and the need to put to a new test the various approaches to these questions.

Until we get ourselves emancipated from the intellectuality of capitalism with its all-pervading mistakes, we are compelled to suspend judgement on all the issues related to the perception, analysis, and organization of reality. As long as we are in the grip of the capitalist intellectual monster, logic and studies of intellectuality and rationality must be confined to the role of showing the poverty and flaws of the capitalist dominant way of thinking, and devoted to the task of emancipation.

This is what the present book is about. Throughout it we must think of the material (reality as such and not as reported by the dominant intellectuality) as an out-of-reach object to recover. We must try to have in the back of our mind, as a background to what is being told here, a mental attitude of leaving nature to itself. We should let the material flow—or not flow—on its own, and imagine we could stand back and let it operate in silence.

To fully understand this book, moments of idle watching the sky, animals and plants, or nothing at all, will help a lot. More help will come from an inward look at how much useless reasoning and artificiality we put in our natural drives (sex, food, and the like) and how we limit ourselves in relation to them, out of purely intellectual reasonings.

This book is not, therefore, for those who hold pets in their homes, or mutilate themselves vis-à-vis nature, such as the nonreligious vegetarians, or those who believe they can locate and even defend a specific natural equilibrium and/or a species or phylum, or those who have ideas of any kind about sex instead of immediate and unquenchable drives. It is not for those who impose their footprints on the snow, or pick flowers, or for those who take out "their" dog to watch it exercise and defecate and think they are loving it.

It is not, in a word, for those who look for a harmony in things, who can express their feelings and even consider them, and seek to forecast what comes next in order to be sure it is something they can guess and insert in its predetermined slot. This is a book for those who like to think that much more than we can tell and predict is out there, and who cannot wait to see it.

In order to develop the argument of the intellectual limitations inherent in the dominant logic of capitalism, we cannot, obviously, start from economics and the social sciences. A more general framework for analysis is needed, that only philosophy can help organize. Our task is to find our way back to the material by means of criticizing, after a careful analysis, capitalism as a mode of production.

We have to tell what it is that capitalism consists in. This in itself presents us with serious difficulties. In fact, capitalism has been analyzed and declared to be a specific mode of production, mainly as an economic system in which commodities and class struggle if you are a Marxist and exchange if you are a mainstream economist, are the basic constituent parts.

That is, capitalist economics and politics have been given a character without minding the connection with the material, and thereby implicating, by default, that what you are talking about is part of the material and follows the general laws of nature. All the items of the capitalist mode of production are taken, and organized, as if they were an actually material part of reality. Many of these items are just borrowed from preceding modes of production, or contrariwise given a suprahistorical universality and distributed back to present, future, and preceding modes of production. The implicated connection with the material, however, is simply not there, as shall be proved in chapters 2 and 3.

The idea of exchange and that of currency are, for two telling instances, compared across history as if the fact that the words that designate them are translatable in modern languages were enough to grant a transhistorical identity to them. In some other cases (the concept of politeia), identicalness is claimed in principle, despite the original thing having been so mistranslated and misunderstood in practice as to make it unrecognizable.

Whatever the wishful thinking implied in history and the social sciences that bring them to work as if there were a continuity and a continuous inter-action between the items of social reality, social reality is only part of a much wider framework. The whole, the material, constitutes such a general frame-work. This could be sufficient as a reason to stop historians and social scien-tists from applying their precooked continuities: the world of the social is held at ransom by the world of nature, where continuities are not granted. More importantly, one rupture is sufficient to annihilate most, or even all, of the continuities that social scientists so painstakingly individuate and pile up for their consolation.

It is just plain wrong to figure out continuities and to work out any system from them. Yet, that is precisely what historians and social scientists do, as we shall see. More tragically and monstrously, that is what underlies the in-tellectuality of capitalism. The material, with its ruptures, is ruled out, and capitalist appreciation of itself winds up into a self-protected and self-isolated bundle of religious-looking aphorisms.

What characterizes capitalism, we shall see, is precisely this self-contained aspect, that the modes of production that preceded it did not have so complete and all-encompassing a degree. What room to escape was available, we have lost.

The "political economy of capitalism" proposed here is, in the Marxist tra-dition but in a much more radical way, a critique of political economy. Find-ing out the flawed logic behind the social sciences, which mirrors and is what takes place within capitalism, is a way to stop their attempt to prevent—by intellectual fiat—the intrusion of the material. It frees capitalism from the prison that prevents its direct contact with nature. The exciting question en-suing from this is: will capitalism survive such an event? If, with Marx's The-sis XI on Feuerbach (1985, 123), the point is to study the world in order to change it, then we will have achieved that: we will have produced a momen-tous change indeed.

In communism, in fact,

> The individuals' consciousness of their mutual relationships will, of course, like-wise become something quite different, and, therefore, will no more be the "prin-ciple of love" or denoument, than it will be egoism. (Marx, Engels 1985, 118)

Both the guiding ethical principles of the liberals and those of the self-avowed socialists (beautifully identified by their unwillingness to pronounce the word communism, for they correctly know it to imply anarchism) are eliminated. We have a weapon to criticize liberals, neoliberals, progressives, socialists, antianarchist communists and all the other types of prophets of proselytism who have poisoned contemporary history.

An intrinsic and powerful conservatism in fact characterizes the social sciences, Marxist and mainstream. If we look, as we shall do in this book, into what they propose, we do not find anything capable of revolutionizing or destroying the fundamental aspects of society as we know it under capitalism.

There is nothing intrinsically wrong with this: we are all entitled to have conservative opinions. What is wrong is the heartbreaking lightheartedness that both mainstream and Marxist social scientists sport while using human lives to further the conservative goals of their agendas. Millions of lives have been wasted on the altars of the liberal and socialist utopias while working precisely at postponing those very utopias into the distant future.

This sad matter of fact turns our attention to the vicious circle implied by the intellectual refusal of allowing direct contact with nature. Safeguarding your system from the variability and unpredictability of nature in fact implies the construction of an ever-complicated intellectual framework, to which ever-complicated institutional setups must correspond.

If we contrast for a minute the stark difference between the frightening power of the material with its unpredictable and "catastrophic" ruptures and the cozy peacefulness of social life as a harmony detached from nature, we glimpse at the powerful banality of how intellectual systems that work are built. The more inexorable the intellectually produced harmony is, the more successful it is.

The need to have an intellectual system to prevent nature from following its course, coupled with the need to have it harmonious to contrast it with the terrifying and catastrophic power of the material, inevitably winds up to produce the obvious result: the prevention of its own underlying utopia. Such intellectual systems cannot, in other words, consummate all of their development possibilities, lest they end up being faced with accomplishment and hence, potentially, end and replacement (this being, needless to say, a natural event).

That is why in practice we are not likely to see capitalism come true as a truly free market system, and that is why orthodox Marxist agitators propose to us socialism instead of communism, which is, and only can be, anarchism. Being based on the surprising schizophrenia free market–national states, it is no wonder that the more tightly capitalism works, the more it is visited by its inevitable existing incubus: that of nationalism with the ensuing evils. We shall see how all this occurs much more systematically than it seems at first sight.

After all this reasoning some might object that there is another, probably more direct, way to look at this. It suffices in fact to observe that human beings are natural and material, and that the senses and the brain, alone and in their combination called rationality, share in the same material as the rest of nature.

Unfortunately, this avenue is precluded to us. The flaws of the dominant mentality dominate our communicative and analytical procedures, preventing us from knowing that we share in the same material as the rest of nature other than by intuition or by those few moments we can steal from the pervasiveness of socialized behavior.

The fact that the natural sciences have stated that both living and dead material bodies are identically composed of atoms, and that the difference is a matter of which combination of atoms goes to compose each entity, is of no use here either. In spite of its aesthetically beautiful materialistic appearance (we are all electromagnetic associations!) the scientific point of view might simply be temporary. This can be both in the Kuhnian sense of being a provisional thesis to be superseded by the next scientific revolution and in the sense proposed here of being just the result of an all-encompassing harmonious mentality that isolates thought and apprehension from a direct contact with reality.

We are thus back to our need to start our quest for the material from a critique of the human sciences and its support of the absurdities of the present mode of production. In doing this we are fortunate enough to have a turning point in European history that gives us the chance to identify the key theoretical question with two related thinkers: Marx's reaction to Hegel's attempt to transform the most "mystically rational" ideas of his time into a philosophical system, harmonious, dialectical, with no exit allowed and far too close in intellectual terms to the actual, but supposedly eternal, institutions of his and our time.

CAPITALISM AS WE KNOW IT

We have been talking, in the two preceding sections, about "capitalism." Despite the various observations that have been put forward to qualify it, most people must have felt comfortable with this word. It constitutes a useful approximation we all resort to when we need to refer to the present social, political, and economic setup with all of the rest that is entailed or which can be attributed to it by all types of syllogisms.

But "capitalism" is no more than a desired object. Not surprisingly, it is desired by those who support it, and even more by those who want to see it disappear. If capitalism were here, we would not have those sedulous fools who help Microsoft. We would have true democracy. We would have a "good life." Instead, not even the rich and powerful enjoy any of that.

Definitions of capitalism are on permanent sale in social sciences. Mainstream economists are masters at the art of producing more and more reductive ones, and Marxists match them in this race, although they keep sticking to a more complex language. Indeed, one cannot refer to present-day reality without being requested to tell what is meant by capitalism.

In the present volume we shall concentrate on capitalism by means of the proxy of the market system. In order to help the reference to reality we shall not deal solely with the market in the mainstream economic sense or the "law of value" with its "process of valorization" in the Marxist sense. I see my work as within the Marxist tradition despite not sharing, as I shall argue in detail, as fundamental a Marxist pillar as the Marxist dialectical fixation. To be complete we need to associate all that to a form of state with its own institutions. By means of discussing these two poles we shall endeavor to see capitalism as a whole, identifying the intellectuality behind the theory and the actual intercourses.

The first thing to do then is to explain why the market figures so prominently everywhere and how it fits our need to have a representative proxy for the whole of capitalism. By outlining what we mean by it we shall also see why capitalism is incomplete, and we shall be able to study the role of the state and of state institutions. That is why in the rest of the book we will always mean "capitalism as we know it" rather than "capitalism." This is a very momentous aspect, with a very important set of consequences, as we shall see in the final chapters of the volume.

A market is a place that exists in fact, as well as a set of rather immaterial actions and reactions. Markets are, at least at this first introductory stage, a most evident instance of the nonexitable game that capitalist relationships come down to. They amount in practice to a lamentable mixture of what they could be—that is, a virtual place where a fair encounter of buyers and sellers takes place—and of what they are—that is, different types of (market) failures. These last, far from being eliminated from the system, remain there.

Failures actually constitute, instead of the exceptions, the very normality of market economies. These last in fact boil down to little more than attempts to adjust, correct, and hope in order that markets allegedly make a bit of progress toward their theoretical fair functioning.

It is well worth emphasizing in this respect that in practice what you look for is not a configuration of reality that approaches the market as it should be (let alone what it is supposed to be in the rarefied pureness of theory). What is meant by adjustments, corrections, development/growth, and reforms is just a progress, however small, from the fully and thoroughly unsatisfactory present state.

The explanation of this ridiculous state of things lies in the manner of functioning that is imposed upon markets in theory and practice. Markets are in fact compelled to work in a step-by-step fashion, with each bit of them relating itself to another or a few other bits. This relationship is expected to bring about a situation in which the bits that have encountered and related to one another move on to a (supposedly) higher status as a result of the relationship.

Such higher status has not actually left the former configuration. It has simply transcended it into a (implicitly and supposedly) revertible new configuration, in which none of the entities involved lose their inner character. The result is, typically, something that presents the characteristics of both the initial entities.

The idea of market as it is exhibited by capitalist apologists is so "democratic" in its reach that it encompasses all forms of noncapitalist and nonmarket production and exchange. It is easy to see why this is so. By the same working logic of the market itself, nonmarket configurations can be inserted in the game any time and in any place, for they cannot (nothing and nobody can) revolutionize an intrinsically moderate set of relations.

We should not be deceived by the empty rhetoric of the language of economic policies. Shock therapy, technological or commercial revolution, survival of the fittest, *homo homini lupus* in the functioning of actual markets and in economic policy making are but vast exaggerations. All they come down to is the normal scrapping of plants and of capitals that takes place all the time, at the different pace circumstances determine. It is not a case of survival of the fittest, but of fitting everyone to survive.

Capitalism's categories are supposed to be universal and applicable to all historical ages: production and exchange, and even money, were allegedly always there. Inserting them in the market is as easy as inserting them in the market. The working logic of mainstream and of much Marxist economic reasonings allows the most acrobatic operations: a primitive man working in a primitive economy becomes a maximizing peasant, with no change whatsoever ever being enforced in his way of life and behaviors—capitalism provides for that too, immaterially but with consequences on selected parts of the material.

If we look at all this we see an inclusive logic that seems to want to prove its inexorable progression all the time, rather than actually progress. The claimed progression itself is not by ruptures and revolutions: it is instead granted by the inclusive logic. That means that all the items at stake participate in the process of realization of the market on Earth, and more in general to the progressive evolution of capitalism toward itself.

There is, obviously and undeniably, a "vulgar" Hegelian dialectical process at work. Its vulgarity is most evident in the thorough and complete disregard for both the actual contents of the Idea and the incidents that nature, with its often nondialectical functioning, might bring about.

Little wonder then that this way of putting things is acritically accepted by the Marxists, and little wonder that, despite its supposed inner logic, the market cannot do without a state and state institutions. This is just like Hegel's organic and ethical state: a way to salvage some typical feudal and precapitalistic items by making them interact with capitalist mechanisms, which are ad hoc given the necessary dialectical features.

But things do happen in practice sometimes. Markets occasionally clear. This or that economic policy has the forecasted effect. This or that production plant or entrepreneur has its peculiar type of commodity absorbed by the market. Even more astonishingly, the stock market and the financial markets in general seem to work with a "normal" degree of imperfection, despite the herd behavior of the majority of the participants and the ensuing possibility, rarely exploited to the full, for individuals to make a rich killing.

The division of labor has given us the working class, Fordism and Taylorism have given us its trade unionization, and the present-day conversion to just-in-time production and the so-called flexibility is making all that disappear. There has been no revolution when the working class was organized and powerful; it has taken no revolution to dispose of it.

Nobody wants out of this dialectical game. All that can happen is that the game itself gets repeated, in a slightly different setting.

Markets are not only a bogus thing in theory. They are a queer thing in practice, and their very existence is easily questionable. What we have instead of their material self is a metaphysics, a reference for the actual goods, money, laborers, capitalists, and victims of the system to know how to predict their fate, and accept it with its consequences, despite its imperfection.

With the market we get a prone kind of mentality, dependent upon the supposed (intellectual) predictability of the system. The items the market processes are drawn from the metaphysics, but such processing can only give known results. The capitalist figures out his way to invest his money and can be right or wrong; nothing will kick him out of the game.

The working class, too, can figure out the way to improve its condition (remember, we are playing a dialectical game, a step-by-step operation with the imprint of moderation) but can go no further than that, and of course it can be wrong. Thus, the proletarians can only choose in between the two stakes of a low-risk bet, with a chance to be slightly better off or worse off at the end. Single results add up in the very long run, pleasing historians but having no consequence on our reasoning.

What we have been sketching amounts to a way to summarize what the social sciences, using the very same working logic of capitalism, tell (and yet often officially deny). The social sciences mirror reality as such, and we shall see this in depth in what follows, because both amount to the same (intellectual) metaphysics. The social sciences do explain capitalist reality, because this whole apparatus works together, reinforcing itself by its actual working. The condition to go on doing so is to keep to the metaphysics—to stick to the harmony, the dialectical. It is the functioning that counts, and not the actual movement of material items.

The most important thing is that the harmonious character is meant to keep the natural off. The market system exists in its perceived isolation from nature, or we would see its absurdity. Hence, the necessity of a complex network of states and state institutions, to make one feel that the primary allegiance of man is to the social, and not to nature.

And in fact "capitalism" is not just the market. Capitalism is that actual thing that conjugates together the market, the state, and the institutional apparatus that goes with it, and also salvages all the bits and pieces that originate in the obsolete, preceding modes of production. The already nonsensical task of alienating individuals from nature is thus further complicated by the need to make room for a set of incongruous and unfitting objects.

Capitalism has at its disposal a set of moderate, harmonious relationships tailored to accommodate whatever can claim an intellectual (true or enforced) homogeneity with the general logic—even parts of nature, as long as they behave. Obsolete social arrangements happily survive, and thrive, in capitalism.

A general logic, however, when it produces an all-encompassing framework for inclusion of anything social (i.e., intellectually identifiable), necessarily must control, and/or often amount to, the emotional reactions. No one could stand the strain of a cozy, harmonious life with no hope of release, unless his emotions are channeled to produce few known reactions.

We can go back to the fools who help Microsoft and to their insane passion for computers. The computer is a powerful metaphor of the whole so far described: it is completely artificial, it has no connection with nature, and it is driven by a metaphysics—that is, an elementary logic whose flaws are visible in their continuous and simply unavoidable breakdowns. Computers are arid, and being so they can supply all sorts of arid quasi-reproductions of any item of reality. You can even use them to reproduce, inventing from borrowed parts and mathematical relations, anything, even so incomparable (and hence not reproducible) a thing as a beautiful girl. You get her, she does not seem real and yet it works, unlike actual chickens in chicken farming and shirts in shirt making, which are material things through and through.

Emotions are fooled and replaced by their articulation in discoursive, communicable terms. It is the inclusive logic of the moderate, dialectical game that dictates these formalized rules of participation (and remember, you cannot opt out). The game is endless because the whole apparatus is intrinsically imperfect: imperfection is the very cause of the persistence of the apparatus itself.

Nonetheless, emotions have to be evoked in the first place, and a system as arid as the one we have been describing could not do it. It needs some evocative items, something that can arouse the social emotions needed, and also claim to be justified by history or the economy. Nothing is easier to get: we have the state (as an Idea) and state institutions, and the past is there to supply that.

Reality has penetrated the theory: the obsolete states that were available when capitalism was dawning have been adapted to the needs of the new production processes and the ensuing social changes. The old national states shed absolute monarchy and accept the rhetoric of the supposed rise to power of the bourgeoisie.

If we look at the early history of capitalism, we notice that the highest point of its political theory debates ends with (just to give a generic indication with no pretence of scientific irrefutability) Rousseau and Montesquieu and the debates on the Venetian and Dutch republics, with their final outcome in the *Federalist Papers.* The coming true of capitalist production hijacked the theoretical debate to a dispute between socialism and a family of liberal and quasi-liberal ideas, and the last forty years have given us only sterile discourses on redistribution and justice, for instance with Rawls and Barry, or the importance of our communitarian heritage (e.g., Sandel, Taylor, Raz).

The bourgeois state—that is, the vast exaggeration of the true phenomenon that has actually taken place—has consolidated itself and wiped away any chance of ever letting capitalist processes work out their own kind of state. We still are not sure as to what kind of political accommodation the unfettered working of the market would bring about. A national state is in open contradiction with the presence of a market. But neither of the two exist, and that is bad news for those liberals who take seriously their cherished idea.

What the presence of obsolete institutional forms of state, with the stunted intellectual debates that go with it, has brought is a set of powerful creators of emotions (first of all patriotism, with all the entailed evils, from racism to fascism, to colonialism, to imperialism). Instead cosmopolitanism, which we should have expected from the working of the market, is nowhere.

This gave us the degeneration of the utopian power of known political philosophies. Liberal ideas have slid into a set of quasi-liberal theories, or even into communitarianism. Marxist-influenced solutions have deteriorated into socialism, or likewise into communitarianism, that perfect link to nationalism all practically minded political philosophies need sooner or later.

The twentieth century, and unfortunately these first years of the new century, witness to the result of this degeneration of capitalism into its present

economically and politically hybrid nature. Nationalism, fascism, imperialism, protectionism, wars, aggressions, carpet bombings, death squads, reset-
tling of populations, and alleged genocides are used to cover up for other, and
true, genocides, terrorism (private and public), and many other hair-raising
phenomena that have made life a hell.

Capitalism has failed to transform itself into that stateless, atheistic worldwide market fairness that was supposedly expected since the times of Adam
Smith. But it has not failed, in its incomplete form, to wreak havoc and nurture perfidy in theory and in practice.

If the economy and politics of capitalism have failed to live up to the expectations, we are left with a mode of production that has in practice evolved
in a direction that is different from that which was envisaged at the beginning
by both social philosophers and common people. There is no characterizing
way to define and analyze it other than its intellectuality, its metaphysical nature we have been introducing here. Capitalism is the intellectuality that has
led us to imagine capitalism that wrong and misleading way. Capitalism can
only be identified by its metaphysics.

This last is the subject matter of the present volume. The working definition of capitalism we needed to put forward is, then, a short one: "capitalism
as we know it." This is what surrounds us and what this book deals with. It
looks horrible, but we are just at the beginning of a long and complex exploration.

THE QUESTION OF REVOLUTION

Everything proposed above points to a very important issue: capitalism as we
know it amounts to an internal solution to itself. The absurd dreams that have
been conceived at the outset of the free market and division of labor adven-
ture have given way to an intellectual nightmare once the development of the
market has crash-landed onto the impossibility to deliver the hopes unleashed. The need to tighten control on internal organization in order to keep
the ever-growing separation from the material has enhanced the metaphysical
features that are the very cause of capitalism's lack of development.

The achievements of capitalism that have been made so much of in the past
200 years amount to sets of quantitative results: from quantities of commodities with their worldwide penetration to average incomes in the developed
countries not imaginable for our ancestors to the growth of Gross National
Product (GNP), the landing on the moon, and the thoroughly assessed
amounts of poverty. This last is a most ironic and pathetic achievement of
capitalism: if we do not think about its causes, we can justly marvel at the precision of the numbers offered.

Nothing epitomizes this better than the so-called, in Marxist parlance, "process of valorization." This represents the essence of capitalist intercourses: anything, comprising abstract entities such as labor power and physical entities such as men and their limbs, has a value. Such a value is always there, even though it is expressed only at the moment the exchange of the items takes place. A man is not compelled to work by the interaction between the system and his own predicament. He sells his "labor power," which is bought by a capitalist who strives to get a markup out of the production process he sets in motion (I find the concept of markup, which has been popularized by post-Keynesian economics, more useful to signify what is involved here and in capitalism in general).

The core assumption for all this, with its jargon, is that anything, anybody, any animal is endowed with a potentially usable value. Beautifully, such value can be stretched (more often than it is redistributed according to Robbins's economic fiction of the scarce resources) to go to the advantage of one or the other side involved in the exchange. We are, as said, in the presence of a quantifiable item. To the delight of the mathematically minded economists, such quantification can take several forms and even produce several results.

The condition for the process of valorization to take place is the surrendering of the person, thing, or animal to the metaphysics. The material body must not be eliminated or forgotten, but transcended. By intellectual fiat, emotions are so channelled as to give the metaphysics power over the concrete. When an inanimated thing is involved, this game takes place in one direction only.

The question of animals, that by being animated would pose some problems to this type of working, is solved in two ways. Some animals are simply deprived of their animal status: take pets, by inclusion into the life of men as outlets for sentimental perversions, and farm animals, by sheer compulsion and alienation. Some other animals, in particular those that need not directly interact with the system, just plainly undergo whatever is decided for them: take quasi-wild animals in reservations, for a disquieting instance.

The winding up of the process of valorization as a purely intellectual operation need not actually take place in a case-by-case fashion, let alone be voluntary. Its very (capitalist intellectual) imaginability enforces its presence on the individual: it is the system itself.

The subject of this process, once alienated from the natural in general, is delivered to the blind rules of profit making. This last bit is what social scientists would say, but it is empty and meaningless if all that has been said above holds. The blind rules of the economy are in fact an encumbering, complex, and emotionally charged set of intellectual functions. It is from this that the power and resilience of what is entailed by the process of valorization ensues.

All the various aspects of capitalist intellectuality, and the mixture of heterogeneous, and at first sight often incompatible items it amounts to, do not have a univocally coherent working logic other than their metaphysical strive to harmony and inclusion. It is precisely this logical incoherence that makes the whole cumbersome and, to the similarly illogical eye of the social philosophers, complex. The great achievement of capitalism as we know it consists precisely in its defective logical connections, which make it a constant work in progress, eternally in need of mending. It is this character that makes it inclusive, a constant emergency necessarily involving all of us.

All this, which is often mistaken for the "invisible hand," is the essence of capitalist harmony with its continuous exceptions. Such rigorless harmony must be sought continuously, subsuming in the process whatever crops up.

The analogy with music is striking and was clear since antiquity. Musical harmony is a set of "linguistic" rules that are supposedly able to express any form of music, comprising what is not part of the canon from which the very linguistic rules themselves originated. Hence the cumbersome way to express things (the pentagram and all that), which musics out of the canon do not need and safely ignore in practice: take the blues.

Yet, ignoring them and going on the old way is not a means to escape inclusion (take the blues again). What you have been doing out of instinct until you have met the canon is now reproduced, and even bettered and refined in technical terms, by the "harmonic" linguistic rules of the canon. Look at the blues once more.

Once the process of valorization is allowed to apply its "linguistic" rules to a subject, there is no going back to the former freedom and spontaneity. You have been conquered by a world made of expressable functions lacking a simple and unequivocal working logic, in constant need of mending. This in turn implies that it is in constant need to express its local or overall working logic, a simply impossible task.

The frantic pace of the succession of emergencies (almost all little, but still emergencies) you have to face leaves you no choice but to counteract, shelter from, or go along with the game.

You can choose an actual productive process, for instance from ore to actual tool, or even select a part of that process (e.g., the mining, or the final industrial processing). But you can equally take a theoretical process, like Sraffa's one commodity model, just to mention one of the most unreal and overestimated. Acquaintance with any of these can take you up a career ladder or make you into a respectable person in casual conversation. In any case it makes you a full part of the goings-on of capitalism as we know it.

This is the essence of the process of valorization. It transforms anything it touches, and that means just anything, into an intellectual item not ready for use in capitalism as we know it but already in use in it. The price to pay is the loss of your natural characteristics. This last is easily summarized by what we shall keep referring to as the capacity to undergo "ruptures and oblivion." Such natural characteristics, needless to say, you have no material power to give up. Hence the strain.

Once there, you cannot work your way back to nature, for there are no fixed logical rules, while a set of praxis-enforced and intellectually purified paths is set for you, which you can follow in any direction, but not leave. Mind you: you certainly can step out, and say "I shall not." But this is meaningless to the general intellectual game, for both are metaphysics, a metaphysics that rules bodies. All you can get is a bout of emotional reactions, but we saw that emotions are governed by the linguistic rules of the metaphysics.

The result should be, and in practice is, a formidable tension in the individuals who undergo this absurdity. They find themselves in between a "natural" drive to fulfill all types of possibility and a "necessary" drive to stick to "dialectical" relationships, as if nature could be kept at bay.

Capitalism is replete with the extreme reactions produced by this formidable tension: these are not, however, the riots and violence that have succeeded each other in modern history, for these are part of institutional normality, like economic crises. They are instead the general climate of oppression by moderation that we all feel all the time, the monotony of always having the same things and witnessing the same reactions.

The result of the tension always goes in the direction of strengthening, by ordering and channeling, the causes of the tensions themselves. The bourgeois institutional setup impinges on our capacity to freely enjoy sex, and we witness a tightening of rules, a pedantic hairsplitting on what sex consists in, and even advice on how to perform it.

Work is boring and makes us feel we are wasting our lives, and we witness a growing insecuritization of work, whose result is our desiring to work as much as possible. Before insecuritization, the answer was even more paradoxical: socialists of all sorts celebrated work as human realization and offered trade unionism instead of emancipation.

Cars' exhausts pollute, and you replace them with devices that do not pollute any longer that way, but just a different way, and meanwhile you have even created (insecure) jobs in the field of replacing the old exhausts. Local natural equilibria (those detectable by normal science) get disrupted, like they always did since the world began, and you find millions volunteering for a replacement, or a reconstitution, of the supposed old state.

Microsoft forces on you its software, and scores of sedulous fools flock to help it run. This is extremely consistent, for Microsoft perfectly embodies the meaning of the metaphysics of capitalism. The market is there as a reference but does not exist in practice, replaced by a set of expressable "imperfect competition" configurations. If you want to succeed you must cry market and not play it; if you are found out, like Microsoft was, you prove the point of the game to everybody, and in the process also can, like many impertinent children, have your cake and eat it. You are a good reminder of what wins, and, in a setup that favors proneness, the direction for the majority to go is clear.

Attempts to see reality are hijacked and turned to the normal routines of capitalist intellectuality.

The mirroring introduced earlier on in this chapter between the intellectuality of capitalism and the methodology of the social sciences cannot produce subversive results. Only justice and injustice are allowed by the analytical and maieutical means of that intellectuality and by the methodology of the social sciences and political and social philosophy that capitalist intellectuality has devised. Powerful thought constructions that could have produced noncapitalist patterns of intellectual activity are bent and denatured to produce justice talks.

The outcome is plain before our eyes. All theories against capitalism, comprising Marxism, have given up philosophical research, flattening themselves upon ethical (bourgeois) issues. Marxism has become a theory of exploitation in search of a bourgeois demonstration (the transformation problem). Therefore, it has wound up into a more and more convoluted theory of how to move from a capitalist configuration to the next.

The one and only point around which the whole intellectual gymnastic of capitalism as we know it revolves—that is, the maiming of man's reason and feelings—is not conceivable for the approaches to the social sciences and political philosophy we know to date. Revolution, the change—in the sense of elimination—of something (intellectual or not) as a whole has been assimilated to its meaning in the empty rhetoric of capitalism as we know it.

Like in the field of technology, revolution has come to mean a change of "paradigm," not in Kuhn's (1969) sense, but in the vulgar, empty sense given to it by economics. It can only lead to imaginable outcomes, such as a (democratic or dictatorial, does not matter) dictatorship of the proletariat. Not only does that happen in practice, which is terrible enough. It happens also in theory. This last is truly unbearable, for it kills hope.

Revolution as elimination (rupture with oblivion) of the existing instead is unconceivable in those capitalist terms. Revolution, however, consists in restoring the connection to the material that capitalist intellectuality has destroyed and in practice forbidden by removing the intellectual means to build it. Materialism (and naturalism, but this aspect is better left to a next volume) is in itself revolution.

The various mainstream Marxisms, by avowing a dialectical method, have assimilated themselves to capitalism as we know it, severing ties with the means to produce a materialism. It is time to make that plain. I shall not dwell here on the repugnant consequences of this move and the unspeakable amounts of human sufferings it has caused. I would like to stress a simple point that needs no extended argument and yet authorizes even more pessimism.

The means to political "struggle" that had erroneously been mistaken by the Marxist as leading to revolution have mutated back into what they have always been: bourgeois tools for proselytism and reciprocal violence. Demonstrations, political showdowns of all sorts, mass uprisings have (justly) been made their own by non-Marxist reformers of capitalism.

The multitudes that used to gather under socialist banners have changed their sociological character. The proletarians, who are typically disappearing, have been replaced by environmentalists, nationalists, pacifists, religious fundamentalists, and about any deplorable category capitalism as we know it can conceive under the collective name of civil society. Their hypocritical Spinozian collective "indignation" never fails to light a spark in the hearts and bodies of those who fully partake of capitalist intellectuality, with the ensuing "uninterrupted procreation, chubby insatiability, freedom as frantic bustle" and their "collective as a blind fury of activity."

"Social violence," as Adorno intuited, under capitalism as we know it, is indeed "unchangeable, as a piece of healthy eternity." It even finds its bards glorifying it, in the right as well as in the left.

One should not be misled by this and throw away the baby with the dirty water. Class struggle does exist, and it does make life unbearable for the majority of us. When the oppressed do not practice it, as they should, to defend themselves, the oppressors do (let me credit Luciano Vasapollo for this way to express a complex issue).

Class struggle is, exactly as Marx had seen, a characterizing routine feature of capitalism. Only, inevitable as it is, and necessary as it is, class struggle has been bent to be a dialectical relationship: a purely capitalist social function. It has nothing to do with revolution. It does not even help toward approaching it.

Revolution instead is emancipation from that intellectuality with its entailed effects on material reality we have called capitalism as we know it. It is a philosophical enterprise, and an eminently individual one. It must emancipate each of us from the intellectual monster that has reduced us all to an arithmetically equal fraction of a homogeneous whole. It is not about proselytism, even less about violence (let alone collective violence). It is the coming about of a point of rupture and oblivion.

Revolution is the act of philosophically getting the relationship with the concrete straight. When it comes about, it can only completely destroy the bases of capitalism as we know it by destroying its intellectual nature. Here capitalist apologists are bound to bark, mockingly, that this is not going to ever happen, for everybody should do it simultaneously, thereby losing their material privileges, however small.

I hope the philosophical reasoning I offer in this volume will prove that their reasoning follows from the misunderstood relationship with the material I am going to show. Those privileges and achievements they give so much importance to are nothing if you are a human. By gaining your self, you lose them.

WHAT IS BEING PROPOSED HERE

What we have been introducing so far is the picture of capitalism as a system that has disattended expectations about its pattern of growth. Instead of taking the free-market path and leaving to the "invisible hand" the issues of fairness and justice, the capitalist mode of production has had its economic and political growth truncated. Those changes in economic terms that have taken place have not been matched by a corresponding evolution of political institutions and political ideas.

The only way to give a definition of capitalism is thus to avoid concentrating only on its strictly economic and political characteristics. What best characterizes capitalism is that everybody is convinced to be living under it. Whole "scientific" apparatuses are put forward to prove just that. Like Voltaire's Pangloss (2003), they mean to unceasingly demonstrate that nothing else could do better.

Some, like mainstream economic theorists, are clever enough to relegate this to the unspoken, and unnecessary to mention, assumptions. Also, and as clever, they limit themselves to schematizing human behavior in as limited and enclosed a way as possible, and by means of convenient proxies (prices). This does not excuse them for their betrayal of the liberal utopia from which they should be drawing. On the contrary, we shall see that behind the mainstream free-market theorization there is the very opposite of a liberal position. Order, discipline, community, and patriotism, however disguised by calling them the rule of the law, are indispensable not just to the practice but also to the very theory of free-market believers.

The Marxists, as usual, make a more complex mistake. We shall see in the course of the book plenty of this kind of "Marxist" theorization. We shall see that the Marxist mainstream shares in the same flaws as the bourgeois mainstream theory, which in turn mirrors the dominant capitalist culture. It is not upon these two approaches that we can rely. We can only turn to philosophy in general.

While, as said, I am perfectly willing to put myself in the widely conceived "Marxist" stream of thought (from which I have been expelled and excommunicated several times by orthodox and unorthodox zealots alike), I feel it imperative to point out that I have no intention to put forward an Epicurean, Feuerbachian, Marxian, or Della Volpean/Collettian point of view. I only intend to give the due credit to the things I have learned from others—whether famous or obscure—or that others have said before and better than myself. Paying respect to the materialist tradition is a duty I very much feel.

The overall purpose of this volume is that of proposing a materialistic, naturalistic, and hence necessarily atheistic approach to the observation of reality. I am simply claiming back my belonging to the material. In order to do so, a path of emancipation from the dominant, antimaterialistic and anti-individualistic culture of capitalism must be open.

This volume will hopefully accomplish this first task, leaving to next works the discussion of emancipation itself and of the details of a materialistic and naturalistic method. Here we shall uncover the true nature of capitalism. This means to both criticize the present approaches in philosophy and the social sciences and to lay bare the structure of capitalism in practice. Fortunately, these two tasks can be pursued together, for capitalism and its assessment corresponds to a single, flawed, intellectuality.

The starting point consists in spelling out the concrete versus intellectual question and finding out its consequences on the thought of economists and social philosophers. In this respect, Hegel and the criticisms of his attempts of philosophical systematization of the state by Feuerbach and Marx are perfect. I shall not conceal from the reader the complexity of this question, whose manifold consequences are dealt with progressively in each chapter. I shall also draw on what a normal social scientist would call "empirical evidence": I shall seek to show glimpses of the actual whenever I can.

Yet the argument is, and remains, theoretical. References to reality are used only to help explain a point or to offer useful glimpses into the material. In order to unfold the complication of the philosophical matter at hand, keeping the attention focused upon capitalism (in order to get to fully explain "capitalism as we know it"), the same references and examples are used throughout the book. For instance, the hybrid and undeveloped nature of capitalism is discussed by means of its most obnoxious and telling consequences: fascism and imperialism. The thorough explanation of these two will be completed with the last chapter.

I seek to offer an inversion of Marx's method in *Capital*. I shall endeavor to prove that commodities are the wrong starting point for studies of capitalism because to do so economic approaches must be used. These are the mirror of the general mentality that makes commodities seem the center of any reasoning and possible description.

We must use philosophy to describe the world and interpret it. We can use it to see reality as it is, directly, without intermediation and without trying to limit it or to prevent it from partaking of the qualities of nature, reality in general. The way to change reality itself is either by returning it to its natural freedom or by intervening on it. Both possibilities are precluded to the economistic method.

What is on offer here is, in other words, the most radical interpretation possible of Marx's Thesis XI on Feuerbach concerning philosophy's task of changing the world (Marx 1985, 123). In fact, today more than ever, unfortunately,

> The standpoint of the old materialism is civil society; the standpoint of the new is human society, or social humanity. (Marx 1985, 123)

We must fill this sentence with meaning, uncovering the emptiness of the concept of civil society.

The result of the world of capitalism as we know it can be summarized with a word that reveals at once the foolishness of the whole enterprise: moderation. The most important result of the present book is in fact the identification of this main characteristic of the general mechanics of capitalist intellectuality. The opposition to the material, the creation of a metaphysical universe in which things work themselves out without the nasty ruptures and oblivions imposed by nature is the result of an unredeemable moderation at the intellectual level.

I am not talking about actual moderation in political and economic ideas, the ideology that always wins in practice in the so-called Western democracies. I intend to refer here to patterns of philosophical thoughts marred by moderation, most aptly epitomized by Hegel's mature philosophy. This is the target of the present book.

Moderation and its cruel consequences take the form of fascism and imperialism, two typical features of capitalism as we know it. But these are not the main target, for our endeavor here is theoretical. Not even capitalism is the actual target. The aim of this book is to practice philosophy as a radical tool for human emancipation.

My favorite way to put this matter is by referring to it as "silence." Recovering a direct link to the material is a form of silence. We are stripping reality of the communication it has been endowed with by nonstrictly materialistic philosophies. Nature does not offer articulated thoughts, nor does it follow articulated patterns, whether dialectical such as in Hegel or mathematical such as in modern physics. Its silent flow and/or lack of flow are what we must seek, and we must do that silently ourselves.

If nature needed our discourses about it, it would be as poor as any human manufact. Human manufacts, being conceived for limited purposes, need endless discourses about them (technical, economic, aesthetical) to keep the boredom off and to enhance the hope that their being humanmade offers more than meets the eye. Once again, the case of computers is telling, but the same can be said about anything.

Manufactured objects follow the laws of physics—that is, a humanmade discipline that deals with a selection of the laws of the material because they have been made in order to do just so. Their interest is limited to the task of mustering physics, chemistry, or whatever other discipline has been used to make them and admire through them the greatness of the achievement.

There is nothing to admire in the material instead, and there is nothing to say about it besides the strictly necessary, except that it has defied every attempt to encapsulate it in a theory or in a theology. From the intellectual point of view, it is completely barren. While scientific attempts to study it should still be pursued, for their application proves itself useful in the world as we know it now, we should not entrust to such attempts any more than that simple task.

Maybe at this point I ought to introduce a suitable quotation from a philosopher, or a poet, to move the reader and drive him/her toward my point. But what I am proposing here is a cold-blooded philosophical argument that needs no enticement of the reader and that cannot be simplified or edulcorated. No feeling is possible vis-à-vis nature other than strictly sensual, whether we take a philosophical point of view or a scientific one. No words are needed to signify our feelings toward it.

Whenever words are uttered to signify our sentiments with respect to nature, they are meant to exorcise those very feelings and what is behind. Whenever the greatness of nature is celebrated, it is either to glorify some god or to prevent participation in nature itself by humiliating man. Our admiration for sunsets, snow, animals, or anything else cheap poets and painters celebrate and exhalt is not to do with nature but with our intellectual apprehension of it. This means making reality other than what it is: such representation gets to be part of the metaphysics in the case of capitalism, or of the dominant culture and its expressive means in all the other cases (see Pardjanadze, Micocci 2000).

Nor are we awed by the material. Whenever we find ourselves in that condition we should remember that whatever it is we are awed by (a landscape of overwhelming beauty, or a dog furiously snarling at us), it shares in the same nature and power as ourselves, and even of single parts of ourselves as such. A hand or a hair of ours are no different, and no less, nor more powerful.

Some allege that our rational faculties set us apart from the rest of nature. Some others enlarge this set of brain-situated qualities to some other "superior" animals. But it is worth meditating that if the argument can be proved that capitalism deranges and limits in a capillary way our rational and sensual faculties (admitting for the sake of discussion that the distinction between the two stands), and we are reduced to the miserable, homogeneous *Homo Oeconomicus*, then such faculties might well be a hindrance rather than an advantage in our relationship with reality. By relying on them only we might be missing a lot.

The present volume is obviously not sufficient to pass judgement on such immense matters. Its purpose is simply to point out that a mode of production like capitalism can be described as an intellectually flawed, self-enclosed, and defensive metaphysics. If an argument can be produced to prove that man is being limited in its material faculties by social constraints that are erroneous, that means at least that a limitation is actually felt at all levels. It might not be the one I propose here, but the sufferings entailed by its existence in everybody, even the staunchest supporters of the status quo, or even those who propose to enforce even more limitations, are there to witness its presence.

The results are at two levels: at the economic, political, and social level, we are deindividualized. We are, as capitalists, only in that we share in the dominant intellectuality, and such dominant intellectuality compels us to be only within it. What is claimed in this book is not completely new, therefore: many, some of whom are discussed in the pages that follow, have put forward similar arguments.

The difference with other, similar efforts is that here a general framework is put forward whereby limitation vis-à-vis the material can be proved to be a general rule of the very existence of capitalism. Capitalism not only debases man's individuality, but simply, and unlike preceding modes of production, is nothing but that debasement itself.

I do not know whether language and its words and the maieutical means of any mode of production can lead us to progress onto the path of knowledge and participation in the material. But I argue here that this is precisely what capitalism's language and intellectual maieutical devices cannot do, and that capitalism exists only in that it homogeneously enforces precisely these limiting tools on everybody.

The second level is that of man's capacity to partake of the material. The grasping of reality to intellectual purposes is in fact second to that first, inevitable condition.

The argument of this book contributes to show that man's relationship to reality must necessarily be brought about by a complete use of all man's faculties, sensual and rational (and so, also of silence and idleness). This is done by showing the damage provoked by privileging only some of these faculties and by annihilating man's individuality in intellectually shared virtues.

Sharing and participation are a pleasure we must choose rather than undergo by an intellectual fiat based on erroneous historical references decided by reasonings misguided by historically determined circumstances and that are hypostatized into eternal truths and natural endowments of man. It is time that we recover that pleasure as individuals.

CONCLUSIONS

The present volume proposes a completely new way to analyze capitalism. An image of capitalism is given that is very different from what the social sciences and social philosophies of the present day have to offer. Many of the illusions they propose are dispelled.

The phenomena that are dealt with here are well known to everybody—as well known as the theories the present volume refers to. What is new is the way to look at them. I have sought to feel free and to follow the various arguments wherever they lead without fear.

This is a radical book, therefore, in which extreme arguments are made because the arguments themselves are pursued to their extreme consequences. I have worked in perfect intellectual silence, observing the bare emptiness of the material, following only my capacity to think and to interpret the thoughts of other people (doing this last did accelerate many apprehension processes).

I believe I have been faithful to the materialist Western tradition. But had I not been, I would feel no regret.

Perhaps I do not have a world to conquer, nor does any of us, I should hope. But most certainly we have nothing to lose but our chains. That is what I have been working at. I do not want to just unlock them, which has been done other times and is no solution. I want to see them disappear for good. This is what radical and extreme means to me.

Chapter Two

The Anti-Hegelian Argument

In order to understand capitalism as a whole, defining its main features for purposes of classificatory comparison with the modes of production that preceded it, one has to necessarily start from the works of those who have set to themselves a similar task. To our purposes here, Marx is the thinker who sought to give a complete overview of capitalism, trying to identify its general categories: historical, economic, and even psychological. While other analysts have concentrated upon, say, sociology (even inventing the very subject to this purpose, with Weber and Durkheim), history, or economics, Marx in fact sought to give a "philosophical" account of what capitalism means in historical terms, with an eye to those shortcomings that might help open the way to its demise. In so doing, Marx faced, but also failed to face in some cases, all of those philosophical issues that will help us, in this and the next two chapters, to start describing capitalism by identifying its most characterizing aspects in comparison with former modes of production.

Let us start from the fact that Marx, as above hinted, was looking for those defects of the capitalist setup that might help hasten its demise. From a general, philosophical perspective, this tells us that Marx did not see capitalism as the final stage of human history but rather as a passage toward something else. This observation is the key for everything that is discussed in this chapter. What is at stake is the idea of change and therefore, also, the idea of revolution as an enforced change of mode of production. I shall endeavor to show that the orthodox Marxists have failed to grasp the fundamental mistakes in their Hegelian dialectical interpretation of Marx's thought, thus preventing change and revolution and joining forces with the capitalist apologists in separating the social and economic from the natural—that is, the material in general, the concrete.

This chapter, in other words, deals with the philosophical questions about the understanding of reality that stem from attributing to Marx's work a pivotal role. The next two will enlarge the reasoning, showing the wide momentum of the discussion pursued here. This presentation is a rethinking and recasting of Micocci (2002a, 2004a, 2004c), whose main lines are nonetheless still perfectly valid.

In order to obtain his philosophical picture of what capitalism is in human terms, in terms, that is, of the degree of fulfillment of human potentialities at the individual level as permitted by the cultural, social, and political setup, Marx had to first of all face the basic question of all such analyses: how does history move? The problem of how it moves of course also determines the direction of the movement, and whether there is a direction at all. Those were the days of Hegel's direct influence on German and European thinkers, and the so-called Young Marx had to take a position vis-à-vis the Hegelian solution to it all: dialectics, or rather, as we shall see, dialectical mysticism.

Thus the Young Marx attacked, using the ammunitions supplied by Feuerbach's critique of Hegel, the idea of dialectics. However, when he stopped being the "Young" Marx he started to write about capitalism in political economy terms, at which point his work started acquiring those apparent dialectical features that have been the overwhelmingly dominant pillar of Marxist intellectual and political activities ever since. The question at stake here, however, is not Marx's coherence. We are embarking upon a journey that leads us well beyond what Marx said or appeared to say. Our main line of inquiry is philosophy, not philosophers.

The basic question that interests us in this chapter is whether dialectical modes of thought can render the way reality as a whole (the natural, the concrete) moves, and if they do not, why that is so and what are the implications of this problem. We shall conclude that dialectical modes of thought cannot be used to describe reality as a whole, for they do not leave to it the needed freedom: the possibility of ruptures, true disappearances.

Here lies the "mystical" aspect of dialectical attitudes: they posit a world whose laws of motion are determined a priori on explicit or implicit metaphysical (religious) grounds and motives. This is most important, for it opens the door to showing the structural analogy between dialectical readings of history and the bourgeois mode of thought. Not only is the intellectual way of working out the structural features of reality mystical but it also perfectly reflects the logic of the actual political, social, and economic dealings of the economics and politics of capitalism.

The whole (reality in general)—that is, the natural—is denied a reality and replaced by an intellectual construction, what we shall call a metaphysics. To this organization correspond those material entities to which the metaphysics itself refers and on which it can exert its coercive power: the material entities that Marx had borrowed from Smith and the other political economists to describe capitalism as a historical era determined by peculiar economic structures.

Things being so, the big questions of change and revolution are answered, by Marxists and bourgeois intellectual endeavors, in the negative. Change and revolution are denied their very determining feature—that of enforcing ruptures. The world is transformed into the paradoxical place that we know so well, inspired by cozy thoughts of harmonic relationships, and therefore condemned to the use of violence and proselytism when a change is perceived as needed, wanted, or simply desired, by somebody or even by the majority. What is recognized as change, and has cost so dearly in human terms, is not change but a mild form of minor evolution (for the better or the worse), a variation on well-rehearsed themes.

HYPOSTATIZATION: THE LOGICAL ARGUMENT

The convenient point from which to start our story is Hegel and the reactions to his system. Rivers of ink have been spilled on this topic, but a systematic account of the debate would be out of place here. We shall open by saying a few words about Feuerbach's "sensualistic" argument, leaving the complete hypostatization critique to Marx and his followers.

In his work Feuerbach had touched on important points that remain a matter of contention to these days. The argument he initiated goes well beyond Hegel and Marx, constituting the starting point and the core of materialism and naturalism.

The central question, in a nutshell, is the sharp tension in between individuality, senses, society, and the philosophies that seek to appraise this very tension in conciliatory terms. There is an undeniable, strong, historically persistent kind of unhappiness in man that seems to depend on the limits set by social life to individual fulfillment. Individual happiness and society seem to constitute two opposite, irreconcilable poles of human history. No philosophy ever solved this problem, but some, we shall see, found its origins in a failure to grasp, appreciate, and assess the concrete, the material.

The modern beginning of this kind of argument is to be found in Feuerbach's hypostatization argument against Hegel's dialectics. This will be discussed in the formulation that Della Volpe drew from Marx (summarized in Micocci 2002a) further on. I shall limit myself here to a few introductory quotations from Feuerbach's last work, to prove the continuity of his thought and the importance of individuality and sensualism within it.

In *Spiritualismo e Materialismo*, Feuerbach asserts that

> the Germans have, up to now and also just for that reason—also not for this rea-
> son alone, as, by the way, is obvious—brought it only to an idealistic freedom,
> because they grasp freedom only in opposition to the quest for happiness, if they
> equally troubled themselves, but in the wrong place and too late, to compensate
> for this opposition. Only that freedom grounded on the quest for happiness, of
> course not just for some but also for all, is a popular and thus irresistible politi-
> cal power. (1993, 68; translation from the German, 1972, by Mark Mascal)

In fact,

> sensualism and individualism are in fact one and the same thing. (101, trans.
> mine) Reason or philosophy isolated from meaning, which denies the truth of
> the senses, not only knows nothing about individuality, but also hates it, as Kant-
> ian, Fichtian, and Hegelian philosophy proves deadly as its natural opponent.
> (101, trans. Mark Mascal)

But attention, general happiness, or sensually based individuality depend
upon a basic principle.

> I am not at all man in a particular form, I am only man as this absolutely defined
> man; being man and being a particular individual is simply indistinguishable in
> me. (101, trans. Mark Mascal)

In other words,

> life, feeling, thought is something absolutely original . . . , inimitable, irreplace-
> able, inalienable—in truth the Absolute—only self-recognizable, but not mysti-
> fied or travestized—of the speculative philosophers and theologians. (127, trans.
> Mark Mascal)

We are now ready to face the diatribe in philosophy and the social sciences
started by Marx about Hegel, in the form of the systematization given to it by
Della Volpe and Colletti.[1]

It is well worth starting our discussion with the so-called Young Marx,
from the *Theses on Feuerbach*. In Thesis VI Marx states that

> Feuerbach resolves the religious essence into the human essence. But the human
> essence is no abstraction inherent in each single individual . . . it is the ensem-
> ble of social relations. (1985, 122)

Thus Feuerbach, continues Marx, is compelled to "abstract from the historical process" presupposing an "abstract, isolated human individual" (1985,

122). Essence is not a "dumb generality which naturally unites the many individuals" (1985, 122).

Here we can place the beginning of that dichotomy in Marx of which so much has been unfortunately made. On the one hand Marx in fact tells us that (Thesis VIII) "social life is essentially practical" so that mysticism is easily dispelled by the "comprehension" of "human practice" (1985, 122). On the other, however, Marx and Engels tell us, very much reducing the import and scope of the above, that "the celebrated unity of man with nature has always existed in industry and has existed in various forms in every epoch" (1985, 62–63).

What must we believe, the general philosophical discourse that leads to Thesis XI[2] ("human practice" as an infinite potential), or the narrow, "Marxist-Leninist" idea that man's essence and potentiality are resolved in his industry and labor? Does the latter follow from the former, like the quoted passage from the German ideology seems to point to, and like Marxist theory and Marxist practice have been insisting upon for so long?

The solution to these questions, if not for Marx, at least for philosophy in general, can be found by following Marx's anti-Hegelian suggestion to its logical consequences, which we shall do from now on while progressing from Della Volpe's Marx to Della Volpe himself to Colletti, and to the conclusions I myself have reached in *Anti-Hegelian Reading of Economic Theory* (2002a).[3] Our main task is to follow Feuerbach and Marx through their critique of the main obstacle to a truly materialistic philosophy: Hegelian dialectics.

Della Volpe starts his discourse from Kant, the true, however incomplete and inadequate, great "returner" to the importance of the senses in the understanding of reality. Kant's attempt, however, amounts to a "Leibnizian-Kantian formula" (1980, 13–14) of very limited import. Hegel did not take heed of this aspect, and went on, as Feuerbach well understood, to assign to dialectics two tasks: that of explaining the transition from the particular to the universal and that of explaining the transition from the thought (universality) of thinghood to the thought of particular things (particularity). Initially, the particular (the discrete, as Della Volpe is wont to describe it) is reduced to the universal as such—that is, the indeterminate.

Della Volpe uncovers a Platonic aspect in Hegel, but weaker than Plato. In this he follows and develops both Feuerbach and Marx:

> Now the discovery by Marx of dialectical "mystification" as the real "secret" of Hegel is of the same order as Aristotle's discovery of the illegitimacy of Plato's diairesis. Hegel's hypostatization—the surreptitious restoration of the empirical world subsequent to its philosophical dissolution—corresponds in substance to Plato's postulation of the (empirical) "species" or "definendium." (1980, 122–123)

In sum, Hegel's universal is not empty, like Feuerbach remarked, but "vitiated," like Marx proposed. The central question then is the role of hypostatization. This, attempting to give substance to the abstract, produces a metaphysics, the "erroneous realism, the (absolute) realism of metaphysicians and apriorists" (1980, 113). Now we have a philosophical problem, a logical mistake. We might simply lay it aside and go on without caring, just saying "If so, Hegel was wrong in general, let us forget about Hegel." Let us see, instead, where this mistake leads Hegel, for Hegel's mistaken reasoning reflected and distilled the common wisdom of his times. This, we shall see, is not all, and is not the most worrying aspect either. In pursuing this line of reasoning, we are compelled to leave Della Volpe behind.

The Idea, to keep to our exemplary target Hegel, is thus translated into the particular. The case of the connection family–civil society–state, like Colletti (1969b) famously explains, is emblematic of the absurd results of Hegelian, mystical dialectics. In Hegel, in fact, the state decomposes itself into family and society, the two ideal spheres of its own concept.

> The Idea thus performs changes on itself: the finite, the object, becomes the ideal, Feuerbach's logical mysticism and yet much more than Feuerbach ever found in it. (Micocci 2002a, 46)

"Empirical reality," Della Volpe (1980) tells us, "is accepted as it is" and even "declared to be rational," for "the empirical fact in its empirical existence has a meaning other than itself" (115, from Marx): it is allegorical.

Already Della Volpe (1997) was clear about this. Let us see what he has to say (in IV, I, *Chiarimenti, Rousseau and Marx*).

> The fault of the (metaphysical) method that leads to such results is—just like the above said Marx insisted—that it *smuggles what it is as the essence of the state*: that is, the metaphysical idealization of real things—far from being able to absolutely transcend them as it intends—undergoes them acritically and therefore ends up proposing as ideal and normative a rough and undigested empirics. (60, emphasis in the original. Translation mine)

Before moving on with the reasoning, it is well worth noticing in the first place that this is not exactly a critique of Hegel on Feuerbachian-Marxian bases, which would require a more detailed and sophisticated analysis of Hegel's work. What Della Volpe, and Marx himself, are doing is observing how the—roughly speaking—logical mistake underlying Hegel's attitude to politics (and history, and the economic, and what we should call in our days the sociological) leads him to logically absurd results. These are, and this is fundamental, not immediately visible unless you question the logic rather than the politics, economics, and sociology themselves.

The second and related observation concerns the last quotation itself. The idealization of real things (*"La idealizzazione delle cose reali"*), which should absolutely transcend it (*"trascendere assolutamente"*), undergoes the real instead, proposing rough, half-baked empirical facts as ideal. This is the "mystical" in its most vulgar form.

The mystical aspect is not solely in the logical apparatus: it is in the intentions and in the deeds themselves (the results of the analysis). Marx greatly insisted on this in his *Critique of Hegel's Philosophy of Right* (1970), and in fact the import and momentum of this aspect are enormous. In practice they are fundamental to capitalism as an intellectual era, a culture. But let us not anticipate.

Closely following in the tracks of the Marx of the 1843–1859 period, Della Volpe moves on to attack political economy. This is an inevitable, immediate next step to what has been argued so far. If political philosophy produces metaphysical idealizations of real things, we must turn to what since Marx's times has been replacing it in many practical tasks, the "queen of the social sciences" of capitalist times.[4]

The hypostatization critique comes to acquire a basic importance. Della Volpe quotes Marx in the *Critique of Hegel's Philosophy of Right* and his noticing that "the assignment of the material to the state is mediated by circumstances." Such "mediations" are actual, but to Hegel they are only appearances, for the actual mediations happen at the level of the Idea: the "mystery of speculation."

> The Idea (the predicate) is made the subject (substantified or hypostatized) and the actual relationship of family and civil society to the state is conceived as its internal imaginary activity. (Della Volpe 1978, 163)

Hegel's concept of state has been transcended into the generic state. The ideal and the actual are conflated together. The abstract idea of state disappears, and so do the actual states of empirical reality. A metaphysical construction replaces them both at the theoretical and practical (economic, social, and political) level. This pseudoideal state is the "Platonic" Idea, which the actual takes after.

In the *Poverty of Philosophy* and the *Contribution to a Critique of Political Economy*, Marx makes the case for showing that Proudhon and political economy in general are based on eternal and generic ideas, which are the result of a process of hypostatization. This is a famous Marx quotation, whose full import has been understood in all its implications only by Della Volpe, from whose work I quote.

> Economists express the relations of bourgeois production, the division of labor, credit, money, etc., as fixed, immutable, eternal categories . . . what they do not explain is how these relationships themselves are produced . . . the moment we cease to pursue the historical movement of production relations . . . the

moment we want to see in these categories no more than ideas . . . independent
of real relations [hence a priori, notices Della Volpe], we are forced to attribute
the origins of this thought to the movement of pure reason. (Della Volpe, 1978,
179, from Marx's *The Poverty of Philosophy*)

Marx's aim, and Della Volpe's, was to extend the criticism of Proudhon to
political economy/economics in general, in order to show the importance of
the hypostatization question for economic theorizations, and bring the "historical" back into the realm of political economy.

The supposed "profundity" of economists lies in this forgetting [the specificity],
when they set out to prove the eternity and harmoniousness of the existing social relations . . . they explain capital as a general, eternal, natural relation.
. . . They tend, in short, to "confuse and eliminate all historical differences," the
specific ones, when they formulate their specific human laws. Thus [J. S. Mill,
for example] presents production as encased in eternal laws independent from
history, at which opportunity bourgeois relations (of production) are then quietly
smuggled in as the inviolable natural laws on which society in the abstract, in
general, is founded. So, they fall continuously into tautologies. (Della Volpe,
1978, 187 and 188, from Marx's *Grundrisse*)

With his characteristic—and typically Italian—verbose way of expressing
himself, Della Volpe called this continuous mediation between the concrete
and the Idea "fraudulent undigested non-mediated concrete quality." Bourgeois social sciences[5] do not have a historical consciousness of their concrete
and given subject, for they cannot distinguish when it begins in thought and
when it begins in reality. Della Volpe had in mind here a whole strategy of replacing Hegelian dialectics, which was then, just like it is now, the gospel behind Marxist theorization, with "a specific logic of a specific object," a
principle-of-non-contradiction-abiding method based on a "general formula
of the materialistic critique of (a priori) pure reason" (1980, 141).[6]

Della Volpe's method[7] is flawed. It ends up reproducing a political economy based on an approximate idea of the discrete/punctual that allows Della
Volpe to keep in place, in his supposedly renewed social science, the empirical evidence of the old. The main fault of Della Volpe's proposal is that his
political economy/materialist science is based on the unproved idea that the
concrete is discrete in the same imprecise sense that is typical of mainstream
social sciences. His dyadic logic replaces, without revolutionizing, the old
Hegelian legacy, placing it within a "proper" (but flawed) historical frame.
The social man of mainstream economics is fully recuperated to a hypostatized, historically circumscribed kind of environment in which change does
not imply ruptures.

Yet, Della Volpe (1978, 1997/1957) himself quotes that "useful appendix" to *The Poverty of Philosophy* constituted by Marx's letter to Annenkov (December 28, 1846), which should have opened his eyes as to the momentum of the reasoning pursued:

> Indeed [Proudhon] does what all good bourgeois do. They all tell you that in principle, that is, considered as abstract ideas, competition, monopoly, etc., are the only basis of life, but that in practice they leave much to be desired. They all want competition without the lethal effects of competition. They all want the impossible, namely, the conditions of bourgeois existence without the necessary consequences of those conditions. None of them understands that the bourgeois form of production is historical and transitory, just as the feudal form was. This mistake arises from the fact that the bourgeois man is to them the only possible basis of every society; thus they cannot imagine a society in which men have ceased to be bourgeois. M. Proudhon is necessarily doctrinaire. (Marx, Engels 1975, 666)

The bourgeois, like the economists (classical and mainstream, as proved by Della Volpe himself in 1967, 1980), tend to see a discrepancy between their "abstract" theories (this roughly means, in mainstream parlance, theoretical) and reality. The origins of such discrepancy, when seen in this way, can only be attributed to the faulty functioning of the "practical," its inherent (Hegelian, Christian, and Platonic) imperfection. This to them can and must be improved: the "practical" must tend to the ideal, the "abstract" ideas of economics. Let me emphasize how the distinction of economists/economic ideas is blurred here: this is easy to understand, by virtue of the "eternity" of economic concepts.

The problem is not simply that economics is ahistorical, which we all know (it is sufficient to open a textbook of economic theory to come across open statements and even theoretical and empirical demonstrations of why this is so). The problem is (and this is only the first stage of a more momentous issue) that economics and the social sciences in general are a hopeless confusion of levels: they hypostatize, confusing the concrete with the abstract, and this confusion creates something in between, a metaphysics that takes over the field, precluding the sight of the two original extremes, the abstract and the material themselves. This is the mystical aspect, which predisposes political economists to posit the eternity and/or naturality of the socioeconomic relations of the capitalist era. In fact, ideas that seem to partake of both an empirical and a theoretical meaning are easily bound to be given an eternal status.

Hegel's idea of state is a most versatile kind of example. It shows that the flawed logical process is not confined to economics, but it is a constituent part of actual economic relationships. To see this we must turn to Colletti, who continues Della Volpe's and Marx's reasoning, sticking to their original logical line.

Colletti (1973, 1975) is explicit in saying that Hegel belongs to the Platonic-Christian tradition, for which determinate objects do not exist and are replaced by the Idea ("the logic inclusion of opposites"). Colletti asserts that this problem is not only a bourgeois one but is also, unfortunately, typical of orthodox Marxist theory.[8] Yet there is much more. Let us start from a well-known summarizing quotation:

> The hypostatization of the Universal, its substantification or reification, does not concern only (or even primarily) Hegel's logic; it concerns reality itself. In short, what the hypostasis of Hegel's Notion refers back to is the hypostasis of capital and the state. (1973, 198)

This perfectly dovetails with what was above announced, the mystical (hypostatized) aspect being a constituent part of actual economic relationships.

The problem is again constituted by dialectics. Colletti (1975) famously points out how even Marxists failed to grasp the difference between real opposition and dialectical contradiction. The former is an opposition without contradiction, compatible with the general principles of formal logic. The latter instead generates a dialectical opposition.

Colletti limits himself to strictly technical considerations on these two poles of the basic question of change (and of revolution). This attracted to him the reaction of other philosophers and of some economists, with the inconclusive debate that followed.[9] Had he looked at the thing with more general, materialistic eyes, he would have seen the immediate connection with the idea of change and revolution, which I shall explain in due course.

In mainstream Marxism (from Plekhanov to Lukács to Mao), Colletti continues,

> Real opposition has been either overlooked, or simply assimilated to dialectical contradiction i.e., described as the existence of two negations within one unity. This goes back to Platonic dialectics, and to the Platonic roots of Hegelian dialectics, which posits that individual ideas are abstractions, whose value is only in their mutual dialectical relationships. Dialectical relationships are mutually inclusive. On the contrary, real opposition is best described as a relation of repugnance (*Realrepugnanz*), that is of mutual exclusion. This last was clearly defined in Marx's mind and used against Hegel in *Critique of Hegel's Philosophy of Right* (1970). (Micocci 2002a, 76)

There are in nature opposing forces (attraction and repulsion for instance) that are real oppositions and confirm the principle of noncontradiction.

To Colletti, dialectical attitudes are a "philosophical romance," "the old metaphysical commonplace" still haunting the workers' movement. What Marxists were describing as contradictions were in fact real oppositions, the waged labor/capital relationship being the most obvious case in point. Interestingly, Colletti limits himself to consider this without seeing that, if this is so, then the whole revolutionary strategy of the communist movements should be rethought. In this work Colletti turns instead, again, to technicalities: that is, the internal coherence of the old versus the mature Marx, well visible in its consequence from the following quotation, whose momentum escaped Colletti himself.

The process of hypostatization, the substantification of the abstract, the inversion of subject and predicate, far from being in Marx's eyes modes of Hegel's logic that were defective in reflecting reality, were in fact processes that he located (or thought he located—the difference is unimportant for the moment) in the structure and mode of functioning of capitalist society itself. (1975, 20)[10]

The whole apparatus of capitalist relations and of the material objects involved in such relations "appear to be upside down"; Hegelian mystical mechanisms are present, only turned upside down. Colletti fails to see the potential of his own argument and limits himself to noticing (I guess that must have been very shocking news for him) that there is an "aporia that marks the history" of the two possible Marxist interpretations of capitalism entailed by the reasoning above. Colletti actually speaks of "two Marxes." The first is the Young Marx, Della Volpe's critic of political economy. The second is the Marx that says that it is not political economy that is upside down, but capitalist reality itself. This last Marx is closer to orthodox Marxism, for in it the contradictions of capitalism (take the mentioned wage labor versus capital one) are not real oppositions but dialectical contradictions.

Colletti is aware, however, that this is not yet orthodox dialectical materialism. For this second Marx reality is "stood on its head," to use Marx's own words, and orthodox dialectical materialism cannot accept that.[11] In fact we have two Marxisms: an anti-Hegelian one which implies the idea of rupture, real opposition—that is, of change as revolution in which something (or everything) is unredeemably lost—and a dialectical Marxism that sees change as a dialectical process. These are two incompatible visions of the world. More precisely, they are two incompatible visions of the material: one is atheistic and materialistic in the strict sense, and the other is a form of mysticism on which a materialistic label has been pasted.

Let us deal with the full meaning of what Colletti had to unwillingly admit and whose consequences he did not fully grasp. The political economy focus in fact helps Colletti elude the enormous problems he had dug up by facing the real opposition/dialectical contradiction question and seeing further than Della Volpe. All he needs in fact is to get his reasoning back to the realm of political economy in the narrow Marxist and non-Marxist senses. Not by chance he goes on rediscovering Gramsci. Not by chance he rests contented with discovering the "two Marxes" aporia, which helps bring this momentous critique home to respectable Gramscism.

Colletti is not alone in criticizing Hegel and Marx from a political economy point of view. Von Mises, in his magnum opus (1949), uses similar arguments, anticipating the anti-Marxist frenzy that will characterize Colletti's mature years:

> There was Hegel. He was a profound thinker . . . but he was laboring under the delusion that Geist revealed itself through his words. There was nothing in the Universe hidden to Hegel. (72)
>   But Marx was better informed about Geist's plans. (74)

In fact, Marx's ". . . is a purely mystical doctrine. The only proof given in its support is the recourse to Hegelian dialectics" (80).

Von Mises is remarkably close to both Gramscist Marxism and Colletti's argument when he says,

> A man perfectly content with the state of his affairs will have no incentives to change things. . . . He would not act. (13)
>   Human action is necessarily always rational. (18)

With the privilege of hindsight we can see that Von Mises (like many others, see Micocci 2002a) was right: "Statolatry owes much to the doctrines of Hegel" (828).

In order to fully grasp the momentum of what is being discussed, we should bear in mind the atrocious images that present-day inverted statolatry of the neoliberal kind produces in terms of human losses caused by wars, economic measures, and political calculations alike.[12]

The agents of the dialectical Marxists and of Von Mises have much in common: their ways part when the mystical Hegelian attitude of the Marxist man pushes him to go about his business as if the *Geist* had in its intentions the evolution of capitalism into socialism. But (we shall come back to this in detail in chapter 3), Von Mises and the Austrian political economists in general had no such illusions. Happiness is not attainable, and all we can do is keep working at our satisfaction in the market, the only way to distribute what wealth is available without messy and violent strategies leading to socialist systems full of "frictions" in their distribution mechanisms.

Colletti moved to this sort of position himself,[13] and it certainly is a possible way to solve the double problem of a mystical bias to be eliminated and a Marxist strategy caught in a tragic impasse: keep the dialectics (the mystic) and turn the world upright by going beyond capitalist social and economic relations by dialectical means, or face the unknown by rejecting the dialectics and the mystic, Platonic-Christian kind of flawed logic.

Let us conclude this section by summing up. If philosophy, with Marx's Thesis XI, must change reality, we must face the real opposition-dialectical contradiction question. This is all the more compelling because dialectical modes of thought have brought about evil results in practice and have led to a true impasse, and entailed crisis, in Marxist theorization.

The question is simple: if we must follow the rules of formal logic, and if we want to recognize all natural phenomena comprising second-order ones such as social and economic phenomena, we must admit of real oppositions. Admitting of their existence gives us a powerful tool to consider all possibilities: from change to rupture and disappearance, or, to put it more precisely, rupture-cum-disappearance. Accepting this, we do not call ourselves out of the Marxist frame. We are simply building upon the so-called Young Marx's criticism of Hegel's philosophical vision and of his theory of the state. Rather, we have made a powerful move toward ridding Marxism, and more in general philosophy and political economy, of one of the main causes of mystical attitudes. This is the first step toward a direct, unmediated apprehension of the concrete, which escaped Della Volpe when he proposed his dyadic dialectics and thereby recuperated bourgeois statistics.[14] But there is much more to it: we can see capitalism the way it actually is.

A WIDER PHILOSOPHICAL FRAMEWORK

Colletti and Della Volpe have not been the only ones to produce a critique of the paradoxical Hegelianism of Marxist theory. John Rosenthal (1998, 1999, 2001) also concentrated on Hegelian dialectics, and so did Mohun (2003), although on a much narrower scale and with scarce results.

Let us start from dwelling some more upon the problem of hypostatization and its importance and consequences. We shall then be able to cast Rosenthal's work, as well as its dialectical opposite by Chris Arthur, in the proper frame. Then we shall see how an anti-Hegelian argument fits in with a materialist, conflictive strand of Western philosophy. Finally, we shall see how the man-society conflict bears upon the task of defining capitalism as a whole.

The best way to start is by a somewhat lengthy quotation from "Why Dialectics? Why Now?" by the well-known Marxist scholar Ollman, in the special issue on dialectics of *Science and Society* volume 62, number 3, 1998.

So why dialectics? Because that's the only sensible way to study a world composed of mutually dependent processes in constant evolution, and also to interpret Marx, who is our leading investigator into this world. Dialectics is necessary just to see capitalism, given its vastness and complexity, and Marxism to help understand it. . . . Capitalism is completely and always dialectical, so that Marxism will always be necessary to make sense of it and dialectics to make correct sense of Marxism. (342)

Not only Ollman asserts things in a dogmatic way ("capitalism is completely and always dialectical"). He just straightforwardly hypostatizes, exactly like those classical political economists criticized by Marx for transforming the categories of their time into eternal objects.

Needless to say, the transformation happens in "the mystery of speculation." "Dialectics is necessary to see capitalism" is in itself a tautology: the world is "composed of mutually dependent processes in constant evolution." This is not another hypostatization of capitalist categories (the harmonious evolution of events in a mathematically continuous world so dear to the neoclassical economists), but an unexplained and undemonstrated restatement of a typically vulgar Hegelian world. If the world is like this, we certainly need dialectics to explain it, and even to change it, because capitalism, like anything else, must necessarily be dialectical. But things are not this way, unless we dream the same harmonious nightmares as the apologists of capitalism.

Despite fully believing that in Hegel's dialectics there is the schematic triad thesis-antithesis-synthesis, Sekine ("The Dialectics of Capital: A Unoist Interpretation," *Science and Society*, same issue) gets close to a more realistic vision of the use of dialectics. To him, the final point/object of dialectics is not the Absolute like in Hegel, nor nature like in Engels, but capital. Capital, unlike nature, can tell its own story.

The dialectics of capital too consists of the three doctrines of circulation, production and distribution. (442)

To Sekine a sector of the whole capitalist setup works (however mechanical Sekine's way to intend Hegelian dialectics is) in a dialectical way. This is relevant, in that Sekine is clear: it is not nature, nor is it the Absolute. Capital belongs to neither of these categories and, being in between nature and the Absolute (the material and the abstract), it is amenable to a dialectical treatment.

One can of course argue that applying dialectics to capital without general philosophical explanations might well hide some kind of ahistorical, hypostatizing reasoning. The main point, however, is the achievement of separating nature and the Absolute from an exclusive relationship to dialectics. To show the value of this achievement, it is sufficient to look at a former issue of the same journal in which Stanley (1997/1998) discusses Marx's critique of Hegel's philosophy of nature. To Stanley, Marx was mainly concerned with the exaggerated power of the Idea in it, for he is perfectly dialectical in his view of nature. Subject and object have a dialectical relationship. Man and nature are, in their connection, the dialectical unity of subject and object.

With Stanley, we have witnessed the mystical drift in action. This has brought us to the dangerous similarities, which we shall see later on, between dialectical views of Marxism and socialist and fascist ideologies. To give the due credit to *Science and Society*, however, I should mention that it published in 1999 an interesting anti-Hegelian paper by John Rosenthal. But we have enough material to continue our discussion of the role of hypostatizations.

A last evidence, this time of the difficulty to proceed onto the anti-Hegelian path, is Pietranera (1966). In the 1960s in Italy Pietranera was considered one of the most distinguished followers of Della Volpe. Himself an economist, he frankly admits to have been, before knowing Della Volpe, under the spell of Croce's Idealism. In fact his work presents all the typical features of an idealistic mentality. Not a single anti-Hegelian consequence is drawn in the whole book. Yet, I must credit him for the coinage of the term *metafisica dell'economia* (the metaphysics of economics). Although the idea behind his term is completely different from mine, the term is his.

What conclusions can we draw from the evidence presented? The dialectical attitude in philosophy not only prevents the vision of nondialectical relationships, or compels its users to mistake nondialectical relationships for dialectical ones (the wage labor versus capital relationship for instance), not only derives, even for Marxist thinkers, from apodyptic statements and undemonstrated general principles, but also, the very statement of these principles and descriptions is intimately bound with hypostatizations. These do not simply follow from dialectical attitudes: dialectical attitudes need hypostatizations to be expressed.

The most important general consequence is that the difference between the categories of reality is blurred. In the most extreme cases, like in Ollman, we are just told that "everything is dialectical." In less extreme cases, like Sekine, dialectics is applied to certain specific aspects of social life. In both cases we face the same problem: we do not and cannot know whether our dialectical, partial landscape belongs to a general dialectical whole. Therefore we cannot see the differences between our variables and the various items that form our picture. We are perfectly impotent to transfer an internal, micro reasoning to the general picture for lack of elements. It goes without saying that this is no problem for Sekine because, despite his protestations about Engels and Hegel, he fully subscribes to the orthodox view that dialectics explains everything.

This last is not a philosophical or scientific statement. In fact, it is rather a statement of purpose: we want dialectics not because reality as a whole (not by chance willingly reduced to Ollman's infantile "the world") can be proved to be dialectical, but because we want our action to be dialectical. The Marxists, just like their free-market counterparts, want their interventions on reality to leave everything in place. Change to them is an interaction of "mutually dependent processes," a continuous weaving of nonresolutive relations that move toward an eventual, almost predetermined, nonoutcome. Capitalist relations are the continuously evolving epitomization of the eternal features of "the world." This is a harmonious view that must be brought to completion, whether it is free market or socialism.

In these conditions, change and revolution as well as, say, innovation à la Schumpeter, can be freely used because they are empty rhetoric, a vast exaggeration. They are powerful shadows used to cover for logically wanting visions of the world. They also serve to lure the practitioner, or the hypocrite who cannot admit of a conservative worldview. John Rosenthal (1998) does not fall in this trap: before analyzing the dialectical features of one peculiar, and special, aspect of capitalism, he takes care to prove that Hegel's dialectics is "quackery."

Rosenthal's approach in fact is based on the demonstration that dialectics is

1. a nonmethod
2. pure mysticism, metaphysics in the same sense as I have put forward here and in *Anti-Hegelian Reading* (2002a).

He then moves on to prove that Marxism's use of dialectics has been a methodological disaster. Then he acknowledges that many of the works of the "mature" Marx seem to present dialectical features. Finally, this is inevitable in that the functioning of some of the fundamental categories of the capitalist social and economic setup present dialectical characteristics: they are mysticism at work. The whole is, therefore, but a necessity due to a question of analogy.

Rosenthal's attack on the absurdity of Hegel's logic takes place in the central part of the book (chapters 8 and 9), after having introduced and criticized "historicist" readings of Marx. His argument has various aspects in common with Colletti's own, but it is pursued independently from him. Like Colletti, Rosenthal starts from the question of the betrayal of the principle of noncontradiction that is apparent in Hegel's Logic.

The Hegelian (or "dialectical") logical canon is, then, exactly the reverse of the customary (or "analytical") one . . . according to the latter a discourse succeeds in grasping its object only to the degree that it avoids contradiction (. . . a necessary condition, though not a sufficient one), according to the former a discourse grasps its object only by precisely exposing the object's essential contradictoriness: hence by itself *pronouncing contradictions* [then goes on] to "sublate" (aufheben) this opposition (or first "negation") in some more concrete determination of which the opposites are now revealed to be "moments" or "aspects." (1998, 95; emphasis in the original for all quotations from Rosenthal here)

This last is the truth of the opposites. This iterative process goes on until the totality is reached, where we have everything, nothing, and each thing is also something else.

The relationship between the particular and the general "*depends upon* his annexing to the logical the theological significations of *body* and *soul*" (1998, 110). Concept and reality in Hegel correspond only in God.

The open secret of Hegel's entire systematic construction is a Christian theological one. (1998, 110)

The supposed "reality" of contradiction, which so many Marxists have taken to be the "rational kernel" of their "dialectical method," is in the original Hegelian context just another instance of precisely the same genre of nonsense. (1998, 113)

As a consequence,

dialectical contradiction is entirely of a piece with Hegel's idealism. (1998, 123) The expression "dialectical materialism" is an oxymoron. (1998)

The question is that Hegel

makes no distinction between the intension of a term or "determination" and its extension. (1998, 125)

This conflation is the "paralogical hinge around which [Hegel's] exposition in general moves. (1998, 127)

Now we can go back to Rosenthal's "Preface" and discover the "paradox and mystery" of the Marx-Hegel relation. Marx is able to "make a rational scientific application precisely of Hegel's 'mysticism'" (1998, X) because money is, "with respect to commodities, just such an 'existent universal' as the Christ is supposed to be with respect to the Christians" (1998). Marx coquetted with a "Hegelian mode of expression" in his analysis of the value-form not out of "methodological choice or predisposition" (1998, 134) but because of the objective character of economic value: "the *Wertgegenständlichkeit* of commodities" (1998).

On page 58 Rosenthal is clear that "as Marx repeatedly emphasized, the very functioning of a generalized exchange economy depends upon abstractions which are real."

This is particularly realistic and feasible, despite the appearances, because the "practical interdependence of the participants in the exchange system and their personal indifference to one another gain expression in the form of 'money'" (1998, 67). Inevitably, Rosenthal converges to the point Della Volpe and Colletti proposed, and I developed in *Anti-Hegelian Reading* (2002a).

> Herein lies the supposed substance of Marx's mature critique of the political economists: namely, that the latter managed theoretically to "naturalize" and hence "eternalize" capitalist production by confusing social form and the material bearer upon which qua private property that form gets impressed. (1998, 85)

It is easy to see that in this framework money is "nothing other than a 'real universal'" (1998, 139), an "ideality realized in material shape" (1998, 85). In fact,

> between the Hegelian "Idea" and the real form of economic value, viz. money, there is an unmistakable isomorphism. The value phenomena . . . happen to exhibit just that structure which Hegel treats as constitutive of objectivity as such. This is a remarkable "accident"—and nothing more than that. (1998, 85)

Here Rosenthal's path parts remarkably from my own. More precisely, he interrupts his analysis and fails to see those logical, general consequences which I have outlined already (Micocci 2002a) and which I shall further develop here.

We can leave aside for the moment the thorough examination of Rosenthal's treatment of money, for we shall be taking it back in due course, and dwell upon the remarkable conclusion he draws after displaying an anti-Hegelian analysis that is in several ways parallel, although from a narrower perspective, to the one I put forward here. Let us start from the reaction that his book elicited from the Marxist milieu.

The exchange between him and Tony Smith that took place in *Historical Materialism* (1999)[15] is most instructive. Rosenthal destroys Smith's attempt to conjugate a Hegelian counterargument with some reproaches and even threats. Smith's counterargument, a "charitable" reading of Hegel, is uncovered (Rosenthal 2001) and shown for what it is: simply inaccurate. In destroying Smith, Rosenthal explicitly states that "as the foregoing reconstruction will have made clear, Hegelian logic is metaphysics" (2001, 136).

This would be no news to Hegel: "Logic therefore coincides with Metaphysics, the science of things set and held in thought—though accredited able to express the essential reality of things" (Hegel 1987, 136).

I cannot say exactly why Rosenthal stops his analysis suddenly, despite some personal correspondence I kept with him. Perhaps the most important reason, which I pointed out to him, lies in his paying not enough attention to Colletti's work and its momentous consequences.

The hypothesis we are going to explore from now on is that the value-form performs its perfectly Hegelian role because the whole of capitalism is analogous to the Hegelian world of flawed relationships that are a priori defined as sharing features with the godly attributes of the universe. The most important consequence of Colletti's reasoning is in fact precisely this: capitalist reality as a whole presents the features of a Hegelian kind of environment.[16] Hence dialectics does apply to capitalist economic, social, and political intercourses.

The material entities, therefore, have importance in their material essence only in that such material existence allows their use to capitalist purposes. And this capitalist use is dependent upon a purely intellectual kind of operation, the deprivation of the material essence from things, its transcendence into universals, the confusion of the general and the particular, the hypostatization that leads to the mystical attitude of being able to consider material and purely intellectual objects alike: the creation of a metaphysics. It is the metaphysics that actually performs the various operations of the capitalist world.[17]

Material entities are central to capitalism only if and when they lose their material character. They must in fact join the metaphysics, the intellectual dance that (we shall develop all this in the rest of this book) leads to the massification and homogenization of the individual.

Let us for the moment concentrate upon the term intellectual, adding some features to what was stated in chapter 1: "The Material: that is, Nature." By this term I shall mean from now on whatever intellectual activity (from syllogisms to wandering thoughts) is performed along the "Hegelian" logical lines delineated so far: that is, those intellectual activities that connect objects and feelings only after having transcended them into participants in this metaphysical game in which the concrete qualities of things do not count other than by contributing to bestowing a name and specific behavioral properties to the objects themselves. Also, and very importantly, such transcended entities with a predetermined set of behavioral characteristics can and often must interact with each other and even have "transitions" going on between (and within!) them that dialectically involve their essence. That is, they are not allowed a break, a rupture, and even less a straightforward disappearance. They can only be, if at all, transmuted.[18]

All this can be expressed, to stay with the jargon of our Hegel-driven discussion, by saying that the mediations (for the functioning of the system is based on nothing else) happen at the level of the Idea. The Idea unfolds itself, also performing changes on itself. No role for man, let alone man's will, is envisaged. That means no role for individuals. Man in the sense of humankind in general is present, but his role is the same as that of the rest of the material, and he exists only *qua* humankind. The question to ask is then: how can such a dehumanizing and dehumanized system as capitalism survive? How can individuals take it?

Here we should not be deceived by the term "mystical" we have been using. The whole, one might in fact superficially say, exists as long as it is mystical. Take the mysticism away, and it falls. But the mysticism is not in the system. As it should be clear by now, the mysticism is the logic of it and constitutes the system itself. It is not something you can eliminate: it will go together with the whole intellectual setup.

There are two things left for this section to do. The first is to actually cast the picture drawn so far into a more general philosophical framework, which I shall call the materialistic conflictive one. The second is to briefly discuss one telling instance of the consequences produced by failing to see the intellectual nature of Hegelian logic: Chris Arthur's version of Hegelian-Marxist dialectics. Let us start from the second.

Arthur is one of the most extreme representatives of an intellectually heterogeneous new tendency of the Marxist establishment, which is variously referred to as "New Hegelian Marxism," "New Dialectics," and "Systematic Dialectics." These thinkers intend to focus "on Hegel's Logic and how this fits the method of Marx's Capital" (Arthur 2003, 3). There is a whole philosophical program in such a statement: forget the grand universal, historical narrative of Hegel's, and replace it, surreptitiously, with the same old thing, only derived from a Hegelian reading of *Capital*. In fact, *Capital* "is a veritable treasure of dialectic . . . not because of the application of an abstract universal method, but because the movement of the material itself requires expression in such logical categories" (Arthur 2003, 3).

Here we are in the presence of another mystical approach. It is not dialectics that applies to everything: it is the functioning of the material that cries for dialectical analyses. In the process, Arthur has moved from *Capital* and therefore the analysis of capitalism as a specific, historically existing mode of production (one in many that have succeeded each other) to the "material" as a whole. This can only derive from a blind, idealistic belief in the "abstract universal method."

And in fact, to Arthur systematic dialectics (2003, 5) is "at the philosophical level a way to keep concepts open and fluid, and above all systematically interconnected." That is, they are not interconnected by virtue of the actual interconnections they have in the concrete: they are interconnected by virtue of bestowing on them such a characteristic. At the methodological level, dialectics emphasizes "a clear order of presentation which is not linear for the starting point is in need of interrogation."

The point is not the actual functioning of the material. Once you have found for yourself a "starting point" you must bestow your empirical analysis with a prepackaged "clear order of presentation." The reason for this is the one above given. "Epistemologically, it insists on the reflexivity of the subject-object relation." This is pure Idealism, and needs no further comment. "Ontologically," it addresses "totalities to be comprehended as 'systematically interconnected categories,' sharply distinguished from historically sequenced orderings." Even the most benevolent reader, willing to ignore the pure Idealism of this statement, would be led to wonder what happens when you find categories that are not "systematically interconnected." Do you just avoid studying them or bestow on them some systematic interconnection, which after all is "required by the material"?

To summarize,

> in a dialectical argument successive stages are introduced because they are demanded by the *logic of the exposition*, and they are so demanded because the exposition itself conceptualizes the internal relations and contradictions essential to the totality. (Arthur 2003, 26, emphasis in the original)

But all orthodox Marxist roads lead to the Rome of proletarian revolution, and Arthur gets there, moving from pure philosophy to actual politics, along the academically distinguished traditional Marxist trajectory. Like all the other dialectical thinkers he is a supporter of class struggle, but unlike his predecessors he has to reckon with the fact that the working class has betrayed him. European and American workers have been voting into power Thatcher, Blair, Bush, Berlusconi, Prodi, and Aznar, who have no intention whatsoever to even care for the socialist revolution Arthur has in mind, however timid, mild, and unsubversive it is.[19] After all, even in times of working-class militancy the Lenins and Gramscis had the problem of convincing the proletarians to gather under their banners. So, the question is "universal."

Here is Arthur's solution:

> Marx here as elsewhere has failed to grasp that the necessary loyalty of individuals to their class cannot be reduced to purely prudential calculation; the individual's identity as a class warrior has to be socially constituted, and instrumental in this is the inculcation of the appropriate values. (Arthur 2003, 238)

This is an astonishing statement. Yet, there are logical reasons why one should bear with it and use it as a springboard for continuing the study we have undertaken here. In the first place, such statements are the obvious outcome of a Hegelian reasoning. If a Hegelian worldview is lacking, then the problem is that those who lack it are not tuned to the "universal method" that is "required by the material." This must be a mistaken form of stubbornness, whose only remedy is the "inculcation" of the right ideas.

Some words of explanation must be anticipated here, that show the abysmal difference in method and conclusions between dialectical and antidialectical approaches. According to the antidialectical logic, capitalism works as a dialectical kind of undertaking. A subset of reality functions by means of transcending all of its primary functions into intellectual activities. That is, the material as a whole, the concrete, is forever out of reach. It exists only in that it has been transformed into its intellectual (metaphysical) counterpart.

Things, to use Marx's words, end up being "other than themselves." Reality is denied, the "world" is reduced to what capitalist intellectuality can deal with, and the whole is blessed with correspondence to the inner laws of the universe. Plus, nothing is allowed forms of conflicts that might imply ruptures. Everything is in a "constant flux"—being, and not being, itself and something else.

This world can only survive by creating "appropriate values," moral entities that ontologically fit the general metaphysics they are devised to support by constituting sets of "must" and "must not." The problem remains, however, that in practice such values must be "inculcated": all political philosophies compatible with dialectical perspectives seem to agree here.[20]

From the anti-Hegelian perspective this is not so: simply, what is described above is an internal problem of the dialectical mind and of the economic and political setup that corresponds to it (in our case capitalism).

All those who have studied philosophy will easily recognize here a whole set of problems that belong to philosophy in general. The philosophical framework of our reasoning, already considerably enlarged in this section, must then be widened further. This is not difficult. We have been considering items that make a discussion of materialism inescapable. Such arguments will be started in the next section, where they will be faced from a Western philosophy perspective. This is not wholly satisfactory to me, but rather constitutes what I can actually do. The inevitable starting point of any Western discussion of materialism and naturalism is Epicurus (see Micocci 2002a, 2004a).

METAPHYSICS VERSUS THE ABSTRACT

The metaphysics question that we have obtained from the anti-Hegelian/ antidialectical argument conceals a number of very important items that help define the main lines of the whole picture, as well as discover the detailed particulars. In fact, if there is such a contrast, and metaphysics (at least in our capitalist times) seems to have the upper hand, we are compelled to wonder how the weight of such an inversion can be born by actual men and women in practice.

The question is the gap, the rift that exists in practice, for each of us, between the perfect freedom and autonomy of the material and the harmonious regularity and predictability of the metaphysical (the social and the intellectual, in our capitalist case). There is a powerful contrast between the concrete, dangerous freedom of the material that might any minute overwhelm and even destroy us, and the arid, limiting, melancholy predictability of the metaphysics with its inbuilt safety and continuity, of which much more later.

A materialistic, concrete-based philosophy simultaneously understands and challenges the existing state of things.[21] Proving the metaphysics wrong can only subvert the political and economic state of things that epitomizes the metaphysics itself. From being a purely philosophical, theoretical kind of task, our search has become the practical application of Marx's Thesis XI on Feuerbach: by philosophically changing that part of the world that most directly concerns man as a sentient and thinking entity we are going to change the whole.

In *Anti-Hegelian Reading* (2002a) I had identified a stream within Western philosophy that presented a materialistic and naturalistic attitude (although not evenly and homogeneously distributed) coupled with a "conflictive" view of the individual versus society problem. The various thinkers I pointed out for consideration there (stretching from ancient to modern philosophy) were by no means amenable to any grouping other than these two loose criteria. I took the ideal ancestor to be Epicurus, for chronological reasons but also because his work presents most completely and fully the various characteristics I was looking for. Also, there is in Epicurus a kind of very poetic vision[22] that sets him apart from the other philosophers and that fits the present argument very much.

The materialistic conflictive thinkers are those who tend to give a primacy to concrete-based explanations of reality. Therefore, they all see the individual-society relation, in fact the whole social life of man, in terms that are centered on the individual. The relationship of man with society is therefore a "conflictive" one. The room that society and societal things occupy in individuals has been stolen from the set of man's potentialities. Social life robs man of his unlimited possibilities. In so doing it is compelled, to insure its very survival, to produce an ever-imposing set of rules and limitations that go way beyond that of regulation, and whose aim is the repression of the emotional side of man.

This complex set of interconnected problems is well represented by the discussion of the cycle theory of political institutions started by Aristotle, continued in Polybius and Livy, and updated by Machiavelli.[23] Man is inherently incapable of standing the limitations imposed on him by society: society must therefore cunningly exploit those very limits in order to ensure for itself the longest possible life span within the cyclical succession of types of polity.

Yet, no form of society can escape ruin and disappearance, due to the comeback of man's animality (his wholeness, in anti-Hegelian terms). Interestingly, the comebacks of animality do not take the individualistic form we should expect from the premises given. Instead, they take the shape of mob action, a kind of human political activity very easy to manipulate. This is what ensures the resuming of the cycle instead of the return to naturality.

This kind of argument is not confined to ancient and Renaissance authors only. We have a most erudite example of cycle theory in Negri (2002).[24] Its most remarkable difference with the materialistic conflictive kind of thought is that Negri has a totally socialized view of man. In his political philosophy man is confused with the "multitude." The multitude replaces individuals in the life cycle of the polity, and even fights the individual. In fact, in Negri's vision of the cycle the role of the villain is given to individual action, to those persons who even when they act together cannot melt into a multitude and are eventually displaced by the multitude itself. This last is taken to be the bearer of the flag of change (meant in the Hegelian, continuous sense).

We cannot include Negri, despite his Marxist past, in the materialistic group, not even from the naturalistic point of view. His naturalism in fact, and indeed his whole argument, is borrowed from Spinoza. Straightforward mysticism, evident in the concept of multitude but present in his general argument too, replaces the mediated, strictly intellectual mysticism of Hegelian approaches. But, most important of all, he sees the individual versus social conflict as a solved problem: institutions are immanent to "the world"; they just can be improved by action pushed by the multitude. Man is a social animal in the sense put forward by Aristotle in *Historia Animalium*: no more than a bee.[25]

Thus, the point of the return to the social after the social has brought itself to destruction by its own devices is also a modern one. We shall see, when discussing socialism and fascism, that this is precisely the main question in contemporary history, the very main characteristic of actual forms of capitalism.

In the dialectical framework we have been exploring here the individual is simply not allowed to exist. The "world" has a predetermined destiny set by the unfolding of the Idea in all its complications. Politics and economics are just what is ratified by rationality in action: only the existing is valid. Paradoxically, the opposite of the existent (say, orthodox Marxist "revolution") is allowed to exist and act, but only as long as it presents the same characteristics as the existent it pretends to discard. The material has no bearing on the whole, except when it is allowed to supply a category for transcension—that is, for action by the metaphysics.

The authors in the materialistic conflictive strand of thought contend in various ways that there is a way out of this, constituted by the main characteristic of the material: its capacity for ruptures and disappearances. We need to add a few words about Epicurus here, in order to set the general tone for the discussion that follows.

The interpretation of Epicurus I first put forward in *Anti-Hegelian Reading* (2002a) was very much influenced by a personal reading that was closer to Cicero's *De Natura Deorum* (1997a) (although Cicero intended to confute Epicurean positions) than to other, more popular readings of Epicurus's thought, first of all Lucretius. My understanding was based on a few fundamental concepts.

In the first place there was the complication of nature, the difficulty to make out specific laws of motion for natural phenomena. This meant that, to my Epicurus, one would be a fool to believe that natural (and socioeconomic) phenomena can be driven back to one or few causes. The complication and uncertainty of nature compels the researcher to always expect complication and unpredictability. Epicurus represented to me the very opposite of Hegelian, and dialectical in general, approaches.

This was also evident in the fact that in Epicurus the logical consequence of this attitude was what we can call in modern terms an "atheist" attitude.[26] Epicurus straightforwardly linked simplistic scientific explanations with vulgar religion. Besides constituting a good anti-Hegelian philosophical precedent, the link also meant that he had grasped the relationship that exists between erroneous, incomplete intellectual frameworks and emotional (mystical) deviations.

The third fundamental feature was the highly poetic version of the general uncertainty of nature that Epicurus puts forward, working Teophrastus's intuitions into a compete and beautiful system in which even gods are perishable. The essential concept of rupture with disappearance is there very clearly.

The fourth aspect was the question of feelings and sex: that is, of the relationships possible among human beings. In Epicurus, friendship and love are treated in a very pragmatic way. The role played by the physical and social constraints determined by the polity was fully acknowledged, and love and friendship were analyzed for what they could be in practice. I would summarize this conception by means of the example of the way animals, say birds and plants, say, those weeds that grow in the interstices of our pavements and walls, have accepted the limitations imposed by the city and yet keep living their way and not the city way. Epicurus's treatment is free from the moralism that goes together with other theories of adaptation.

The last important point was Epicurus's treatment of the question of work and money. I read in his writings a sort of communist blueprint. I take it he meant that wealth and labor are two inevitable things that should be practiced and possessed only as a guarantee for actual survival, and only up to the point when a comfortable level of welfare is reached.

Readers from Mediterranean and Latin environments have been pointing out to me that I heavily interpret Epicurus. I simply believe that there is not enough material by, and about, Epicurus to assess how far I or anybody else, for that matter, has strayed from the orthodoxy.

Second, I simply do not trust the most commonly used reference for Epicurus's philosophy, Lucretius's *De Rerum Natura* (1992). This in fact, by its very un-Epicurean nature of a work for the public at large, and by means of Cicero's probably heavy editing hand (which can fairly be supposed to have been anti-Epicurean and traditionalist), cannot be trusted.

I do not in any way want to give the impression that I am building an Epicurean argument, but there is one further aspect that I feel the need to discuss, whose importance will be evident later on. The best way to introduce it is by using Diogenes Laertius, for its actual origin is to be found in Pyrrho, whom Laertius discusses in chapter 11, Book IX (Epicurus is in Book X). The question is composite, for it involves the notion of *prolepsis* (and *katalepsis* and *ipolepsis*) and the very question of language itself, and of its relationship with a concrete-based, materialistic apprehension of nature. I do not aim at solving the question of the interpretation of Epicurus on this score but simply to use this problem as a springboard for my materialistic proposal.

Diogenes Laertius (2002, 31–32, 33), while explaining Epicurus's philosophy, says that in the *Canon.*

> the criteria of truth are the perceptions (with sense and/or intelligence: αισθήσειζ), the anticipations (προλήψειζ) and the feelings that are passively received (πάθη) to which the Epicureans add the direct apprehension of the representation of thought. Such statements can be found in Epistula ad Erodotum and in the *Capital Maxims.* (Diogenes Laertius, 31, all translations from the Greek mine)

Sensations are a-logical and memory-less. Reason depends "absolutely" on sensations, whose truthfulness is insured by the actual existence of immediate perceptions. All our notions derive from sensations in various guises, with some collaboration from reasoning.

Prolepsis, anticipation, is "almost (quasi) a cognition or immediate apprehension of the real (katalepsis)" (translation mine). It can even be thought of as a "universal idea that is inside us," inherent to our nature: that is, "the memory of what appeared often outside of us" (412), just like when we say "here is a man." In fact, when pronouncing the word *man*, "immediately also his appearance presents itself to our thought because of prolepsis, under the preliminary guidance of our senses" (412). In other words, every statement we make of the "that is a horse, man, etc." sort depends on the existence in us of prolepsis. "We can give things a name because of prolepsis" (412). Even new opinions depend on them.

Ipolepsis is supposition, and pathe is divided into two, pleasure and pain. These last determine preference and aversion.

There are two types of investigation, one relative to things, the other relative to pure and simple words. (Diogenes Laertius, 34)

In *Epistula ad Erodotum* (Diogenes Laertius, 38), Epicurus insists on the importance of not indulging in "vain words": the original thought that is in every word must be picked up at once. And to do so (in order to avoid scientific mistakes) we must understand that notions derive their existence from "similarity" or "analogy" or "union" (Laertius, 32, 412). Even the visions of crazy people, as well as dreams, are true, because they "move our minds" (Diogenes Laertius, 32, 412). Only what is not cannot move our minds.

What Epicurus calls "empty talking (words)" can be likened to what I call the (flawed) dominant culture. Only a direct, sense-based observation of the concrete grants veridicity to what is studied. But the concrete is not what Hegelians or mainstream, dialectical Marxists would call so. It is comprehensive of what is capable of striking one's mind, from concrete objects to dreams and abstract reasonings. Here the substantial impossibility to distinguish between prolepsis and katalepsis and its consequences on ipolepsis is fundamental.

Moderns tend to confuse prolepsis with prescience, the Idea, Platonic knowledge and the like, which is a mistake of the same kind as that which produced Hegelian and Marxist dialectics. Epicurus intended a purely materialistic kind of thing: the inevitable presence in the mind of images of material things caused by the inevitability of seeing, looking, feeling, and being told while being nurtured and the impossibility to determine which is first in going to constitute the "notion" of a thing. This in fact is dependent on a word/term when it is to be used in science, but is, and remains, a mixture of sensation and reasoning when left in a, so to speak, blank mind, a mind without intention to communicate. Images and representations of things are in our mind even before we acquire language.

The "notion" is little more than name-giving, the translation in the elementarity and sociality of words, languages, and articulated thoughts of a complex set of interconnections that is perfectly grasped by the sense-mind coordination but can be expressed only by transcension.

To complicate things for us, but to simplify them in practice for humankind about their daily businesses, there is the question, often hinted at by Epicurus but evident in the anti-Hegelian proposal, that the most common things of life, and in particular the socioeconomic things, have little or no variability and unpredictability. They are amenable to dialectical treatment because they are amenable to the simplifying transcension implied by their translation into language. This, it is worth repeating it, is dependent upon a complex core (the prolepsis-katalepsis-reason-pathe relation) that presents, to the dialectical or capitalistic mind, a chicken-and-egg difficulty that is only apparent.

If sense-based understanding is truthful (I would rather say immediate), and if whatever moves your mind is an existent thing, there is simply no need to disentangle that relation. It follows that ipolepsis is an intellectual apprehension of things, false because indirect and therefore detached from the concrete. Dialectical mental processes are based upon ipolepsis. Ipolepsis is handed out to the public as a ready-for-use method of thinking. Yet the process behind this, the actual making of this apparent ipolepsis, originates in the mixture of prolepsis-katalepsis-reason-pathe we have introduced.

This kind of approach to materialism calls into question language. Language itself can in fact take completely different kinds of meanings and roles, when it is used from a materialistic or (to summarize) a dialectical (but we shall see that "socialized" is a preferable term) perspective. We shall come back on this in the course of the book, although it is not something we can and must solve here.

We shall see the consequences of considering senses, mind, and language in this way in the next chapters, at almost every step. This kind of approach is not present in its straightforward way in the materialistic conflictive tradition. Rousseau at times gets close to it (see his *Discourses*) for an important instance. Thomas Aquinas also would need to be discussed, and Meister Eckhart who, however, does not belong in the group. We must defer the argument to a next volume.

A last item that must be mentioned in the present treatment of Epicurus is John Bellamy Foster's surprising insertion of Epicurus in *Marx's Ecology* (2000).[27] Foster gives a prominent role to Epicurus in Marx's philosophy. In fact, he seeks to identify a whole philosophical trajectory that is supposed to lead to Marx the ecologist.[28] Thus, he moves from Epicurus to prove that, like in a game of Chinese boxes, we can reach Marx by piling, each inside the next, the various boxes constituted by Epicurus, the Enlightenment French sensists (De la Mettrie, D'Holbach), Darwin, and Engels. We can go even as far as Lenin.

His understanding of Marxist theory is dialectical, and this reduces the importance of his work to having pointed out the importance of Epicurus for Marxism. In this respect, it needs emphasis that his focus is on ecology, and on Marx's ecology. He does not take the inusitate step for an Anglo-Saxon of giving Epicurus a role to play in political philosophy. Also (34), Foster's Epicurus is almost exclusively reliant on Lucretius's *De Rerum Natura* (1992). and owes very little to other authors and to the other extant writings of Epicurus himself.

There also are some problems with Foster's attempt to attribute to Marx a Darwinian-Epicurean-Engelsian dialectical frame of mind.

Marx was deeply influenced by the non-deterministic materialism that he thought he had found in Epicurus . . . absorbing it within his larger dialectical synthesis, which also included Hegel, political economy, French socialism and nineteenth-century evolutionary science. (Foster 2000, 256)

Bellamy Foster's interpretations are questionable, often a bit too superficial, and he produces sweeping generalizations. Nonetheless, he put Epicurus back into the discussion. This is in itself an achievement, and a step forward toward returning this thinker to the prominence he deserves.

RUPTURES AND OBLIVION

It is time now to develop the question of the metaphysics versus the abstract in its relationship with the capitalist mode of production. This will expand and clarify the question of ruptures and disappearance and that of the natural flowing of things. This in turn will lead us back to the social question and to capitalism.

We had started by displaying a generic critique of dialectical modes of thought that had become with Colletti a critique of the mode of operation of capitalism itself. It is important to point out that Colletti's intention was not to criticize capitalism, especially in such a radical way, but to make some supposed aporias in Marx's own thought evident. Rosenthal (1998, 2001) independently adds the very good example of the functioning of the question of value. Unfortunately, he takes the dialectical functioning of the question of value to be (as seen in the preceding section) an accidental analogy instead of a constituent feature of capitalism.

The compelling force of the anti-Hegelian argument of the Feuerbach–Marx–Della Volpe–Colletti line instead unequivocally points to the fact that dialectical modes of thought are an intrinsic character of modern times. Hegel's systematization simply distilled into a grand system the systematic hypostatizations of modern intellectuality. Marx proved that this was true in general and especially for the political economy case, and Della Volpe proved that what Marx said for political economy remained valid for present-day social sciences in general.

The antidialectical critique implies a sense-based approach to the grasp of the concrete. While the problem of constructing a concrete-based approach is taken care of by the use of those tools of logic that dialectical modes of thought have denied, if not in theory at least in practice, we remain with the question of the determination, at the individual level, of the effectiveness of a sense-based approach. This is a theoretical task. We cannot rely any more on predetermined intellectual frames such as the dialectical modes of thought. We are alone with our quest for an immediate, logic-bound apprehension of reality that reduces the use of rationality to the organization of the cultural heritage on the one hand (which must be constantly subject to a critical scrutiny, and considered vis-à-vis the basic tool of the direct apprehension of reality), and on the other hand the actual set of images (our days, obsessed by computer-derived language and by the empty rhetoric of market exchanges, call this "information").

One should not be deceived by words: when I say "reduce the use of rationality" I obviously mean it in relation to the present abuse of such use for purposes that are flawed and mystical, as earlier argued—that is, merely intellectual.[29] In capitalism, as a consequence of the hypostatization argument, mysticism takes the form of ipolepsis, a mistaken and exaggerated use of a schematic rationality that replaces both the direct use of the senses and the use, and the effects, of spontaneous emotions. The actual abuse of this intellectual method in the form of ipolepsis tends in fact (I am anticipating here, for the sake of clarity) to replace the direct interaction sense—emotion with the indirect, mediated form of discourses about senses and emotions. This is an evident corollary of the argument of this chapter.

I should add here that for the present purposes we can leave sense and emotions to their intuitive meaning. In fact, if the argument about the intellectuality of capitalism is correct, before defining them we must go through the whole process of liberation from the dominant flawed logic. Vice versa, if we are not liberated, then sense and emotions take a meaning that is within the reach of the dominant intellectuality, that of a simplified, politically usable concept. A definition here is therefore pointless.

This is just another way to look at the multifaceted metaphysics versus the abstract argument. It is true that it coincides with the material, historical form taken by capitalism. But it would be wrong to identify the abstract versus metaphysics with the case study of capitalism. Being an intellectual kind of thing, it obviously is a general, timeless question. The fact that it finds its most complete and abherrant expression under capitalism is just a further complication that must not be mistaken with the philosophical core of the problem. The study of capitalism serves only to clarify issues that are philosophical.

We have to discuss and define now the problem of the direct apprehension of the concrete, for which we have a powerful tool in Epicurus's discussion of prolepsis and the ruptures and oblivion. We shall introduce the topic here. The consequences will be developed throughout the whole book.

The complex and thorny problem of Epicurus's prolepsis and all that is connected to it is indeed a central question for a materialism that must be effectively concrete-based and reliant on the senses (i.e., naturalistic). The issue is momentous not only because it constitutes the core of any form of materialism but also because it brings in its wake a whole set of important side effects. The most important side effect is the implicit attack on the dominant theories of intellectuality, be they political, cognitive, psychological, or language-based.

If a sense-based materialism can be produced, culture-based theories of human understanding must be rejected on the grounds of their being dependent, in their form and analytical method, on the historical circumstances of their birth. They deal with the "political animal," with merely an aspect of man, and an aspect that is the apex of alienation of man from himself and his fellow human beings, to use the expression Colletti borrowed from Marx. The "political animal" is the result of the intellectuality so far criticized. Man as such then is to be explored by means of a materialistic, sense-based method.

The first and foremost consequence is that we are talking of understanding reality as an individual task. There is no way other than individual for sense-based understandings of reality. Yet, this cannot be the whole story.

Man is not alone, even if it were for the simple reason that he is born from other men and needs parental care in childhood. Man's understanding of the concrete is intimately bound up with the presence of other men, with forms of organization that do not originate with the individual. With birth, one is to face the splitting question of the presence of the metaphysics, the predetermined vision of reality with inner laws that human civilizations have been producing.[30]

Thus the direct apprehension of the concrete on the one hand comes to represent the conflict that we all face, whether we like it or not, between the abstract (our free thought) and the metaphysics, the ipolepsis of Epicurus. On the other hand, there is not, and cannot be, a "pure" phenomenon of apprehension, for there is no such thing as a blank mind with reasoning capacities.

Here comes the precision with which Epicurus identified the problem by means of his discussion of ipolepsis, katalepsis, and so on. It is clear that there is a "quasi-" condition to all the operations of the mind that are sense-based, and consequently a quasi-impossibility to precisely assess the impact of preexistent aids to understanding: not to understanding as reaction, however, which needs no mental processing,[31] (I am putting forward a limited case for explanatory purposes) but to an understanding that can be shared with other fellow human beings through the basic means of bestowing names at first, and on to the more complex communication tasks. It is at this level that the perverse operations of the metaphysics[32] begin, vastly exaggerating the binding capacity of the presumed laws of behavior of the subject under study.

It is at this level that we must operate if we want to achieve a materialistic, concrete-based method that is independent in emotional and intellectual terms from the socializing dominant mode of thought. In fact, in intellectual terms we can, by operating with the anti-Hegelian method I propose, reason in a nonsocialized way, achieving both a materialistic method and an analysis of capitalism. Here the intervention of the emotional side is important.

The materialistic process begins at the level of perception, at the point in time when we decide to pursue our analysis without fear and call ourselves off from the rest of the people, those who—willingly or out of laziness—accept to think along the ipolepsis lines, with suppositions along a priori designed (presumed) laws of behavior. I shall call the choice to proceed along the subversive path to materialism "detachment," and the condition of remaining within the frame of purely intellectual understandings of reality "socialized" forms of thought.

We can now introduce the rupture and oblivion topic. This theme will recur throughout the whole book, along with the metaphysics versus the abstract question. The case here seems to be easier. It suffices to point at the stringent logic of the anti-Hegelian argument and corroborate that by pointing at nature "out there." There is indeed an important and impressive list of ruptures-cum-disappearances "out there." Think of the Neanderthal men, the mammoths, the Plantagenets, the secularization of politics versus the Middle Age preponderance of divine political theories, our past feelings for this or that girl. The list could go on and on, with the only discussions being linked to assessing the precision with which this or that case fits the bill.

But things are not so simple. If we look at the recent production in mathematics, philosophy, epistemology, and in the natural, social, and historical disciplines, we do not find a clear conceptualization of ruptures and disappearances. This is only logical, from the anti-Hegelian perspective: dominant science is just unable to produce such definitions. Not that they have not tried. But all these studies share in the attempt to identify an algorithm, a law of behavior and a role to assign to ruptures and disappearances within some general flow. Not by chance Thom (1978) refers to such a concept as "catastrophes"—a literary-theatrical term that indicates determining (teleological) turning points in the development of a story.

The dominant culture of capitalism produces, instead of ruptures, denouement and overturns episodes along its continuous, uninterrupted imagined history of the world, of the universe, and of mankind. The various forms of Hegelian Idea that are at work in it can only produce a priori schemes even for terminal events, whose momentum is, like everything else, played down and reduced to a step along a predetermined path of human elevation. Not only the meaning of rupture and that of oblivion is lost. The whole empirical aspect of the analysis is, as a consequence, played down and/or, at least, heavily distorted. Dominant social and natural sciences do not look at the concrete (reality, in common parlance). They rather select, in their observations, whatever aspect is relevant for their theory and cover the bones with flesh,[33] inventing the rest of the story.

The main, but not the only, issue at stake here is that of continuity. This can be taken in a mathematical sense, like economists explicitly do since Mill's time, or in the vulgar evolutionary sense (in natural as well as social sciences), or by proxy. We have very important examples by eminent authors of mistakes due to implicit continuity. I shall mention here two similar instances: Adam Smith's *Wealth of Nations* (1999) and John Maynard Keynes on ancient currencies (1982b). While Smith embarks upon a cross-time comparison of the prices of wheat in historical and present-day value from the year 1202 to 1740 (359–367), Keynes considers currencies since Babilonian times, focusing on "standards" from the times of Solon and Pheidon onwards. He implies that from Nebuchadnezzar onwards economic activities have been based on exchange, and worse still, that the role of money/coinage has been the same since.

In order to avoid such evidently preposterous mistakes, we must properly consider ruptures and disappearance/oblivion. We must take an open, direct relation to what scientists call the empirical material. Let us start from the first.

Rupture is here meant in the sense that the word indicates: a *caesura*, a rift, an almost (we are applying here the Epicurean "quasi") impassable gap that has taken place in between two phenomena or sets of phenomena. This can be cultural as well as chronological or chemical/physical (say, the disappearance of a species, or its impossibility to interbreed with other, similar organisms). A rupture can bring disappearance and/or oblivion. There is a difference between the two: disappearance means that something is irretrievably gone (say, Genkhis Khan's empire). Oblivion might refer to disappearance, and is intended to mean some unrepeatable phenomena whose reproduction is impossible, and on whose existence there is no certainty. One example could be the supposed artefacts of Neanderthalers or of more primitive species; another could be the influence of religion on political institutions: the Azteca case seems gone forever, the Christian one is more controversially so.

Coming to the attitude towards the empirical, we can only refer back to what has so far been said in this chapter about our materialistic, sense- and concrete-based method. This will be explained in the rest of the book. Also, we shall see the relationship between the method here introduced and the existing social sciences.

Those who accept the dialectical method (the proof, to be completed next chapter, of the strict connection dialectics has to capitalism, makes this whole reasoning more dramatic), in Epicurean terms those who reason in terms of suppositions, ipolepsis, can be compared to the typical childish way to look

at things. In trying to make sense along the lines of what adults seem to think
of how things and animals behave, children attribute to them a purposeful
mind. Cars "go," "want," "intend," even "feel." And so do the unitary entity
of horse and rider, or a plane comprising into one entity the actual aircraft, the
pilot, and the passengers. So do cats, chicks, houses, and what have you. They
have a formally purposeful behavior which in fact just follows the simplified
lines set by a child's enforced understanding of the behavior of reality out
there.

   This is exactly what happens when interpreting reality with dialectical
eyes. Entities "do" things along elementary, predetermined sets of lines that
can always be traced back to the stylization of everything's and everybody's
behavior supplied by the socialized, vulgar, and only apparently common
sense view of each epoch. They can even undergo fatal accidents, for they
emerge from them unscathed (the continuity), like animated cartoon films.
When proposed and practiced by grown-up men, a childish analysis is infantile. In this sense I shall use the term from now on.

CONCLUSIONS

The construction of a materialistic method starts from acknowledging that we
are in the presence of a contrast between an abstract, logically correct mode
of thought and the metaphysics produced by the dialectical method with its
omnipresent hypostatizations. While the first is to be recovered philosophically, the second is the dominant one even among those who do not care to
admit it. The first allows for ruptures/disappearances, thus covering the whole
range of natural phenomena, while the second refuses to acknowledge in
practice the presence of ruptures, creating a world ruled by a priori laws and
impermeable to the concrete.

   In this kind of framework a main role in the search for a direct apprehension of the concrete is played by the senses. This poses important questions
on the relationship, when senses are mainly relied upon, between senses, rationality, language, and the role of culture/nurture. The key for the solution of
this problem is to be found in the development of the Epicurean notion of prolepsis. The big question at stake, it is well worth reminding, is the recovery
of man's individuality on materialistic grounds. This passes through the recovery of a direct, sense-based relationship with nature.

   The other, and last, main philosophical question is that of detachment from
the oppressive role of society, and the return to the beautiful uncertainty of
nature, with its ruptures and disappearances. This from the point of view of
the reconstruction of the social sciences from a materialistic basis poses the

problem of the relationship with the empirical material. Once again, we cannot resort to just the logical part of the anti-Hegelian proposal. It is necessary to use the whole set of philosophical arguments so far put forward in this chapter.

The next task is to demonstrate that dialectical modes of thought, with all their negative consequences in political terms (in terms, that is, of human emancipation), perfectly identify the mode of production we call capitalism. They not only identify and characterize capitalism as a concept, but they also do so for the actual thing we imprecisely call capitalism, the present state of economic, social, and political things at the world level. This will be done in chapter 3.

NOTES

1. What follows is a development of Micocci (2002a).

2. "The philosophers have only interpreted the world, in various ways; the point is to change it" (1985, 123).

3. Such conclusion is clearly hinted at in Thesis V ("Feuerbach . . . does not conceive sensuousness as practical, human sensuous activity"), VII ("Feuerbach . . . does not see that the religious sentiment is itself a social product, and that the abstract individual whom he analyzes belongs to a particular form of society" [122]), XI ("contemplative materialism [not comprehending] sensuousness as practical activity is the contemplation of single individuals and of civil society" [123]). But we shall expand on this throughout the whole book.

4. We will face these themes in the rest of this chapter and in the book. See also Micocci (2004c, 2002a, 2004a, 2005c, 2007b). In our days the term political economy is desueted and left to a minority of traditionalists and to the Marxists. Yet its current replacement, the ideologically monolithic "economics," despite its intellectual poverty, is explicitly hailed by its practitioners as the heir of the former science, political economy.

5. See also Della Volpe (1967), in which a critique of sociology can be found.

6. "The positivity and indispensability of matter itself as an element of knowledge follows from the very defectiveness and sterility of any (a prioristic) reasoning that takes no account of the material, of the extra-rational. This may be termed the non-dogmatic, gnoseological and methodological axiom of matter and therefore of the matter-reason relationship as a relationship of heterogeneities" (1980, 141).

7. I proved that in *Anti-Hegelian Reading* (2002a).

8. See *Anti-Hegelian Reading* (2002a), in which the argument is dealt with in a more diffused way. Colletti attacks in particular—and I find this plausible—Engels and Plekhanov.

9. This is well summarized in Napoleoni (1985). See also A. A. Smith (1986).

10. Mohun (2003) quotes the very same passage, but is unable to see its subversive power. Part of this is due to his inability to grasp the crucial difference between real opposition and dialectical contradiction.

11. See Rees (1998) and the special issue of *Science and Society* 3 (1998) for two typical examples of the Marxist dialectical way of thinking that reflect very well the mentality of Marxist activists everywhere.

12. We shall see this later on. It suffices to point out here how devastating wars and pauperizing economic maneuvers can only be enforced in countries where statolatry has worked its evil as far as the minds of the poor and the lower classes in general. This is best done with the help of Marxist, and progressive in general, movements. Economists are grasping at last at the state-centered features of the so-called minimal state, however. See for instance Chang Ha-Joon (2002).

13. For humanitarian reasons I omit to talk about Colletti's late folly that brought him to join Berlusconi's party. He has been punished enough, for nobody deserves to be called by Berlusconi, once dead and hence unable to defend himself, a friend.

14. See Micocci (2002a).

15. See Micocci (2002c), Smith (1999), Rosenthal (2001).

16. Of which Rosenthal has only the intuition.

17. This is a very complex point, whose various aspects will be dealt with in detail in the course of the book. For a preliminary, general treatment, see Micocci (2002a, 2006b).

18. Just like Christ in Christian religion, Rosenthal and Marx would point out.

19. One should also add that the working class is disappearing due to the deindustrialization of the West, but this is another matter altogether. Most Marxists tend to replace it with all other sorts of oppressed groups available, thus keeping the flame.

20. I have faced this subject at greater length in Micocci (2002a): here I shall redefine the general lines of the argument, adding some new concepts and thoughts.

21. We have been equating, so far, the metaphysics with capitalism on the grounds of continuity with the approach of the anti-Hegelian Feuerbach and Marx. In the next chapter we shall demonstrate, by analyzing political economy, how this identification can be proved correct in general.

22. See also Micocci (2000a, 2004a, 2002a).

23. Whose reciprocal and complementary part is constituted by the philosophical vision of the poet and philologist Leopardi. See Micocci (2000c) and Biscuso (1999).

24. See Micocci (2004f).

25. For an interpretation of this aspect in Aristotle, see Micocci 2002a.

26. Epicurus did believe, or pretended to believe, in the gods. Only, he insisted that they be given more ineffable features. Epicurus's famous argument (see for instance Cicero 1997a, 55–56, 133) that applying "normal" kinds of reasoning to the analysis of nature engenders the fear of God, indeed the very hypothesis and consequent belief that the gods create things and intervene in man's business. "Impious is not who eliminates the gods of the common people, but who attributes to the gods the opinions of common people. That is because the statements of common people on the gods are not prolepsis or true pre-notions or anticipations, but ipolepsis or false suppositions" (Diogenes Laertius 2002, 124, 440, trans. mine).

27. Without Alex Callinicos's mentioning the book many times to me, and his actual sending it to me eventually, I would not have read it, due to life circumstances.

28. It is well worth stating that I deem Foster's analysis of Marx's ecology correct, or at least coinciding with what I would myself say on the topic.

29. Here I am answering Tassone's concerns, vented in "An Objection to Andrea Micocci" (1999), a reply to Micocci (1999a).

30. With different degrees of pervasiveness, of course. Also, it must be pointed out that the metaphysics need not be a complete form of culture. A name bestowed on an object is sufficient to set in motion the whole set of (right or wrong, it does not matter here) syllogisms that constitute the rationale as well as the thinking and analytical methodology behind such a name. Anybody who has been rearing children or remembers something from his early years knows this.

31. Inferior animals live perfectly and reproduce even in the absence of a brain by simply combining a stimulus-reaction mechanism. They understand their environment and collaborate with it, with means (chemical operations) identical to our sense-based operations.

32. Of which Hegelian and dialectical methods are only a most recent, and particularly virulent, instance.

33. A perfect case in point is the—admirable from other perspectives—historical work on the transition by Brenner (1977) (see Aston, Philpin, eds., 1985). In it, as said, Brenner looks for instances of class struggle in times when the term cannot and must not apply. So ingrained is the belief in the continuity of reality that such a mistake went almost unnoticed, and Brenner was criticized only for his excessive Marxist schematism and dogmatism.

Chapter Three

Political Economy of Capitalism

The metaphysics represents the dominant functional mechanism of capitalism. This determines some very typical and interesting features of institutionalized society. We need to explore how a flawed intellectual schema manages to escape the scrutiny—and the inevitable opposition—of individual minds. We have an indication, already, in what Marx and more in general Epicurus and the materialistic conflictive thinkers say about the hypostatization mistake. This in fact goes to constitute "processes that [Marx] located . . . in the structure and mode of functioning of capitalist society itself" (Colletti, quoted in chapter 2).

That is why political economists can get away with inventing ahistorical categories, whose harmonious relationships are then, as we saw with Marx in the preceding chapter, "smuggled as the inviolable natural laws on which society in the abstract, in general, is founded." It is in the reciprocal correspondence between economic theories and actual capitalist relations that we must find the demonstration of the fact that capitalism is the most perfect instance of the metaphysical nature of social, economic, and political relations.

This chapter serves to show the mirroring, and actual reciprocal immediate identification, in between dialectical modes of thought, political economy, and actual capitalist relations and institutions. At the end of this chapter the intellectual nature of the capitalist mode of production should be clearly established, thus leaving to the next chapter the task of investigating the possibility that this intellectuality has to innovate/change.

MAINSTREAM ECONOMIC THEORY

In this section we shall study mainstream economic theory, considering both the orthodoxy and the so-called heterodoxy. Considering the two together is possible in that there is little the heterodoxy could do, and indeed intends to do, to change the situation of the discipline as a whole. The heterodox authors simply focus on specific aspects of the theory, offering specific recipes geared to correct those aspects. Even those who seem to adumbrate a type of critique that involves the whole of the orthodox mainstream system end up being unable, or perhaps unwilling, to put forward an alternative: Garegnani and Lawson are formidable cases in point.[1]

Before entering the core of mainstream economic theory it must be acknowledged that, however rare such events are, some mainstream economists consider philosophical and logical aspects. In the preceding chapter we mentioned Mohun (2003) and Barkley Rosser (1991, 1999, 2000). Here, we go back to the *Cambridge Journal of Economics* to see that Setterfield (2003) directly faces the issue of dialectics, claiming that it does exist, both in Marx and in Keynes (or, more likely, the Keynesians). Starting from the well-known Keynesian topic of uncertainty and probability, Setterfield argues that one can see attempts to get some order and predictability in reality (say, by enforcing routines), making uncertainty less uncertain. This is the realm of dialectics.

All this would seem to square with what I say here and in *Anti-Hegelian Reading* (2002a, 2005d). Yet, Setterfield makes some confusions that are typical of how dialectics is understood in political economy.

> Dialectical processes involve actual contradictions—tensions, or, more precisely, Kantian real oppositions between the component parts of a system— which create transformatory change at the level of the system as a whole. Dialectics therefore provides a theory of historical motion, which can be applied to the study of actual social phenomena that are known to evolve through time. (374)

Nondialectical occurrences produce events that proceed dialectically and can be studied accordingly.

This is not the case of someone who has not done his homework. As argued in Micocci (2002a) and in the preceding chapter, there seems to be a complete subservience to the dominant mentality that allows for the same interpretation to be repeated over and over and applied to everything. Economics is, and we come to the central question of this section, the most perfect epitomization of such mentality. Let us see how.

The theoretical core of mainstream economic theory, that contains all of the more philosophical debates, is the market.[2] From Adam Smith onward, the market supplies a tool for riding history back and forth, for it embodies the presumed natural tendencies of man and his social activities. Smith himself, however, in (1999) realizes that the natural, eternal human characters that lead to the "invisible hand" are not sufficient theoretically, and he desperately seeks indicators that point to a continuous evolution of history: the discussion about the amount of gold/silver in coinage (see e.g., Book I, chapter 4 or chapter 9) is a most important instance, as well as the "natural progress of opulence" discussion (Book III, 479 ff.), or the tables in Book II (359–67) on the prices of wheat.

It is on top of this historical continuity that the naturality of "eternal" social, political, and economic relations is in fact predicated. In this case apparent common sense can acquire the enormously convincing power it has in our days:

> The quantity of every commodity brought to market naturally suits itself to the effectual demand. It is not in the interest of all [who bring] any commodity to market that the quantity never should exceed the effectual demand, and it is in the interest of all other people that it never should fall short of that demand. (160)

When things do not work out that way, a safety valve of almost infinite power is available: "enhancements of the market price are evidently the effect of particular accidents, of which, however, the operation may sometimes last for many years together" (1999, 163).[3]

Markets work precisely because most of the time they do not, due to the force of the imperfection of the actual. The very "imperfections" of the actual constitute the mechanisms whereby such events are absorbed in the metaphysics, the eternal categories of the "invisible hand." It matters little more than that, like Napoleoni notices,

> The economic theory that appears after 1870 starting from Jevons, Menger, and Walras, has as its starting point the refusal of the concept of net product of the Classicals and the aim to build an image of the economic process in which the distribution of income is totally reduced within the process of value formation, in the sense that the income available to the various subjects is nothing else than the price paid for the factors of production of which each is the sole owner. (1976, 103, trans. mine)

The key is in the possibility to conceive economic and historical events as categories that fit the (flawed) logic of the general flow without discontinuities.

The logic itself, however, is never made explicit. In this framework one can produce any kind of theory, from the elegant neoclassical construction to the cumbersome apparatus of the various Marxisms. Implicitly, and sometimes even explicitly, economists position themselves outside the philosophically abstract world they pretend to come from, transcending those very categories they are using, finding out or making up metaphysical eternal entities: hypostatizations.

That this could pass unnoticed can be explained only by admitting that it is the whole of (capitalist) reality that is dialectically upside down. Writers as clever as Hutchison (1992) would not, otherwise, write that economics, however defendable from the charge of being a positivistic discipline, is about predictions. To Hutchison, in fact, economics from Petty to Marshall has a history of attempts to ground the discipline on "facts." Still, in a changeable world the economists' predictions are "highly imprecise" (87): but they could, potentially, be used to avert crises as devastating and global as "the monstrous catastrophe" of 1930 to 1932 (87). If only Hutchison substituted the word "facts" with "metaphysics" he would be just right, even in saying (but we shall find that out from chapter 4 onward) that predictions can be useful.

Shackle (1972), because of his more varied economic preparation, is aware of the ahistorical, hypostatized character of economic variables.

"[In economics] *the business of life is thus seen in some degree* sub specie aeternitatis." (446, emphasis in the original)

In fact, the tools of economics such as game theory

assume away the whole of that aspect of business, science, art and contest, which allows originative genius to exist. It assumes that business, and life at large . . . are a game with rules [known and understood by the players]. (422)

But earlier on he had generalized this statement of economics as a whole by saying

the rational ideal is the conception of man's conduct as a part and aspect of the orderliness of Nature. (122)

And this is not simply in theory:

[Economies and hence governments] in aiming to control the average and the mass [wish] only to know about the average and the mass. It is statistical in its measurements as well as its aims. (362)

    The reifying of "consumption," "investment," "capital," "general output," "gross national product," "the capital-output ratio" and a dozen or so other vast and looming phantoms . . . when they are constructed these unrealities are treated as objects of worship. Their precise meaning is believed in. (362)

In order to demonstrate the tight correspondence between the hypostatized entities of the theory and the hypostatized entities of reality introduced in the preceding chapter, we can focus upon a pillar of market theory, the question of value formation. While classical approaches posited a labor theory of value, mainstream economics uses a utility approach. Both approaches seek to solve the chicken-and-egg problem of what came first between market prices and market environment by means of their ahistorical theorization and implicit continuity of history we saw. Mainstream economics takes care of the questions of value formation, and of everything else, by means of its well-known aseptic set of assumptions about man and economic intercourse and its "scientific" methodological structure. This permits it to pretend to isolate itself from the general metaphysics it belongs to. Economics can thus look like a "scientific" discipline that studies the world with detached eyes. It still partakes of all the faults of the metaphysics, but—simply—it needs not mention them.

Differently from the Austrians, the mainstream economists (both in the orthodox and the heterodox camps) do not venture into explicitly positing (or denying) a relationship between the market and the form of the actually existing political institutions. Economists expound the virtues of the market for the final—and, depending on possibility, present—happiness of mankind mainly in the microeconomic terms of availability to the individual. They perceive their job to be the perfecting of market theorization. Economic intercourses, and this is fundamental, are only very rarely classifiable as market intercourses. Yet the theory, orthodox and heterodox, can only treat them with the language and tools of market theory.[4]

No mainstream economist would be so foolish as to deny truthfulness to Shackle's statement that

the dependence of an exchange medium as such [reference to Keynes's General Theory] . . . upon convention is, after all, a very old and long-recognized truth. (1972, 219)

In this long-recognized truth we find the mechanism that grants the functioning of value formation and of economic theory in general. Economics is, and cannot be otherwise, the self-confessed mirror of a hardly meditated acknowledgement of a number of platitudes about the (eternal) mechanisms of economic reality. These have their deep roots in those supposedly eternal conventions that shape social and political reality and the modes, and rationale, of exchanges among men. This need not be discussed, only every now and then admitted.[5]

It is at this junction that we can see the importance of the "scientific" method, the attempt to put economics on equal ground with the hard sciences. Such equality is a way to maintain economics' neutrality, simultaneously delimiting the realm of economics itself. This is crucial: the other social sciences must be left free to roam in the rather vast territory whose landscape is too vague for the simplified tools of the economics method. It is the other social sciences that supply all those relaxing "long-recognized" truths, and they must do so with a language, and a method, that economists could safely reject, should the need to do so occur.

Millions of sheets of paper have been wasted arguing whether the "scientific" methodology of mainstream economics exists in practice, whether it is of any use in economic analysis, whether it reflects positivism or rather the swift opportunism of the founding fathers of the discipline. This, there is almost no need to say here, does not matter. Whatever method is used, the crucial point that grants the success of the undertaking is that there is an original mirroring: the structural identity between the way theory is built and actual intercourses are operated. Plus, even noncontinuous approaches are reduced to dialectical versions, thus allowing subsumption under the overall intellectuality.

The general intellectual nature of the mirroring question has been explained in chapter 2. Both economic theory and actual capitalist intercourses share in the dominant logic, a common intellectual nature (a culture) that is easily driven back to, and represented by, "Hegelian" dialectics and its copies of all kinds. What we must do here is, therefore, to study the relationship between the much vented neutrality of the method and the actual role economics plays in capitalism.

In order to do so, we must necessarily divide the mainstream according to an intellectual criterion. In fact, the "utopia" behind market theory is a liberal one, which in its pure form could potentially clash with the dialectical mode of reasoning of economics and actual capitalism. We must read economics as the best example of this unsolvable tension. The majority of mainstream practitioners and the Austrians represent the two poles we are interested in.

The implicit liberal utopia of mainstream theories can be found in the assumptions behind market theorization. These can, and actually are, traced back to Adam Smith, David Ricardo, and John Stuart Mill. The liberal approach is based on the neutrality of individuals to each other. All individuals are identical in terms of feelings and interests, and inert, in political terms and during economic intercourses, to each other. Without such inertness, no valorization could take place.[6] This allows for all sorts of political and philosophical liberal theories to be compatible with economics in the sense that they can be used by it. Economics, however, remains free to pretend its independence (its neutrality) from such theories.

The possibility, present in the utopian formulation of liberal theories, to withdraw within one's *hortus conclusus*, avoiding contamination by the general metaphysics, vanishes at once when the issues of inequality and distribution are brought in. This in fact entails the necessity of considering wider metaphysical bases and methods of reasoning. Justice, fairness, and distribution are granted in the theory by neutral intercourses, but in practice they need the presence of all we actually have: state, polity, community, language, culture, and the like.

Political and economic theories of liberalism in fact are incompatible with the very type of justice that they claim they can enforce. Callinicos (2001) (see also Callinicos 2003) makes this very clear: despite the mighty efforts of liberal thinkers of the caliber of Rawls and Sen, the fixing of inequality in liberal terms can only produce a final crisis of liberalism itself.[7]

There is thus room for the Hegels of all kinds to point out the eternal character of the institutions of capitalism. This also explains why liberalism is often accused of being cold and inhuman. Tellingly, these accusations come from the moderate left, orthodox Marxism, and the fascist right alike. The inevitable result of all this is an economic theory that necessarily has to keep itself aloof from theoretical debates, not to join a political-philosophical theory that turns into evident and explicit metaphysical conundrums every time it deals with ethical topics related to actual reality (fairness, justice), and an actual, capitalist reality that is best represented as the epitomization of that very fall into metaphysics.

In sum, behind economics lies an unexplicited, unspelled-out liberal utopia that cannot be used other than by just hinting at its existence. Economics's "scientific" apparatus is compelled, as pointed out by Marx and Della Volpe (as seen in chapter 2), to recur to hypostatizations whenever it needs to display its grand theory arguments. But even when not attempting grand theories, or when simply setting the range of variables needed for the actual microtheorization, mainstream economics and its ancestors produce some dangerous theoretical hybrids.

Such theoretical hybrids (that are perceived by mainstream practitioners as the theoretical referring to the empirical) can best be rendered as bridges, because of their technical position in between the "scientific" wishful thinking of economics, the unsuccessful attempt to stay aloof from metaphysics,[8] and the metaphysics of actual social, political, and economic intercourses. Take Adam Smith's "wealth of society," a most typical instance of mistaking,[9] and interexchanging, the individual and the social. This mistake is also typical of the never resolved micro- to macropassage in modern mainstream economic theory.

To show the momentum of this problem, it is well worth reporting some telling quotations from other eminent economists. Mill's *Principles of Political Economy* (1998) reads like this:

> in every state except total solitude, any disposal whatever of [wealth] can only take place with the consent of society, or rather of those who dispose of its active force.
>
> The rules by which [distribution of wealth] is determined, are what the opinions and feelings of the ruling portion of the community make them, and are very different in different ages and countries. (6)

Let us not be deceived by Mill's sensitivity about the "ruling portion" (a merely technical consideration) and above all the "different opinions and feelings." In fact "these are consequences of the fundamental laws of human nature, combined with the existing state of knowledge and experience, and the existing conditions of social institutions and intellectual and moral culture" (6).

Eternal categories not only exist in theory, practice, and intellectual feeling. The "primary and fundamental institution on which . . . the economical arrangements of society have always rested . . . [is] the institution of private property" (7). All this is amenable to Marx's and Della Volpe's critique of political economy[10] seen in chapter 2. Marshall brings the question to modern, neoclassical times, for he is a rare one among the neoclassical founding fathers to tackle difficult issues of this type.[11]

In his *Principles of Economics* (1910) Marshall notices that

> ethical forces are among those of which the economist has to take account. Attempts have indeed been made to construct an abstract science . . . of an "economic man" who is under no ethical influences. (XIII–XIV)

But

> there seems to be no good reason against including them: and in the present book normal action is taken . . . [that of] the members of an industrial group. (XIII–XIV)

In fact,

> man's character has been moulded by his every-day work . . . more than by any other influence unless it be that of religious ideals; and the two great forming agencies of the world's history have been the religious and the economic. (1)

Eternal categories, eternal ideas, natural institutions and the like make up the whole set of hypostatized, ahistorical pillars of economics. It is sufficient now to refer the reader to any of the textbooks that go around in the monolithic world of mainstream economics to find out a whole list of implicit bridges launched, despite their non-necessity, toward the metaphysics of capitalist reality. In fact, the mirroring earlier described would be sufficient to grant relevance to economics.[12]

The role of the bridges is different from the apparent one of connecting to actual (social, hypostatized) reality. This connection itself is a methodological problem for mainstream economics, for it suspends its concepts right in between a fully theoretical conception and a reference to, and contamination with, the imperfect items of reality. This, paradoxically, is actively sought by economists. The ensuing ambiguity mars the whole of the theory, yet allows it to escape its fate by alternatively pretending, as suits their purposes, theoretical and empirical bases.

The Austrians cling to their utopian liberal purity a bit longer than their neoclassical colleagues before, however, succumbing to the need of bridges just like them. Like for the neoclassical, their theories mirror capitalist reality in intellectual structure in the first place. Let us start from the mirroring, then.

Menger (1937/1882), one of the founders of both Austrian and neoclassical economics, is justly polemic against the German Historical School, Comte, and organic visions of society. His liberal mind leads him to distinguish between historical and theoretical sciences (and practical too, but this need not detain us): political economy belongs to the latter. Yet, the "laws of nature" are "exact laws," while we should not seek exactitude in economic reasonings. The key to understanding reality is repetition: exact operations are for the theory, just like pure substances and reactions are for theoretical chemistry.

Also, Menger (132) attacks Smith's ahistoricity, his letting it slip that institutions come as the production of collective will: Menger prefers Burke's approach. Yet, Appendix 8 seems to make clear that the beautiful liberal vision he displays in theory founders when legal matters are considered. In fact, to Menger tight legal arrangements are fundamental. This throws the whole story back to the beginning, to Marx and Della Volpe.

Von Mises (1949) is very serious in his liberal attempt to separate individual and society, avoiding the treatment of society as a whole in economics. Economics as "Catallactics" is nothing but "Praxeology." The action of individuals builds up to a joint social effort because men are naturally social and the inevitable outcome of their actions is social.

As a thinking and acting being man emerges from his pre-human existence already as a social being. The evolution of reason, language and cooperation is the outcome of the same process. . . . But the process took place in individuals. (43)
   But men are not like animals, yielding "to the impulse that prevails at the moment." (16)
   Man is a being capable of subduing his instincts, emotions and impulses. (16)
   Human action is necessarily always rational. The term rational is therefore pleonastic. (18)

And that is why

all the praxeological categories are eternal and unchangeable as they are uniquely determined by the logical structure of the human mind and by the natural conditions of man's existence. (199)

This slip is only apparently mitigated by the acknowledgement that

the market economy is the social system of the division of labor under private ownership of the means of production. Everybody acts on his own behalf. . . . Everybody in acting serves his fellow citizens. (258–59)

In fact,

the teaching of catallactics do not refer to a definite epoch of history, but to all actions characterized by . . . *private ownership of the means of production* and *division of labor* . . . the real action of real men. (647, emphasis in the original)

Therefore, for instance,

[the Roman civilization] perished because it did not adjust its moral code and its legal system to the requirements of the market economy. (763)

Despite his understanding of the faults of classical political economy ("Ricardo failed to free himself from the Mercantilist image of the Volkwirtschaft," page 633), Von Mises presents all the faults so far attributed to mainstream economics.
   The case of Hayek is difficult to render. He seems to approve of everything Von Mises and Menger have said. Only, in his work there is a true fixation with the power of the market to deliver justice and fairness in the long run. Even enormous inequality should be looked at with benevolence, and left untouched, for the market will correct it in the future. In fact, to Hayek the social sciences have an enormous power:

[*social sciences*] are not about the social wholes as wholes; they do not pretend to discover by empirical observation laws of behavior or change of these wholes. Their task is rather, if I may so call it, to *constitute* such wholes, to provide schemes of structural relationships. (1948, 72, emphasis in the original)

One could comment that this idea is a step forward, in a liberal direction, from the tyranny of the socially determined and socially based theories (the hypostatized ones). It reveals an absolute, abstract belief in the market as an independently conceived pure idea. This is in fact a most important aspect of Hayek's mind, visible in his works of 1948, 1960, 1978. It squares with his belief in the microfoundations of economics and in the compulsory nonintervention of governments.

But it clashes against, and founders upon, the question on which Hayek is most adamant in all of his writings: the rule of law. This theme is treated in all of his works.

In a chapter titled "The Errors of Constructivism" (1978), he equates civilization to reason/loss of instincts, and (surprisingly, for a reasoning man should need no rule) moves on to discuss once again the importance of rules. These are of three kinds: given by social habit, not stated in words, aimless. He is even more specific in 1948, when he explicitly states in ("Individualism: True and False" that laws have to be "abstract." It is not what is "expedient" that can generate order, but what comes from a supposed higher authority: use, time, tradition, the eternal tendencies and characteristics of human beings and human society. That is why, in *The Constitution of Liberty* (1960), free market explicitly means freedom (freedom is explained as the presence of free market). The rule of law is independent from the inherent imperfection of man.

The conclusion to this section is as obvious as it is telling. There is no value formation, even in the ideal world of mainstream and Austrian economic theories, that can do without the presence of the metaphysics. This is introduced surreptitiously, and always inconsistently, in the liberal utopia behind market theory that should be exempt from it.

But, as we saw in the last chapter, in practice there is no liberal utopia behind political economy and economics: only hypostatizations, and a mirroring of the intellectual structures of capitalism. The attempts to construe a neutral, "scientific" method are now observable for what they are: attempts to cover up for the theoretical metaphysics with bridges thrown toward the more "empirical" metaphysics of the eternal institutions of the social.

MARXIST THEORY

Dialectical Marxist theories are similar to bourgeois economics. In the hands of dialectical Marxists, value and class are perfectly bourgeois concepts.

Let us recall how the process of valorization works.

Now, both the practical interdependence of the participants in the exchange system and their personal indifference to one another gain expression in the form of money. (Rosenthal, 1998, 67, emphasis in the original)

In fact, Rosenthal quotes Marx to the effect that

the sphere of circulation or commodity exchange is in fact a very Eden of the innate rights of man. Here alone reign Freedom, Equality, Property and Bentham. (from *Capital*, vol. I, in Rosenthal 1998, 78)

Rosenthal is clear that this involves, in Marx, a critique of political economy.

Herein lies the actual substance of Marx's mature critique of the political economists: [they] managed theoretically to "naturalize" and hence "eternalize" capitalist production by confusing social form and the material bearer upon which qua private property that form gets impressed. (Rosenthal 1998, 85)

Thus

physical items are placed in the value-relation by virtue of a certain sort of social practice. (163)

The situation is simple, when considering value formation.

Recall Marx's observation: This inversion, whereby the sensate-concrete counts only as the form of appearance of the abstract-universal, and not, on the contrary, the abstract-universal as the property of the concrete, characterize the value-expression. (163)

Thus,

what Marx calls the value-relation is, in effect, just the ratio at which different categories of marketable goods exchange. (163)

Therefore,

to belong to a society in which commodity-exchange has become the dominant form of sociality, viz. a capitalist society, is tantamount to participating in the network of exchanges. (144–45)

The conclusion is evident:

actual transactions serve merely to confirm the value-relation, the prevalence of which is precisely the condition of the possibility not so much of their occurrence as such . . . but of their orderly occurrence . . . the coherence of each exchange in the context of the totality of exchanges. (165)

the proposition that money is the empirical universality of commodities is neither curiosity nor mystification. It is correct. (188)

This is a perfectly Hegelian environment. Marxists acknowledge that this is so, only from the wrong end of the argument. To them, there is nothing wrong with the whole being Hegelian. On the contrary, this proves to them that dialectics is a pillar of materialism. They move from a criticism of political economy back to political economy.

The capitalist process is described in the way it works, which is just like the bourgeois economists say it does (only, the Marxists use a different language and pretend to abhor what they describe). Economics is not criticized in Marx's sense of a critique of political economy. On the contrary, it is given a complementary explanation, a reinforcement. Plus, the practice itself is not criticized: it is given the "eternity" and naturality discussed in chapter 2.

The rationale for revolution, then, can only be sought for in the "injustice" that the processes of value formation imply and determine. If revolution is a business of the proletarians or in general of those who are exploited, then it must take the form of class struggle. But having taken a dialectical stance, orthodox Marxism has deprived class struggle of any revolutionary power.[13] Workers are condemned to interact with the system and the classes in power.[14]

There is another, and as bad, outcome: the Soviet solution. Soviet-style systems have terrible problems when seeking to explain the differences between capitalism and their solution to the economic problem, such as why they have prices. There is a law of value at work, and a huge waged class.[15]

Wilczynsky (1973), the author of a very well-known and widely translated Soviet-style textbook, claims (22, 23) that the "general characteristics" that distinguish a socialist from a capitalist system are four:

1. concentration of power in the hands of the party, the representative of the working classes;
2. social ownership of the means of production (state and cooperatives own the productive sector);
3. centralized economic planning;
4. distribution of the national income on bases of social justice.

We are facing the same bankrupt mixture of pretended "scientific" claims and bridges disguised as "the empirical" in practice. The whole is theoretically and practically a metaphysics.

In chapter 15 ("Socialism and Capitalism") Wilczynsky expounds the "advantages and defects of the socialist system" (258, 259). The following are the superior aspects of socialism:

1. economic activity is the expression of the whole of society;
2. full employment is guaranteed;
3. rates of growth have proved very high;
4. workers are not disjointed from the place of work that they somehow co-own, getting pride from their work;
5. national income is well distributed in that wages are the only source of income;
6. costs and social benefits are well balanced;
7. some wastes are prevented (those related to market functioning, say, forced obsolescence of products);
8. vitality (they have been able to adjust to the different situations history brought about).

The disadvantages (261, 263) are an "undue" dominance of politics and ideology over economics, the power of the bureaucracy and the consequent rigidity, microeconomic phenomena are not given due prominence, large scale errors are possible, a "manageable and rational system of prices has not been elaborated yet," "competition is too limited," current consumption is not given due consideration, and last, the masses are alienated from the system.

Whether he is talking about the advantages or the disadvantages, Wilczynsky not only is practicing a mode of thought typical of capitalist intellectuality as explained in Chapter 2 but also throwing away those actual bridges we saw earlier on in this chapter and that are needed to correct those few moments in which the theoretical hypostatizations disguise themselves as methodological/scientific method.

In fact, Wilczynsky (265, 271) suspects that Tinbergen (1961) might have a point with his "convergence hypothesis." "In the last few years" socialist countries have enhanced their attention for the microeconomic sphere, while the capitalists have had Keynesianism.

Centralized planning (in Wilczynsky's times) was being slowly decentralized, while limited forms of planning were practiced in the West. Property and management were getting separated in the West, and the managers were increasingly monopolizing management in the East. Financial incentives and disincentives were being applied in the East, where monetary policy was gaining new importance, while in the West monetary policy was losing ground to fiscal policy and banks. Profit was being accepted in the East and losing importance in the West. Property rights show the same pattern, like income distribution and social structure. The law of value was being extended in the East and distorted in the West (e.g., by monopolies). The role of the consumer was converging, international trade increasingly favoring reciprocal amalgamation.

Let us see what Martov, a libertarian, nonphilosophical Marxist, has to say.[16]

Martov (1980) accuses the Bolsheviks of having privileged "class hatred," transforming the working class into a group dedicated to "social patriotism" or "anarcho-jacobinism" (13). But he knows better than that:

> the working class is a product of capitalist society. It follows that its thought is dominated by that society. Its conscience develops under the pressure of its bourgeois oppressors: school and church, barrack and factory, press and social life, all the factors in sum that form the conscience of proletarian masses are powerful vehicles for the influence of the ideas and of the mentality bourgeois. This is obvious. (43, trans. mine)

But this does not lead Martov to question the Hegelian influence. On pages 48 and 49 he insists on the importance of the working class as the "makers of the new society" and the paramount role played by the alliance (a necessary thing) with other classes (say, the intellectuals, indispensable to make the economy work). He is taken by the dilemma that must have held in its grip many a Marxist revolutionary.

> If we consider Marx's and Engels's opinions on dictatorship, democratic republic and "evil state," we can only conclude that the problem of the conquest of political power has been reduced by them to the "breaking" of the bureaucratic and military machine that despite democratic parliamentarism is the master of the bourgeois state, and to the elaboration of its own state machine, based on a coherently applied democracy, universal suffrage, the amplest possible self-management, on the condition that it is the proletariat that actually leads the majority of the population. (61)
>
> But it is also doubtless that in the political writings of Marx and Engels we find traces of . . . the forms and institutions . . . of the political power of the proletariat, the character of a completely new thing, opposed in principle to the forms of institutions of the political dominance of the bourgeoisie, a thing contrary in principle to the state. The examination of these traces of another level of thought deserves a tractation in itself. (61, 62)

This could not work because, Martov claims on pages 72 and 73, the working class could defeat the complex and organized bourgeois state only by means of an organization as complex and tight—just exactly what we meant to demonstrate. Marxist orthodoxy is a form of bourgeois thought, and not, according to Martov, because it deals with a bourgeois world. The reasons are discussed in chapter 2.

Maurice Dobb is in the same kind of predicament. The perceived need to throw up bridges with the supposedly actual, present-day reality that derives from the Hegelian stance (the incapacity to see the homology between the metaphysics of the theory and that of capitalist reality) draws him to conclusions that are similar to those of Martov. In "A Socialist Economy" (1978), chapter 7 he says,

> In the terminology of contemporary discussion in those countries, the precise relation between plan and market remains undetermined. (127)

He continues:

> two things, however, it seems safe to postulate about market relations in a socialist economy; drawing again upon socialist tradition and upon the practice of socialist countries to date. In the first place, the retail market for consumers' goods . . . must normally be a market in the full sense . . . This we shall see has certain implications for price policy in this market and indirectly for input policy as well.
>
> At the other end of the economic process there are some analogous characteristics in the manner in which labor is engaged and wage-differentials for various occupations are formed. (127)

This is truly astonishing, but is not all.

> Differences in income will . . . be necessary to achieve Adam Smith's "quality of net advantages" as between different occupations. (128)
>
> Perhaps a combination of moral inducement and propaganda might reduce the need for such additional differentials . . . but this is hardly likely to dispense with them entirely. (128)

And finally,

> the existence of such inequalities is fully consonant with the distinction that Marx had made in a famous passage of his *Critique of the Gotha Programme* of 1875 between the two stages of socialism. (129)

The most remarkable thing here is the transformation of the market of the theory into a real thing, which not even the most rabid free-marketeer has ever attempted, and in a real thing that actually works! Not only the theory of market works in theory, which many a mainstream economist have doubted. It also works in practice. Even more astonishing, it exists, and its implementation presents no difficulty worth mentioning. All this is conveniently drowned in a "vulgar Hegelian" amniotic liquid, where incentives, inducements, and the various stages of socialism are as real as the market.

It is evident that the conception of socialism and communism that was, and is, in the minds of dialectical Marxists of all kinds is but the twin brother of the bourgeois institutional setup. This is only logical, because of the considerations developed in chapter 2. Here we notice the relevance of the bridges to supposed reality for Marxist theory.

This is not to mean, it goes without saying, that the discussion of economic planning is useless, or worse, obsolete. On the contrary, I agree with Callinicos (2003) that it is time to at last define what economic planning can do. But that is another story. There is much else that the Marxists do, in theory and in practice. Many perform a commendable work of analysis of the mechanisms of the capitalist economy. One instance will suffice, in that the argument is well defined and clear already.

A recent book that has made a certain amount of noise is Brenner (1998). An extended debate has followed on the pages of *Historical Materialism*.[17] Brenner's work and the debate that followed (and that involved some of the names already quoted and discussed in the present book) show all the characteristics that we have been seeing in this and the preceding chapter. Brenner analyzes capitalist crises using the tools of a Marxist with "analytical Marxist" leanings. The market, and the other concepts and empirical facts, are given a life of their own and thrown into the flow of the continuous, dialectical historical development we saw.

The bridges that we talk about in this section are mainly in the form of empirical variables treated as if they could be directly linked to the whole, which is itself attributed an existence and precise features. The result is that the study is made of simple, even univocal causes, and the various characters and institutions appear to be nothing else than what their description (direct and indirect) offers: poor, arid, simplified objects with one or few roles and influence.

Another most important application of Marxist or quasi-Marxist theory is to the question of uneven development on a world scale.[18] In the 1960s and 1970s a large number of development economists engaged in this kind of pursuit, producing a literature that had very precise characteristics. Their approach proposed that international economic relations are biased toward the advantage of the rich nations. This had already been said on empirical grounds by structuralists (Prebisch and Singer) in the 1950s, but got a more theoretical treatment by Marxist authors. Amin (1976, but see his 2005 work too, that shows the coherence of his thought) and Emmanuel (1972) are the most famous cases.

The theoretical models and empirical observations put forward by Amin and Emmanuel in fact were similar. Emmanuel in particular produced a theoretical model that for its undeniable sophistication had an enduring fortune and is still widely studied. The question is that behind Emmanuel's and Amin's models there is nothing else than the mainstream conception of international trade, the so-called Ricardo-Heckscher-Ohlin-Samuelson model. Orati (2003) makes a compelling case for this possibility.

The Ricardo model in itself is a typical example of mainstream theory with a bridge. Recall Von Mises from the preceding section (see Micocci 2004b): "Ricardo failed to free himself from the Mercantilist image of the Volkwirtschaft" (Von Mises 1949, 633). In a nonliberal environment, nations engage in international trade, confident in the superiority of comparative advantages to allocate production, resources, and income. This implies a sort of final worldwide outcome, a distribution of roles Emmanuel and Amin have immediately picked up.

Starting from, as Orati proves, the Ricardo model, they set out to prove the inherent injustice of the patterns of international trade. It is another and blatant case of bridges linked to the supposed reality within the (unperceived and unsuspected) general metaphysics fueled by the hypostatization mistake.

CAPITALISM, ECONOMICS, THE ECONOMY

The various questions we have been posing here and in the preceding chapter were not unknown to the practitioners, even in the early days of modern economics. Nor were they underestimated. A professor of political economy by the name of Max Weber invented a whole new discipline to mend and fill the gaps provoked by these very problems. But having been invented using the same methodological framework, which entails the presence of the same general intellectuality, sociology did not solve any of the problems posed by economics.

Turning to the "social" variables and concentrating upon empirical analyses rather than theoretical models is not a solution to the hypostatization, let alone the ahistoricity, of the social sciences.[19] It is well worth starting by quoting at length Weber's intuitions on economic theory, the functioning of capitalist relationships, and the correspondence between the two. Weber is merciless in his precision.

> The fantastic claim has occasionally been made for economic theories—e.g., the abstract theories of price, interest, rent, etc.,—that they can, by ostensibly following the analogy of physical science propositions, be validly applied to the derivation of economic behavior with respect to means is unambiguously "de-

termined." This claim fails to observe that in order to be able to reach this result even in the simplest case, the totality of the existing historical reality including every one of its causal relationships must be assumed as "given" and presupposed as known. But if this type of knowledge were accessible to the finite mind of man, abstract theory would have no cognitive value whatsoever. (1999, 246, from "The Methodology of Social Sciences," 1904)[20]

Weber is saying here that reality is far too complex for the methodology of economics and its model-building working habit. In doing this, however, he says much more than he would like to say: he contrasts the infinity (or at least the numerical vastness and complexity) of "causal relationships" to the capacity of the human mind. One is brought to hypothesize that he has in mind exactly what we have been discussing so far. Weber needs not dwell on ruptures and oblivions, given that he chooses to concentrate upon the social rather than the real (the concrete, in our philosophical language).

While his observations on the limits of economic methodology bring no new light on our methodological argument, it is well worth noticing Weber's attention to the connection, explicit in those days and unchanged—although implicit—in ours, between the natural and the social sciences. In fact, he continues,

The naturalistic prejudice that every concept in the cultural sciences should be similar to those in the exact natural sciences led in consequence to the misunderstanding of the meaning of this theoretical construction. . . . It has been believed that is it a matter of the psychological isolation of a specific "impulse," the acquisitive impulse, or of the isolated study of a specific maxim of human conduct, the so-called economic principle. Abstract theory purported to be based on psychological *axioms*. . . . (1999, 246, emphasis in the original)

Weber takes the momentous and dangerous step of not only noticing that reality is complex and social reality is different in a very substantial way from it. Also, in his whole paper he explicitly and unambiguously links human individual and social psychology with "the natural," reality as a whole.

He did not pursue this line of thought further. But the question remains that we are talking of a problem that was, and is, clear. But let us go on following this line of thought in Weber, for we are in for some surprises.

Another lengthy quotation is necessary.

Marginal utility theory and economic "theory" generally do this not, say, in the manner and with the orientation of psychology but rather pretty much in opposite ways. Economic theory does not, one may say, break down *internal* experimental correlates of everyday experience into psychical or psychophysical "elements" ("stimuli," "sensations," "reactions," "automatisms," "feelings," and so on). Instead, it seeks to "understand" certain "adaptations" of man's "external" behavior to conditions of existence of a quite specific sort that are *outside* man himself." (256, emphasis in the original)

The determinants of man's behavior in society (i.e., of economic behavior) are external to man himself. We must couple this with the fact we have seen earlier that they also are rather schematic and simplifying.

Weber is proposing, without explicitly admitting it, that economic theorizations do not simply fail to cover all the possible occurrences of reality. Also, they are intellectually conceived to stand in between a purely conceived theoretical construction and an empirically determined model, thus posing themselves precisely in that position where we saw metaphysics produced. But there is more to come.

Weber continues, on the next page, drawing inferences from this general reasoning.

> The general theorems that economic theory sets up are simply constructions that state what consequences the action of the individual man in its intertwinings with the action of all others would have to produce, *on the assumption that* everyone was to share his conduct . . . exclusively according to the principles of commercial bookkeeping—and, in *this* sense, "rationally." . . . [T]he assumption does not hold. Yet, the historical peculiarity of the capitalist epoch, and thereby also the significance of marginal utility theory (as of every economic theory of value) for the understanding of this epoch, rests on the circumstances that— while the economic history of some epochs of the past has not without reason been designated as "history of non-economic conditions"—under today's conditions of existence the approximations of reality to the theoretical propositions of economics has been a *constantly increasing* one. It is an approximation to reality that has implicated the destiny of ever-wider layers of humanity. And it will hold more and more broadly, as far as our horizon allows us to see. (257, emphasis in the original)

Weber continues stating that the significance of economics "*rests on this* cultural historical *fact*" (257). Also, he notices that the stock exchange constitutes the best instance of this, in the sense of being the most straightforward application of "rationality." This is so because

> action on the stock exchange is economically rational in especially high degree—or can be so. (257)

Before we end up attributing too much of farsightedness to Weber, we should consider that in this particular work the object of his attack is not the epistemological state of economics but the hybrid connection between economics, the natural sciences, and Brentano's psychology.

Reality appears to resemble more and more the predictions of economics's absurd theories. This is what we argued in the preceding chapter: the connections between theory and reality, and the tendency both have, in capitalism, to move toward metaphysics in practice.

The sad part of this story is that this was, and is, well-known to the practitioners of the social sciences. For instance, it has been one of the main preoccupations of Schumpeter throughout his whole life. It bothered Shackle, and also Keynes. In these days it worries very much Tony Lawson (1998, 2003, 2006). Yet, none of these scholars has been able to tackle the question from a general point of view, for this entails the concrete possibility that economics and the other social sciences are challenged to their bases.

Even Napoleoni, who was conversant with Colletti's and Della Volpe's argument about dialectics and was steeped in philosophy, shrank from drawing the necessary conclusions from the issue. Napoleoni (1976) has written with philosophical purposes in mind, to account for the meaning of the theory (better said, theories) of value. We quoted in the introduction to chapter 3 his starting point. Yet neoclassical theory is not a psychological but a technical discipline.

Napoleoni's discussion gets interesting when he comes to talk of the differences between plan and market, for this gives him a chance to admit that economic activities are by their own nature repetitive. As in Weber, the economy does entail the potentially infinite range of occurrences that may derive from man's actions. After claiming (Napoleoni 149, 150) that Schumpeter inserted innovation, entrepreneurship, and revolution in the endlessly repeating cycles/processes of Walras and von Neumann, and having earlier said that Soviet institutions shared the same theory of value as the bourgeois economists, he can only conclude that

> concerning the equilibrium situation, the difference between market and plan is substantially evanescent: when events repeat themselves immutable, and therefore when decisions, once taken, must only be repeated infinite times, the *way* they initially got formed, if from the centre or from the periphery, loses importance. (154, emphasis in the original. Translation mine)

It is well worth meditating upon the complementary function with the same conclusions reached by Dobb and discussed earlier. Napoleoni's discussion of Colletti limits itself to relegating the argument to erudition.[21] Colletti himself, as argued, did not realize the full import of his observation, especially when it comes to the iterativeness of the functioning of the economy. Napoleoni instead, like Schumpeter, sees this iterativeness, its relationship with equilibrium, and the similarity with Soviet systems. But he does not pursue the argument at all. Indeed, it is hard to think of a philosopher or economist who has followed the iterativeness argument to its momentous consequences.[22]

Part of the reason for the absence of this kind of discussion in economics as well as in philosophy is the fact that most scholars are shy to engage the natural-social dichotomy openly. Any time this is done accusations of "Rousseauian utopianism," and above all of "not being realistic" drop like rain. There is an unspoken consensus over the fact that man's social accretions cannot be shed. This simply misses the point: discussing the "natural" as opposed to the social man is simply a device to discuss politics and economics posing man—and not politics and economics—at the center.

Perhaps what these scholars are afraid of is the "subversive" consequences of such analyses: the ruptures and oblivions entailed.[23]

Hong Hoon (2002) mentions the social-natural man distinction, which he nobilitates by using the *physis* and *nomos* terminology. He deals with Marx and Hayek whom, he claims, conflate the two things by positing a natural-social (naturally social and socially natural) man. To him, for these two authors capitalism makes the natural-social distinction disappear through, for instance, fetishism-of-commodities and the value-form. Obviously, this is a rather strong approximation of the thought of Hayek, and even more so for Marx. One should nonetheless praise Hong Hoon's courage, which shows that the problem exists, it is felt by social scientists, and it keeps cropping up every now and then.

It is worth now having a second look at the liberal stream of thought. This in fact has a potentially strong utopian character that might well make room for the question of ruptures and oblivion. This is not the case, however, and why do liberal thinkers get entangled with discussions that imply the ahistoricity and eternity of institutions?

Charles McCann Jr. makes the point we need here in a general and useful way.[24] McCann (2004) conducted a thorough and exhaustive study of a well-chosen line of thought within liberal theory. After a discussion of the main questions at stake in the application of liberalism to actual society, and of communitarianism, he analyzes the thought of, and relationship between, Mill, Stephen, Spencer (I find this choice, that might raise some eyebrows, quite felicitous and sensible), Sumner, Mises, and Hayek. His aim is to prove that liberalism has consistently been misunderstood as a

philosophy of detachment, egoism, greed, individualism, isolation, laissez-faire, self-interest, and selfishness . . . denigrated as providing the intellectual foundation of capitalism, fostering a free market mentality . . . engendering commodification and exploitation . . . to favour the personal over the social, to favour process over result. (1)

But

as one proceeds through the philosophies of the writers presented herein, the themes of society and connectedness will become clear. (5)

And clear they are, in fact. McCann acknowledges that he should talk about liberalism only limited to the thinkers considered. He is, however, adamant that

> liberalism is much richer as a political philosophy than its detractors might be willing to acknowledge, as it is capable of incorporating those very elements of community said to be essential in the conservative and communitarian views to the existence of the good society. (35)

But this is precisely the problem. There is a rift between a theory that is austere and extreme in its theoretical purity and envisages a society in which there is no need of all those devices that actual societies enact to preserve the social order, and its referring to actual societies as embodiments of its ideas. Such devices are those we saw when we discussed Hayek: a strict application of metaphysics. There is no need to go over them again. The question is rather why scholars seem to prefer bending a theory, transforming it from a logical and cogent possibility (a utopia, in common parlance) into a metaphysics.

The core of the problem here is the concept of possibility. Scholars of all sorts devote themselves to bending and hybridizing (or simply avoiding, or forsaking, coherence) the theory they intend to work with in the name of what is "possible." These wise men, who modestly appoint themselves the saviors of humanity from its own foolishness, decide what is possible and go on to distort and denature the theory they choose to update to reality, to "what can be done."

But in the light of the hypostatization theory put forward in the preceding chapter, what they do is simply to take what they have and project it onto the "feasible future." To them the possible, by intellectual fiat, is what they already have, and not what can happen. Lenin looked at czarist Russia with hatred but consistently refused any opening toward communism and anarchy; Mussolini took Italian nationalism, corporatism, and idealism and transformed it into fascism. Smith could not help resorting to the "wealth of society," while Mill put his trust in "community."

McCann acknowledges that

> while liberalism shares with conservatism and communitarianism this understanding of the essential communal nature of man, both conservatism and communitarianism are constructed as to avoid what they perceive to be the chief conflicts of liberalism. (214)

What he has in mind is that

> by accepting as a premise the social nature of being, the liberal as here contemplated needs not posit a *social* ontology [apart from Spencer] . . . to the others it is enough to accept an *individual* ontology, with all the misunderstandings that in-

dividuals are socially constituted, i.e., they are social beings relationally bound
to others. A society, then, is comprised of individuals *and* their relations to one
another, where relations include duties and obligations, predicated on benevolence, solidarity, and sociality. (215, emphasis in the original)

The solution McCann has devised is hinged on that emphasized *and*, which
connects not simply individuals and social relationships but also liberalism
and nonliberal positions. These cannot be trusted to wishful thinking, or to the
undeniable observation that the most important liberal thinkers have been
"coquetting" with them.

The problem remains of the "compatibility" of these two sets of ideas.
If such compatibility might be possible in practice (within the view of
"possibility" earlier explained) due to the capacity of dialectical intellectual processes to connect anything to anything else, in theory we face a different case.

An "ontology of sociality" is needed, which destroys the logical bases of
liberalism; or, the powerful limitation to the potential of liberal thinking constituted by the acknowledgement of present-day institutions, social relations,
and intellectual processes will have to be accepted. Both ways mean giving
up on liberalism and giving in to the absurd idea of "possibility" that derives
from hypostatization.

Another problem, which we are going to face in the rest of the present
book, is the question of the relationship with empirical reality. In fact, theories can be logical and elegant, but they have to reckon with the fact that the
actual, the concrete, might seem reluctant to follow the course that the theory
indicates. That is why we need a theory that goes straight to the concrete,
without contamination during the various phases of its invention, articulation,
extension, and application/verification. Such a theory could prove right or,
simply, wrong.

The importance of the logical argument in the social sciences is thus fundamental in the widest possible way. If linked to, and starting from, the concrete, ideas can actually change the world, as Marx argued in his Thesis XI
on Feuerbach, and also allow precision and hence brevity.

There seems to be a way, for dialectical approaches, to set up a two-way
exchange with both reality as such and reality as perceived by the dialectical
thinkers (the metaphysics). These two dimensions seem to overlap completely. The relationship is possible because we are dealing with items that are
supposed to share a common nature. Writers of all orientations have gotten
entangled in this sort of interpolation.

We can call such interpolation the expanding power of metaphysics. The
hypostatizing powers of the dominant intellectual mode homogenize whatever they come to handle, separating it, in the process, from both the concrete

and the abstract. We have witnessed a story of bridges being built to a reality that was only imagined by those engaged in the bridge-building enterprise. And yet, this imagined reality more and more seems to shape of itself the lives and destinies of the vast majority of the world population, as pointed out by Weber.

Capitalism resembles an anti-individualistic hell, where persons are prisoners of an elementary method of functioning of society. This crippling way of thinking can only be identified with the intellectual method that shapes both the participants in actual life and those who study it. Let us recall, to conclude this section, the discussion in chapter 2, "Metaphysics versus the Abstract," concerning Epicurus's distinction between prolepsis and ipolepsis.

If we are to continue our attempt to detach ourselves from the capitalist dominant, dialectical mode of though, it is crucial to be precise with the idea of prolepsis. We are about to give names to things we have been witnessing since our birth and that look immediate and like a "second skin." The central point is to use prolepsis without disentangling the mind maze. And now, on to discover the dialectical character of actual commercial and economic transactions.

METAPHYSICS VERSUS THE CONCRETE

Capitalist intercourses are perfectly rendered by economics and political economy of both mainstream kinds (bourgeois and Marxist), which reason in a dialectical way. Such a situation leads to the impossibility to move away from the metaphysics that is created any time a description of, or a judgement about, "reality" is uttered. Also, there are undue contaminations between (supposed) items of reality and the theory: bridges are built, by means, for instance, of "ethical" positions, or of actual institutions.

The question is that there is a misuse of the combination of words, theoretical discourses, and observations that go to constitute the expression of sensual perception. Discourses have the lion's share and are the place where the dialectical attitude and the hypostatizations are found. This is not the case, as Epicurus would put it for his own time, of a straightforward substitution of ipolepsis for prolepsis. Rather, it is in a great number of cases a mishandling of prolepsis.

To Epicurus dreams and the delusions of madmen are true because they are produced by sensation through a form of analogy aided by reasoning (Diogenes Laertius 2002, 412); any form of dialectics must be avoided to let prolepsis, aesthesis (perception by means of senses and intelligence) and pathe work themselves through our brain. That is why he also had room for "direct apprehension of the representation of thought." (Diogenes Laertius 2002, 411) Fundamentally, however, we saw that

> there are two species of investigation, one relative to things, the other related to pure and simple words. (Diogenes Laertius 2002, 412)

It is conflating these two that makes one think that whatever can be said in words and articulated in discourse must be put at the same cognitive level as the concrete and the abstract, the two levels that analysis is about.

What happens in practice is that the schematic logical structures of the dominant mentality cannot be completely isolated from reality. This last is constituted both by the social aspect and by the unavoidable influence of reality as a whole on it, which with its mixture of dialectical contradiction and real opposition multiplies the occurrence of what we call "the empirical."

The predominance of discourses, and their dialectical, harmonic character ruled by grammar and syntax and structurally deprived of ruptures and oblivions, leads to the mistaken, facile use of a counterfeited prolepsis. To take the usual illustration, the state's institutions and the state itself are generally taken as if they could be understood by means of prolepsis.

In this framework, the dominant intellectuality works at various levels simultaneously, erecting bridges in the social sciences and operating the prolepsis-katalepsis-reason-pathe relationship. These two modalities are fundamentally similar and the difference between the two blurs in the practice of life under capitalism as we know it.

This is what harmonious thinking, dialectical mentalities do. No interest in actual materiality and in logical soundness is shown. As long as a thing can be said and articulated in discourse, it is worth enrolling it among the items philosophical and scientific analysis can study. The category of exchange for instance, which is composed of a number of concrete objects and acts, as well as generous doses of wishful thinking, is transcended into a (metaphysical) concept that is in the process mistaken as an object. It therefore is studied as such and even identified across eras and geographical distances.

The presence of a "system of prices," for another instance, must imply a conception of value in practice. But prices are not, and cannot be, a "system" other than within institutionalized settings (the five-year plan of the USSR, or the "free market" regulations of the West). Yet, the existence of value is taken for granted and around it the very existence of economics and Marxist political economy is put at stake.

Categories (value, exchange, and the like) born out of misguided intellectual operations become—within the misleading picture of the whole, the metaphysics—apparently as concrete as the concrete itself. This goes back to feed another round of mistaken appraisals, in a never ending game.

The particularity of this situation is that you do not need to go through the various misleading intellectual operations. It is sufficient to "pretend": take the category, use it like the others do, and nobody will notice. The metaphysical part of life is parasitic on the concrete, which supports its operations supplying the material means it holds in store for the endless corrections that are needed.

The most relevant conclusion social scientists can draw is that if categories of the "real" under capitalism can consist in mistaken theoretical reasonings and yet work with the rest like the rest, then the concrete need not be the beginning of scientific investigations. The perception of the concrete, the so-called physical reality, can merrily be misunderstood, as sometimes it is in natural sciences, or just neglected, like in economics.[25]

If the concrete can be neglected in basic reasonings, and be studied only when, and if, some of its elements crop up, the most important thing for capitalism in general and for us is the intellectual aspect. Capitalism is an intellectually based system. Let us go back to the case of value.

Value is the turning point around which everything revolves both in mainstream economics and mainstream Marxism. Without value there would be no exchange, and no equilibrium could be sought. Without value, prices are unable to form. Napoleoni (1976) traces the problem of value back to the physiocrats and follows the development of the question as far as Sraffa. With this latter, he claims, the problem has not been solved but simply "suppressed" (96). But do we perceive value when we lead our daily lives? Or do we just pay money, its easy and multiform proxy?

Karatani (2003) comes close to what we are developing here:

Marx's insight as that the capitalist economy is a system of illusion, that is driven by the movement M-C-M, and that at its fountainhead is the drive to accumulate money . . . in distinction from the wants and desire to achieve wealth. To achieve this objective, he returned to the "value form." Therefore, *Capital*'s similarity to the Hegelian system should not confuse us. (159)

In fact,

The commodity economy is that which organizes objects and their production with its fictitious institution, thus giving them commodity form. . . . what we grasp as objects of the political economy are never the "things in themselves" but only the "phenomena" . . . i.e., the commodity economy. [This] discovers its limits in those things it cannot organize at its disposal [the natural environment, human beings]. (198)[26]

I could not think of anything a mainstream economist could find to comment upon or oppose in the quotation above, once it has been translated into the simplified language economists are used to. The whole thing is in fact but one of the many tautologies economics itself is made of.

In fact, the description of the formation of prices within a system seeking a mainstream or Marxist equilibrium matters as long as we accept the presence of (fictitious) "institutions." Not only is there no way to disentangle the two: also, without the institutions properly limiting our field of action we would not be able to produce the solvable set of equations we need to work-out our equilibrium. What we need to have, as Rosenthal (1998) puts it when defining money, is

> an economic system distinguished by the fact that the range of productive activities it comprises are only articulated into an interconnected whole a posteriori through exchange. (55)

Money, although conceived of as an "abstraction," in fact "constitutes" the empirical-concrete of capitalism.

> As Marx repeatedly emphasized, the very functioning of a generalized exchange economy depends upon abstractions *which are real*. (58, emphasis in the original)

Here is the substance of Marx's critique of political economists (Rosenthal does not develop this), who naturalized and eternalized capitalist production "by confusing social form and the material bearer upon which qua private property that forms gets impressed" (85). This does not help us progress, however, in understanding what we need equilibrium for and why the conceptualization of equilibrium is behind any attempt, Marxist and mainstream, to explain exchange, value, and prices.

Textbooks of economics use equilibrium all the time. But what is an equilibrium?[27]

Equilibrium is the process of approaching the static state of a system. It only exists when it is mentioned and made explicit, and its most common representation is the meeting of two curves on a Cartesian quadrant. It is the most perfect example of an abstraction that is real. We draw a supply and a demand curve, notice that they end up meeting somewhere, notice that the point where they meet holds the property of balancing the satisfaction and dissatisfaction of suppliers and demanders, and armed with this result we proceed to apply it to various cases, first of all those determined by the possible shapes and slopes of the curves.

Strong with its applicability, we turn to "reality," and notice that yes, it is possible after all to conceptualize prices as going up and down according to the availability of the goods supplied and demanded. At that point, we can even guess that this "abstraction" fits reality: our "abstraction" has gone to constitute "the empirical-concrete of capitalism."

But here, mysteriously, everything vanishes in the haze of empirical studies, and equilibrium resurfaces only in the introduction of papers and in sophisticated theoretical discussions. The "normality" of the economics profession is punctuated by the confusing presence of the bridges to empirical reality, a need that finds no justification and yet is felt by most practitioners.

Both Marxist and mainstream equilibrium[28] are just the requirement of a tautological theory. You cannot match prices, values, production, and the like and bring them to a point of visibility unless they are static: in equilibrium. Once you have done that, of course you have to go the other way around and look for dynamism again, like Schumpeter attempted. You have to show that entrepreneurs go where profit rates are higher, and you have to do that by means of a succession of equilibrium points. But in so doing, you have abolished the fact that

> *physical items are placed in the value-relation by virtue of a certain sort of social practice.* (Rosenthal 1998, 163, emphasis in the original)
>
> Actual transactions serve merely to confirm the value-relation, the prevalence of which is precisely the condition . . . of their *orderly* occurrence—of, in brief, the coherence of each exchange in the context of the totality of exchanges. (165, emphasis in the original)

Rosenthal understands the important role money has to hold together coherently all these metaphysical exchanges. He puts it in a way that I can only commend: the money-commodity is isomorphic with the Hegelian "empirical universal," perfectly so. (See especially 192–93.)

Not taking the anti-Hegelian argument to its logical conclusions brings Rosenthal to a description of economic phenomena that is critical of them but cannot replace anything in the sense of Marx's Thesis XI. It suffices to notice for our purposes here that we have found out a well-known though never admitted old truth—that is, that the reasoning of economics produce metaphysics, and that the question of value, that is the origin of the whole exchange system in practice, in the concrete of actual exchanges, is metaphysics at work.

Concrete objects, from our bodies to coins to commodities, labor, and so forth, are moved around by the sheer power of metaphysics, as long as there is a coherent environment for all this to happen without anybody shouting, "The king is naked!" Those portions of the concrete that fall under the spell of the law of value get for a while suspended from Earth and from the material, converted into metaphysics. The only properties of their material nature that cannot be suspended are those of, say, natural decay and obsolescence.

Commodities, or labor, are given a value that has no ground other than social convention, which itself follows the same rules as the theory. Equilibrium is being worked out when prices change in relation to the fluctuations in supply and demand. But it is the very presence of those parts of the concrete that are out of control (Adam Smith's "enhancements of market prices") that leaves a possibility to both approximate as much as possible equilibrium and escape it, making, say, "windfall" profits.

The whole thing is a system based on the exceptions to the rule. If there were no exceptions it would not work for long, as Schumpeter was fully aware: only imagining it as a continuously revolutionizing (à la Schumpeter) process can we imagine it will endure.

But Schumpeter's "revolutions" have not saved capitalism from its endemic crises, nor have they changed it. Technology has not moved forward for a very long time now. Gordon (2000) is quite convincing when he notices how few of the great inventions of the past and present can be considered revolutionary. The debates on the transition from feudalism to capitalism and on the Industrial Revolution point to the role of "important" technical changes and inventions (crop rotations, the steam engine, the division of labor, sanitation) in comparison to which recent inventions (Taylorism, Fordism, nuclear power) pale or look ridiculous (take computers).

We can only infer that the needed exceptions to the rules must come from either the nonconformity of the system to its logic (say, the markets not working, the cases of mono- and oligopolies, which seem in fact the rule at all levels of capitalism), or the presence of constraints that obstruct the functioning of the system itself. While the first case can be, given the correspondence between theory and reality discussed so far, dealt with quickly by referring the reader to the literature of economics and the other social sciences (which in such cases, simply, apply), the second leads us back to the problem of the bridges, Hayek's solution, and McCann's reading of his sample of liberal thinkers.

We must consider the actual way whereby what I have been calling so far "metaphysics" expresses itself in practice. We are clear that it is a kind of intellectual attitude sustained by a flawed logic, and it is detached from the concrete without being fully abstract either. We have also seen, very importantly, that we have a "faked prolepsis" going on. That is, the relationship between some concepts of actual social life taken as "the fundamental ones" and the immediate presence of their image in the human mind is considered, in fact faked, as a prolepsis.

While, however, light, or a horse, or any material object (or absence of visible objects) are easily imprinted in the mind of the infant, this is certainly not the case with "concepts" such as state, law, duty, and the like. These, we saw, derive from an intellectual operation and not a straightforward one: they derive from a socially determined type of intellectual operation, the kind that is pursued in children (and adults) only after the first order type of logical inferences are developed by nature and, inevitably, by nurture.

It is here that the bridges work their way into the dominant mentality, complicating the faked prolepsis and gaining that respectability that legitimates them in the social sciences. If social life is held together by a (dialectical) intellectual metaphysics that searches and finds its counterpart in the actual relationship of reality, then it is evident that the handling of the social concepts by the social sciences and the public at large is just an intellectual game with words. It is the second species of investigation Epicurus talks about: that about words.

It is in fact words that constitute the variables in the game, the metaphysics of social life. Words are vested with the whole burden of what we have called the metaphysics. Propositions such as "the presence of state and/or society is self-evident," or "it is natural to man to live in society" are extreme examples of the complex process we saw.

But the most important thing is that in the "orderly occurrence" of the "social practice" Rosenthal talks about, or the "system of illusions" Karatani has in mind, actual intellectual processes can be skipped in practice and replaced by ready-made result. Words at the social level signify "discourse." Culture determines the way words are composed into discourses. That is, to use a more common but imprecise term, language (language as such might in fact exist even without this or that culture) is the mirror of the time we live in.

This is no news: Marcuse's *One-Dimensional Man* (1967) is a desperate observation of this sad fact, just like Adorno (1989) and Adorno/Horkheimer (1979). A more complex and ambitious attempt is that of Debord's *Society of the Spectacle* (1983, 1989), worth a more diffused look, as well as a defense against enthusiastic exegetes and self-appointed "situationists."

We can see very clearly now that when we mention, say, "market," we are not dealing, whatever the circumstances in which we need that word, with anything else than the word itself. Whether we said it in the context of launching a new product, of a classroom presentation, in the heat of a political meeting of anticapitalist activists, it is the empty word we are referring to. This is what even those who have a developed sense of the logical shortcomings of capitalism and its dialectical mechanisms, like Karatani or Rosenthal, do not see, at least in its full import. They still attribute to it some philosophical meaning, or at least a certain amount of reasoning.

This simple matter has always been very clear. For instance, Erasmus says,

When the people of Rome were ready to rebel, what recalled them to a sense of civic duty? A philosophical oration? Hardly. Rather, a childish cock-and-bull story about the belly and the other parts of the body. A similar fable of Themistocles about the fox and the hedgehog had the same effect. What wiseman's oration would ever accomplish as much as that imaginary hind of Sertorius . . . Spartan Lycurgus. . . . To say nothing of Minos or Numa, both of whom controlled the foolish crowd by making up fables. Such trifles as these have an effect on that enormous and powerful monster, the mob. (Desiderius Erasmus 2003, 40)

Only, what in ancient eras was expressed with stories and anecdotes under capitalism is more succinctly replaced by words evoking the metaphysics, such as market, or value, or exchange. These in fact cover up for an implicit reasoning that is taken for understood in normal usage and that is nothing but the occasional epitomization of the dialectical, hypostatizing logic. Here is the formidable advantage of capitalism: in normal social intercourses, which also comprise the endless exceptions to the rules, there is no need to resort to the (flawed) general logic, for this is homogeneous and inescapable.

Both the exceptions and the rule exist precisely because of the presence of what is supposed to signify them: their fall could come only once the hidden logic is called into question by a sufficient majority, an almost impossible event in normal circumstances.[29] Critics of economic theory and of political philosophy who think to be working for change are mistaken: they are, at least in the short-medium run, just inconsequential.

We are dealing with a coldly rational kind of psychology based only on those syllogisms that can handle the dialectical features of the relationships among the words/concepts we use. These represent and in fact constitute the facts with which we are pretending to deal.

We now see the correspondence between the actual mechanisms of social intercourses and the intellectual mechanisms of society that correspond to it, both at the level of everyday life and of economics and the other social sciences. We have reached a turning point of our general presentation of the metaphysics and the dialectics of capitalism.

RUPTURES AND DYNAMISM

We can now see in a different light what we have called "bridges" and methodological incoherences in the liberal thinkers, comprising the Austrians. Their attachment to state authority and the nation-state, and their insistence on a framework of rules predicated upon ethics, traditions, and culture, is not a complete betrayal of their ideas. Although the incoherence on logical grounds remains, they are simply inserting in the right slot those "words" for which their chosen field makes room.

McCann (2004) puts it perfectly:

While liberalism shares with conservatism and communitarianism this understanding of the essential communal nature of man, both conservatism and communitarianism are constructed so as to avoid what they perceive to be the chief
conflicts of liberalism. (214)

Yet he is very aware of the true danger:

By accepting as a premise the social nature of being, the liberal as here con-
templated needs not posit a *social* ontology. Of those with whom we have dealt,
Spencer comes closest to such a reification of society. . . . As to the others, it is
enough to accept an *individual* ontology, with the understanding that individuals are socially constituted. . . . A society, then, is comprised of individuals *and*
their relations to one another. (215, emphasis in the original)

McCann sees the fundamental point of what he calls, along with the dominant jargon, the "conflicts" inherent to the liberal idea of freedom. He also
sees the danger of reifying society if a "social ontology" is accepted. His solution is as brilliant as a solution within the mainstream could be: an individual ontology with a socially constituted individual.

This solves McCann's contingent problem but breaks the path to a whole
set of new problems. One is constituted by the paradoxes considered by Alex
Callinicos's *Inequality* (2001). The other, more momentous, is the reification
of the socially constituted self. This not only concerns the argument unfolded
in these first two chapters. It also takes us to organic visions of society—that
is, to positions analogous to those of Spencer. We must not be shy to call such
positions by their names: fascism and socialism.

The most pressing thing here is the complex question related to the idea of
"conflict" that bothers so much the conservatives, the communitarians, and
even the liberals themselves. Conflicts contain a whole range of possibilities,
comprising the nondialectical kinds. Think of all those instances when society impinges upon the rights of the individual to pursue its own idea of the
good life. But more than these kinds of oppositions, which are amenable to
be reduced, edulcorated, and denatured in theory as well as in practice, in capitalism we find potential real opposition.

Take, in economics, the disappearance of inadequate firms, entrepreneurs,
products, machinery. In a homogeneous capitalist environment (no underdevelopment, no oligo-monopolies, all market laws in their place and working),
the "inadequate" entrepreneurs, factories or, say, products, would be scrapped
at once by the market system. They should disappear with all the entailed endowment of techniques, knowledge, means of production, and the like.

The market then would indeed be, like Walras stated very clearly, a static thing, if it worked. A world of homogeneous capitalism, of a liberal sort, would be condemned to a perfectly static condition, with resources shifting only from a market to another, and equilibria being only temporarily upset as a consequence.

Here comes the splendidly lucky fact[30] that

1. Since Adam Smith, economics and Marxist political economy are built around the existence, and acceptance in the theory, of the nation-state, or just any sort of state, given that the state is unexplicited in mainstream economics and community or society can do instead of it.
2. The world is extremely far from even approaching capitalism, even in the so-called developed countries. Present-day capitalism lives precisely out of this international inequality among nation-states. There is no need to discommode development economics and the theories of underdevelopment: it is sufficient to point out that the very theory of "international" trade is hinged upon David Ricardo's comparative advantages (the Heckscher-Ohlin-Samuelson model)—that is, the resurrection of the *Volkwirtschaft* pointed out by Von Mises (1949, 633. See also Micocci 2004b).

It is only because of this incomplete (and uneven, and unjust, and disgusting) state of things that "capitalist" theories—liberal, communitarian, conservative, but also Marxist—can survive in their logical and epistemological confusion, and the mechanisms that rescue everybody and do not let anybody out of the game can work. Economics works despite its internal contradictions and incoherences because it resembles the very same inconsistencies that are present in reality. The "words" are the things, and the things themselves are only accessory to the metaphysics.

Did Marx get things wrong in *Capital*, then, when he started his tractation from commodities? Yes and no. Commodities are in fact, in the framework here sketched (but we shall complete the description in the rest of the book), second-order categories in the functioning of capitalist society. This is even more so in our days of "advanced" capitalism, in which production of material goods has come to be regarded as the obsolete sector of the economy. (See e.g., Sylos Labini, 2004; Vasapollo 2003a, 2003b.)

But in starting from commodities Marx was also right because of his own Thesis XI: he did not just intend to interpret the world. If a revolution is to be pursued, then you have to, first and foremost, start from the material and look for those tendencies in the material that lead to real oppositions, ruptures, and disappearances. Commodities are concrete things; the point is rather that they should be placed within a nondialectical framework.

In fact, the image of capitalism we have been delineating is that of a place where there is no room for real oppositions. Only dialectical relations of reciprocal influence are at work, in a vulgar Hegelian framework where relationships between incoherent entities and realms (the material and the abstract) are possible because these two realms are superseded in the metaphysics. Let us stay a bit with dialectical Hegelian authors to see in some detail how this takes place.

Paul Diesing[31] (1999, 7) starts by saying that his work will be most useful to "political economists and philosophers who think in terms of dynamic social processes . . . rather than static abstract models." Claiming that theoretical models are abstract is a statement of great momentum: it fixes in one stroke all of those interpolations among incompatible worlds that make up dialectical theories and realities. To him

culture, then, is the objective *Geist,* as in *Geistwissenschaften,* cultural sciences. . . . The spirit has issued forth . . . and embodied itself in an external and outward world . . . the world of *institutions,* . . . laws, society, state, customs, manners. (10, emphasis in the original)

In fact,

remember, present society and culture grows out of the past and carries its past with it. (22)

No ruptures, let alone disappearances, are permissible:

That's dialectic! Everything internal, like love, gets externalized, and everything external gets internalized. So love implies its opposite, furniture, *our* shared capital. The family is actual . . . furniture and housing are the material base of the family. . . . The family and its material base change together. (49, emphasis in the original)

This example (I wish to Diesing he got a better deal from love) is absolutely perfect in embodying the transference that dialectics can operate from material objects to words (the vulgarization of the metaphysics).

[Economists] have discovered general principles operating in the mass of daily life details.

But notice that these principles are

a show of rationality; they deal with appearances, market transactions. Hegel wants to go beyond these . . . without rejecting the work of economists . . . [to

see] how the universal mediates the particulars, changes them by inducing them
to adapt to one another and become more and more interdependent. (52)

Indeed,

the particular buyers and sellers, and their differences, are mediated by the universal: exchange-value. The market also develops . . . during this process; it
doesn't just exist. (52)

In fact,

Socialism must grow within capitalist development, if at all, just as capitalism
slowly grew within feudalism. . . . One way to start is by looking for signs of a
reversal of domination. (169)

But there is more to Diesing that must be pointed out.

New institutions grow slowly out of the old ones, and the old persist in revised
form (*aufgehoben*) in the new. Changes in Eastern Europe are the latest example. (173)

The old "authorities" and "structures" persist.

Hegel learned this from the French revolution, but failed to convey it persua-
sively enough; utopian thinking persists. Progress comes slowly, if at all. (173)

Even Hegel slipped into some utopianism!
Unlike Diesing, Arthur (2003) is committed to dialectics to the point of in-
tolerance of any strategy that contains even a hint of a rupture or disappearance, even microscopic instances of it. Take, to start with, the fact that

the value form of the commodity becomes actually established as a concretely
universal determination. (34)

Arthur does not see that the capitalist qualities of commodities are embodied in the word and its syntax. They are established as a concretely universal
determination: at last Geist has embodied itself in the proper form, and we
can move on. Marx's M-C-M movement is "so to speak, 'absolute form'"
(103).

A mode of production is an organic whole that reproduces itself almost automatically. It can only be replaced by violent socialist revolution. (213)

In chapter 11 Arthur introduces the example of victims of capitalism who
steal books. This to him is anathema:

I have shown that obedience to the rationality of the system on the one hand, and particular negations of its norms (constituted by acts of self-assertion on the part of disadvantaged sections) on the other, are both equally valid, that this contradiction cannot be resolved in theory if it expresses the structure of a material situation. It follows that only a practical transformation of that reality is capable of resolving it. (229)

If this were not clear enough,

the point [is] the failure of abstract reason to relate to practice. (230)

In order to understand completely we must go back to page 228. Arthur is not particularly interested in arguing a philosophical opposition. His main concern is not philosophy but reality as a Hegelian structure: he is concerned ·with society as we have it and its "transformation." You must ban acts of rupture, however small, such as in the case of people stealing books from bookshops and libraries, because

the anti-social consequences of such an act cannot be ignored. A bookstore might be forced to close altogether to the net loss of everybody. Whatever ground for each offence there may have been the overall effect is to promote insecurity. . . . One cannot justify directly an infringement of an existing social practice by reference to the allegedly superior quality of non-existent alternative practices because, for practical purposes, it is the meaning of the action within the existing system that determines the kind of act that it is.

All that has been said about dialectical approaches is condensed in this last sentence. An action that is not determined by the existing system is not. Mind you—it just is not. Here is the key to understanding the power of that translation of facts, relations, and actions into words. If that translation does not take place, things, actions, and relations are not.

Ruptures and disappearances, being not part of the system, are as a consequence ruled out. The question is then whether this is possible in practice— that is, in general.

We have seen in chapter 2 an introductory definition of rupture. We can add here a description of how it works and a distinction between noncontrollable and controllable ruptures. We shall thus come to start seeing what dynamism is. Let us begin from the second aspect, which involves important considerations.

Distinguishing between "natural" and "social" ruptures/disappearances, say, earthquakes and the like on the one hand and on the other hand the disappearance of Neanderthal men would be, simply, wrong. A distinction between natural and social in the framework so far developed can make sense only at a superficial, descriptive level, to keep a communicative connection with the mainstream social sciences.

The reason is that even intellectually limiting capitalist acts are "natural." They are just attempts to limit the unknown potential of the naturality of the mind to one, or a set, of syllogisms from which a manageable range of consequences can be obtained for life in society (true, imagined, or sought for). The social is meant as a subset of the natural that is determined by the application of limiting mechanisms.

Thus we can talk also of controllable and noncontrollable ruptures. Coming to the announced description of how ruptures work, we must first of all acknowledge a difficulty in our plans. While there are grand ruptures we can use as examples and images of what is meant, such as the Neanderthal case, we cannot claim we can safely define them as ruptures. We can approximately describe them as ruptures because there are in them a number of aspects related to disappearances and gaps; but we do not know what and even if Neanderthalers have bequeathed anything to us.[32]

If capitalism stands on a dialectical mentality that substitutes things with metaphysics, then the kinds of ruptures we are interested in are intellectual. They are individual acts of full, nonlimited intellectuality. They are an instrument to break with capitalism, to make a revolution rather than "revolutionize capitalism," and they are not amenable to proselytism and, contrary to Arthur, violence.

In economics, and in the social sciences in general, dynamism is meant to be the capacity to follow in detail, without giving up the theoretical strictures of the method, the supposed "innovative" capacity of capitalism. It is decided a priori that capitalism is dynamic/innovative, so that the social sciences can go and search for instances of dynamism and innovation, with a chance to redefine the objects of one's search as suited. Marxist political economy does not make this mistake, for it is fully aware that the dynamism of capital consists of its capacity to create itself from the historically given conditions. The problem is that orthodox Marxism follows an impossible dialectical path to do this, thus losing sight of its own object.

A dynamic approach is instead an approach that, being logically sound, is capable of conceiving, and making room, for ruptures and disappearances. The study of reality is organized starting from the concrete. Social rules and behaviors become instances of peculiar ways to prevent ruptures. The laws of the social or that mirror it are therefore not useful to study it. We need "extraneous standards."[33] These we are in the process to obtain with the rest of the argument in the present book.

CONCLUSIONS

This chapter has taken us through a number of conceptual developments that go against the grain of the common sense of life under capitalism. The potential developments of all that has been said are even more unsettling in this sense. I shall not conceal the fact that the emotional corollaries of this might prevent a number of readers from fully grasping the meaning and import of what is unfolding here.

Let us put some order in the things that have been said. We have given some general reasons for the social sciences to represent what they are meant to scientifically analyze. We have found out that this is due to a hypostatizing, dialectical mentality that is identically present at the level of the method of the social sciences and of the actual intercourses of capitalist societies. This has created a general, metaphysical framework in which actual things, actions, and relationships are substituted by the words, and relative syntax, that are supposed to signify them.

Syllogisms replace reasoning and observation. Things, actions, and relationships do not exist unless they are put in the shape of syllogisms of the elementary, flawed type we saw. This whole setup is therefore unable to transcend itself, and even less to leave itself. No exit is conceived. This whole thing takes place at the intellectual level. Dynamism is misconceived as the actual functioning of a system that bans disappearances and ruptures. Capitalism amounts to an intellectual game aiming at settling with the standard set by the developed countries, crystallizing it. This is mistakenly identified as capitalism *tout court*, with a typical tautology. All material acts are moved by this, and only this.

This looks, and is, truly terrible. Like all terrible things, it enrolls in the group of its defenders precisely those who have some clues as to its atrocity. To stand back and look at it, avoiding emotional reactions, we have to take "extraneous standards": we must detach ourselves.

Those readers who feel uncomfortable with what is being said should think of the present book as a thought experiment. If they think that what I say is wicked (some told me so), then they should liken their reading to that time when they tried acid or cocaine or immoral acts just to see what it is like (I hope they have done something of the sort). Once brings no addiction; yet, doing it, going beyond the boundaries, is an emotion worth feeling, even to go back within the boundaries.

Those who have felt emotional unease during our journey so far should prepare themselves for further traumas. I wish you could share my thrill at moving forward.

NOTES

1. Garegnani (see for instance 1981) has been pretending to criticize the whole of economics, going no further than a snail-paced production on the subject. This has also slowed down the work of all those who recognize him as a schoolmaster, and, in a sort of tide typical of the clientelism of Italian academia, of whosoever was considering Garegnani and his clients their reference point. For the grouping together of orthodoxy and heterodoxy, see Micocci (2002a, 2003b, 2004c, 2005a, 2005b, 2005c). For a critique of Lawson's critique of economics, see Micocci (2004d).

2. I shall take for granted here that the potential reader of this knows what the market is in mainstream economic theory. Readers who are not sure they remember it perfectly are advised to take a second look at it before continuing reading. Any textbook of economics (they are all the same) can be consulted for this purpose.

3. Smith's is a classical vision. The difference with modern mainstream visions is unimportant, however, to the purposes of the present discussion.

4. One should not be deceived by (especially heterodox) cries of "here the market does not work," or "does not exist."

5. Such admission is left to heterodox practitioners like Shackle, or "multidisciplinary" kinds of guys. Thus, the sacred neutrality of economics is left to its purity.

6. This brings us back to Marx and Rosenthal on the value form. Here Marxist and mainstream theories coincide in the analysis, disagreeing on the consequences. But we shall see the whole in chapter 7.

7. Callinicos does not see that the same can be said for Marxism. In fact, he concedes that ethical arguments have an importance. Both liberalism and Marxism are incompatible with such arguments, which drag them back inside the complications and incoherences of the metaphysics of reality in general.

8. The aloofness itself is useless anyway, in that it is at the level of the hypostatization mistake that economic theories, classical and neoclassical, fall (see chapter 2, and Micocci 2002a, 2003b, 2005c).

9. A most revealing instance is on page 459 (Book II, chapter V, "Of the Different Employment of Capitals"), on the type of capital that adds to the wealth of society. That is why in Book III, chapter I, he (but so do his epigones, too) can then talk about "The Natural Progress of Opulence."

10. See also Micocci (2002a, 2004a).

11. Menger, whom we shall discuss later on, had the same courage as Marshall.

12. I argue this in Micocci (2003b, 2004a, 2004d, 2005c).

13. See chapter 2 and Micocci (2002a, 2003b).

14. This interaction can take the form of organized violence, or of reformism.

15. This was faced in the 1920s by Preobrazhensky, who gained admission to the group of the victims of the regime but not to the hall of fame of the rehabilitated, like his sycophant Bukharin. See Micocci (2002a). See also Scarfoglio (1941), a most interesting early appraisal of the Soviet experiment by a sympathetic and ironic observer.

16. The West is replete with publications by Soviet dissidents, from Soljenitsin to Sakharov to the Medvedev brothers to Kagarlitsky. None of them shows any theoret-

ical inclination. Those who worked on theory, such as Meszaros and Baran, showed instead a wholehearted commitment to the Marxist-Leninist orthodoxy.

17. See Micocci (2002d).

18. This question had a thick Marxist moment, went back to more generically progressive positions, and eventually disappeared due to the normalization that has taken place in development economics.

19. See Micocci, 2002a, where I develop the methodological argument.

20. I want to thank Charles McCann Jr. for sending me this anthology, which prompted fresh thinking about Weber.

21. Napoleoni (1976) misunderstands crucial points about the dialectics. See also Micocci (2002a).

22. Hints of the iterativeness questions can be found in the political writings of Debord, whose Marxist orthodoxy has been constantly neglected by commentators. See Micocci (2002a). Schumpeter had it in mind too (see Micocci 2001c).

23. I thank Massimiliano Biscuso's patience in bearing my insistence in discussing this topic. By the way, I could not convince him of my ideas, which substitute the usual disclaimers.

24. He obviously objects strongly to the conclusions I infer from his work. We have been discussing the topic for a long time now.

25. Lawson (1998, 2003) is the most respected scholar who bases his reasonings on the assertion that economics has nothing or little to do with reality. His mainstream readers, however, know very well that it does not matter (it is in fact a favorite subject for those jokes about the profession that economists are so fond of telling each other at congresses).

26. Karatani uses this insight to pursue his Kantian *Transcritique*. See Micocci (2006a).

27. Modern introductory textbooks just start from actual equilibrium (Begg et al. 2003; Zamagni 1987; Schiller 2002). So I went to good old Allen (1960), only to be as frustrated.

28. While in mainstream economics equilibrium is a completely theoretical construct, most Marxist attempts at equilibrium start from a sort of classical *tableau economique* (the Departments I and II), which might be accounted an essential moment of the "materialist" method.

29. Normal circumstances being precisely those when the explicitation and discussion is not needed.

30. See Micocci 2004b.

31. I would like to express my gratitude to him for an unexpected review of Micocci (2002a) and for his sending me his *Hegel's Dialectical Political Economy* (1999).

32. We also, conversely, presume to know what the Romans bequeathed on us, but this presumption should be challenged as well.

33. See Marx and Engels (1985): "History must, therefore, always be written according to an extraneous standard . . . [not to] share the illusions of that epoch" (59–60).

Chapter Four

The Iterative Nature of Capitalism

Capitalism's elementary, simplified logic can only produce operations that resemble each other: capitalism is a boring, repetitive place. The aim of this chapter is precisely that of showing this aspect of the inner nature of capitalism.

Capitalism as we know it keeps going endlessly without evolving and without allowing any entry or exit. It is constantly in danger of contamination/puncturing by the whole of reality—that is, the naked concrete, the material. Therefore its only hope to survive is by consolidating its hold on itself: its isolation from reality as such with its complexity. The material is just incidental to the functioning of capitalism. The driving force of its isolation mechanisms is intellectual homogeneity. Material or material-related entities such as commodities, or exchange, are second-order variables. Social intercourses determine their effect on commodities by means of their homogeneity with the dominant intellectuality.

The functioning of capitalism, I shall argue, is "iterative." Iterative does not mean repetitive: iteration indicates a series of operations that must be necessarily repeated, although not necessarily in the same order or in the same quantitative and qualitative terms. Many operations of normal life are iterative in nature: for instance, those that have to do with fitting something into a predetermined frame, shape, or object. One has to try an adjustment, check if it works, than take the thing back for a further adjustment (which changes slightly the thing's aspect), for an indefinite number of times, until the two fit each other.

Capitalism's iterative functioning, and its apologists are right to point it out, causes a degree of movement all the time. Only, they mistake iteration with innovation and change. Every iteration is hailed and saluted as "evolution," or even revolution. This process has a further complication: given the continuous degrees of variation (the iteration), the solution, the final perfection, is unreachable.

Capitalism can only adjust; it cannot change or, even less, evolve, even into what its celebrators claim it is set to become. Capitalism as we know it is extremely far from its supposed final, definite form. Most importantly, in its present, imperfect situation it in fact borrows features from supposedly anticapitalist ideologies and practices, first of all fascism. The iterations might one day stop, like all historical things. The survival of capitalism is thus entrusted to the intellectual whole that creates and protects the bubble capitalism comes down to in practice and that can only be beaten by "extraneous standards."

CAPITALISM AS A CULTURAL FRAME

Let us start by going over the question of what it is that we, often lightheartedly, define as capitalism. The issue is simultaneously very simple and very complex. We could just say that capitalism is what is unanimously called so by both mainstream and Marxist social sciences.

But we have seen that the most peculiar and determining pillar of capitalism is its intellectual nature. Not only does capitalism correspond to a dialectical frame of mind that constitutes the rationale and the driving force for all its actual, material, and institutional parts and movements. Also, to this general intellectuality there corresponds a simultaneous apprehension of what capitalism is supposed to be. This is constantly revised and revisable.

Here is the cause of the complexity we witness, as well as the cause of the very perseverance that is typical of capitalist intellectuality. The most striking and comprehensive aspect of such perseverance is the intellectual mirroring between Marxist and bourgeois social sciences. This also illustrates, by causing it, the more general, practical perseverance of everyday life that goes on despite the atrocities we witness every day.

The need to continuously assess, apprehend, and act in practice keeping within the general framework that is being assessed can only refer to reality as it is perceived: the metaphysics. Items that hang between the concrete and the abstract come to depend on the maieutical capacity of the current period. This is the mechanism of actual socialization. As long as they can be socialized, capitalist items can undergo the intellectual maieutic of the process of valorization, or any other process (say, that which leads to belief in nationalism, or in socialism), and the "business as usual" of capitalism can go on within the metaphysics.

The erecting of bridges that we have seen in the preceding chapter is an inevitable part of this process. Put this together with the intrinsic continuity of the intellectual processes (one cannot stop thinking) and you see an ongoing, "only apparently changing" world. Everything moves, because even when material entities do not move (say, commodities in the typical glut situation of economic crises) the intellectual activity of which they are nonetheless a part keeps going on: the metaphysics never rests.

All the rest, like nationalism, or the participation in the process of valorization as if that was natural, which when described amounts (we saw it last chapter) to a complicated and apparent faked prolepsis, follows from this main feature. The intellectual (flawed) nature of the metaphysics determines its continuous motion. We should, therefore, look at capitalism minding the gap between the unlimited world of material entities and the limited logic of the metaphysics itself.

The most relevant consequence of all this is that capitalism constantly disattends the expectations implied by the apprehension and assessment activities. Capitalism must continuously settle accounts with the descriptions of itself that it uses as a reference for keeping its intellectual nature going. It has been shown in chapter 2 that we are in the presence of an economic theory that mirrors the actual economic processes, whose intellectual nature it shares. Capitalism is constantly talking of itself with its own syntax and words and must endlessly justify itself vis-à-vis the variety of the material.

Let us go back to the need—the inevitability—to build those bridges to the supposedly empirical that the preceding chapter has revealed. This operation, given that capitalism always disattends its apprehension processes, ends up recuperating the noncapitalist features of capitalism in reality. This gives capitalist intellectuality the chance to overcome for a while its limited and limiting character.

Capitalism as we know it is a maze of interconnections between laws, institutions, ideologies, limits to commerce, limits to material production and the distribution of products, the presence of the "market of the theory," and of what we call "actual" markets, which happen in the limbo of the metaphysics. We have seen that this maze works because it shares a common intellectual culture (a flawed method and structure) that acts as a maieutical device and constitutes the only evolving part.[1]

Reality has taken care of the gap between the utopia of the theory, the fairness of the invisible hand, and the powerfully limited intellectual means of reality. It has done so by transcending not only the material, like some of the Marxist vulgata would have it. It has transcended utopia itself (any utopia, liberal as well as communist) "downwards," transforming its logical rigor (its perfect abstractness) into the metaphysics we have learned to identify. The outcome is capitalism as we know it today.

Among the practical consequences on normal life of this debasing of the intellectual abstract, we can single out for explanatory purposes nationalism, the presence of oligopoly at the national and the international levels, the nation-state with its inescapable role in the management of markets,[2] the (growing) presence of religion in state matters, and the idea of "community." All these were ideas that were present *in nuce* since Adam Smith and were well developed in Mill's times.[3] If we put them together, adding the spice of the recurrent cries against the injustice of capitalism, we can see the seeds of fascism[4] and of the other types of chauvinism and jingoism that have marked the twentieth century, and seem to have made a powerful comeback in the twenty-first.

This is fundamental. If we look with open and unprejudiced eyes at what we call capitalism we see that there is no trace of that benevolent isolation of individuals that was deemed to be the core of the "fairness for everybody" of liberalism. What McCann (2004) sees in his chosen field of theory is even more evident in practice. Nation, ethnicity, religion, economic barriers, and even imperialism (and the resistance to it!) present the same structural characteristics. It is not difficult to understand why their clashes are characterized by the blind violence we are all witnessing.

Here we see the power of the hypostatizing dominant intellectuality of capitalism to absorb everything, erecting bridges not only to actual capitalist (perceived) facts but also toward facts and ideas that are not capitalist. The imperialist drive that has brought the USA to invade Iraq, and Afghanistan, Grenada, Panama, Vietnam, Cambodia, and Laos before finds a true plethora of explanations that put together, without any qualm, what should not be together. Precapitalistic aspects (conquest of territory, religious conflicts, nationalism, just to mention a few) are dialectically reabsorbed within the general frame of capitalism as we know it, and in the process are deprived of their former abstract features—that is, further debased. Economic concepts that were meant to signify ideas and facts born out of a historical rupture are bent to the need of dialectically preventing ruptures and oblivion, keeping the bubble going.

With this last observation we have reached an important result in our investigation of the dominant intellectuality of capitalism. This not only is perfectly fit to deal only with itself (the bubble). It also has inglobated, and harmoniously dealt with, all of those precapitalist features of reality (especially of the political kind) that have survived undisturbed since the Industrial Revolution. Liberals like those discussed in McCann (2004), pseudo-Marxists like Negri (2002), Negri/Hardt (2001), and Lenin (1972/1916), take it for granted that the institutional frame they deal with is just capitalism. They do not see that the dominant mentality they rely upon has made bridges to facts and concepts that come from different, preceding eras. Such concepts have not been kept in their former intellectual mode, nor have they been given capitalist (metaphysical) natures. They have only been debased, reduced to a tool you can use whenever you want to.

While in fact economics is a discipline born out of a completely new kind of historical situation, the applied disciplines of politics, law, and related subjects are instead direct descendants of noncapitalist debates and historically actual situations.[5] It suffices for the purposes of the present chapter to recall the continuity between the medieval, Renaissance, and Enlightenment political debates and the reliance posed by the makers of the American and French constitutions precisely on such debates. This aspect impinges upon the dominant, hypostatizing mentality.

The iterative process of the dominant Hegelian-dialectical intellectuality at work in capitalist intercourses and relations must take into account the presence of these bridges. These act as a further complication not only in that they force the dialectical process to accept the presence of obsolete entities that can be used or disregarded at will. They actually powerfully help the dominant intellectuality to tighten its grip on capitalist reality by supplying all of those concepts and related individual and mass emotions that a mystical rationality needs: "the historical continuity" needed to justify political action. In fact, there is no mysticism without mystical concepts, and things such as the idea of nation or of institution are as amenable to mystical treatments as one might possibly want.[6]

All this compels us to discuss those scholars who do have a logical and historical method in mind and tend to be considered on the edge of, if not outside, the mainstream. Let us take Schumpeter and his former pupil Sylos Labini.

All students of Schumpeter agree that one of his main objectives was the creation of a liberal economic alternative to Marx's historical method. Also, it is undeniable that Schumpeter (1987) was very pessimistic about the future of capitalism. A further complication is that he saw with clarity some of the precapitalist features of capitalism.[7]

Sylos Labini (2004) is less pessimistic about the destiny of capitalism (although he was desperate about the destiny of democracy, which he repeatedly pointed out to me in private conversations), even though he believes Marx to be a wrong starting point for a socialist revolution (see the essays in Sylos Labini 1974). His liberal outlook makes him a biased observer of what he often calls, in Sylos Labini (2004), "phases" of capitalism that will come and go.

Both scholars have concentrated their efforts on questions to do with the presence of oligopolies (the most evident imperfection of actual markets) and with the role of innovations in fostering capitalist dynamics. This last we shall take up and engage more thoroughly and technically in the second and third part of this chapter.

The degree of detachment they obtain from their historical attitude should help them see the historical "incoherence" of capitalism: both its incomplete rupture with the past and its use of precapitalist concepts. Indeed, Schumpeter (1951) sees some of it. Unfortunately, these are just episodes. Both authors remain within the purview of economic theory and are at pains in inserting in it their respectively pessimistic and optimistic historical insights.

We are in the presence of a dialectical, capitalist mentality, a dominant intellectuality homogeneous to the functioning of the new economic structure brought about by the Industrial Revolution and open to contamination with intellectually different, yet translatable, items. We also have, in practice as well as in the intellectual framework, the presence of noncapitalist matters of fact, from material entities to ideologies to institutions. These are not simply dialectically inglobated in the bubble and smoothly inserted in its homogeneous working. Such straightforward possibility is prevented precisely by the limited and limiting characteristics of capitalist intellectuality that cannot take external words and standards as such but must transcend them, transforming them into the rational mysticism that is its salient general working feature.

The example of religion is obvious. Other examples are the role of money through known history, the role of trade in the making of an individual, the changes in the use and meaning of language feared by Marcuse (1967) and Adorno (see Micocci 2002a), or the question of community already repeatedly mentioned. The noncapitalist aspects, and the bridges that are built toward them, are moments of slippage in the otherwise smooth (although variable in speed) repetitive functioning of the dialectical intellectuality of capitalism. Before a solution is found for fitting the obstacle smoothly in the flow, a hesitation has taken place into an otherwise continuous mechanism.[8]

This is the device that grants the iterative functioning to capitalist intellectual perseverance. The endless spinning of the limited and limiting capitalist mantra has to be restated on new bases every time it comes upon one of these slippage points. Each slippage constitutes an occasion to reorganize the same old thing from a slightly different position from before. In *Anti-Hegelian Reading* (2002a) I had compared this to the positioning of a tachymeter in field surveys in topography, without considering the fundamental part above.

There is, in other words, in capitalism a general iterativeness, to which a form of "smaller" iterativeness must be added. This is the kind deriving from the necessarily cyclical movement of market equilibrium, the one dealt with by Schumpeter, Sylos Labini, and all the other economists.

A kind of iterativeness is typical of all forms of institutional life, from precapitalist times.[9] There is no denying in fact that any kind of political institution must necessarily work in an iterative way. There is a cunning in mainstream economics and social sciences, which refers to this inevitable iterativeness without mentioning it and that is part of the ahistorical features of the mainstream.

But we must not be deceived by superficial analogies such as this. Capitalism actually uses precisely this kind of bridge to show its dialectical continuity with whatever is around it. The iterativeness of capitalism is not the same as the iterativeness intrinsic to any form of institutionalized polity. It derives from capitalism's intellectual nature of a "rational mysticism," which is a characteristic of capitalism only.

This of course does not prevent the presence of the "institutional" iterativeness and of the iterativeness typical of the functioning of markets. We shall study in the second half of the present chapter the cases of firm management and marketing of products, which are instances of this type. What we must establish here is that capitalism would be iterative even if "the market" did not operate at all.

Part of the cunning of the social sciences lies in the fact that this whole movement is understood as "change" and therefore it seems to imply a degree of "innovation." A phenomenon of "routinization" of the "change and innovation" process is at work. The "routinization" of change and innovation that Schumpeter (1971, 1987) as well as the lesser economists talk about (Gordon, 2000) not only covers a vast array of different phenomena and trains of causes. It also, in so doing, accomplishes the task of hiding the wiser cunning mentioned above behind the suggestiveness of this "local" type of cunning.

Discussing the routinization of change and innovation by letting the items involved in the first type of cunning peep through the folds of the argument simultaneously shows — without a chance of digging it up — the "local" type of cunning. This is part of the functioning of economics and the other social sciences: they offer to the willing a glimpse of the wide, unresolved philosophical and human questions that are behind them. It is precisely this that misleads some of those willing to go beyond the social sciences.

The followers of ontological realism in economics[10] are a perfect example: they attribute an ontology, and a dialectics, to the metaphysics. The cultural, hypostatized frame is taken to be material, or rather to constitute an intrinsic, nonseparable part of the structure of the material. Their descriptions of the polity end up resembling those infantile descriptions of community that we find in children's fairy tales.

We can now reconsider some features of capitalism in a new light. The common wisdom of the mainstream and of Marxism has it that capitalism exists and develops precisely because it innovates and revolutionizes itself as well as the rest of the world. The rhetoric of this kind of (unanimous) attitude can take the tones of Schumpeter's abused "creative destruction," or the messianic language of dialectical Marxism. Almost every day brings about a new classification of some supposed technological or productive "revolutions," expressed in the terms of one of the highly technical jargons of the various branches of economics, business, and sociology.

Schumpeter himself was very pessimistic about capitalism precisely because he did not see a sustainable chance to keep the revolutionary mechanism of creative destruction going. His ambivalence about the "social and cultural role" of innovation and revolution, and the role of the entrepreneur in it, founders in Schumpeter (1987, 132, 133), where he explicitly realizes that the flow of "economic change," when institutionalized, is bound to become "depersonalized and automatized" (133).[11]

This question is more complex for Marx, who is justly praised for his admiring descriptions and analyses of the engineering aspects of capitalism. The "heavy artillery" of commodities that tear down all Chinese walls is the outcome of a portentous advance in technological dynamism.

At the risk of simplifying a bit, we must argue in the first place that Marx was considering technology as part of the Industrial Revolution and of mass production. This was a historical turning point, from a mode of production to the next. The characterizing aspect of capitalism was not technical progress as such, but its use in mass production: hence he made commodities his starting point in *Capital*. Technical progress made capitalism what it was, once and for all: hence, the possibility to describe it by means of the *tableau economique* of departments I and II.

Secondly, Marxism has produced, together with a heap of technology admirers, a whole tradition of prophets of doom for technological advancement. The most egregious case is obviously that of Lenin (1972/1916) who in his prophesized the end of progress and the decadence of capitalism, brought about by one of the many sorts of underconsumptionist arguments.

Brenner (1998), in his analysis of the recent crisis, talks about, among other things, many of which I disagree with (see Micocci 2002d), the endless process of the scrapping of old plants and the importance of its pace. In fact, what is usually passed as innovation, change, and even revolution in the economics of capitalism usually amounts to a faster pace of plant scrapping and a faster flow of commodities and commercial brands in the markets.

The division of labor, Taylorism, Fordism, the present drive to the precarization of labor associated with privatization and deregulation, the computerization of productive processes, the "quality circles" Japan exported to the West in the 1970s, robotization, the *maquiladoras*, and what have you, give an image of the poverty of change, innovation, evolution, and revolution in the capitalist economy and polity. Hybrid seeds, genetically modified organisms, agricultural machinery, chemical fertilizers and pesticides, and organic farming have depredated agriculture without revolutionizing it, just helping install a new iteration in the plunder of the natural. They represent some of the long-wave iterations that have characterized capitalism as we know it.

THE PHILOSOPHICAL EXPLANATION

We are bound not to understand the importance of the present argument if we do not fully understand the repetitiveness of capitalism and the iterative functioning of such repetitivity together. Most people, especially economists, have some kind of strong emotional resistance to this.[12] This is one more manifestation of the infantile traits that the profession allows, and probably nurtures, in its practitioners. Their emotional resistance to a change in the way they see reality amounts to little else than tantrums. Surely an environment with parental care, magically arriving presents, and no risk is comfortable. But growing up brings, with the risks involved, far better things: sex, individuality, liberties, alcohol, for some telling instances.

In the general framework of capitalism described so far the very idea of novelty is simply banished. Anything that changes the rules of the game — say, anarchism or communism (the two are the same to me, but not to the communists) — is simply unthinkable in theory and in practice. Conversely, even a hermit, or a stylite of any new kind, just cannot escape acting this part of his/her within capitalism, however intensely he/she believes to be, or seeks to be, out of the game. The same holds for terrorists, or for all the types of self-inflicted amputations, starting from the nonreligious vegetarians, which accompany capitalism. All of these, and anything else that can be summarized and defined, however imprecisely, in words, is within capitalism. "Extraneous standards" are possible but must be sought in a different raw material (the concrete) with a different mental structure.

In *Anti-Hegelian Reading* (2002a) I described the operation of capitalism as an iterative redressing of the same old items. That was sufficient for the provisional, limited definition and bounds of iterativeness I gave there, very much focused on what we have called in this chapter small iterativeness. But here we are talking about something inbuilt in the hypostatizing, dialectical, general intellectual structure of capitalism: something that pertains to the realm of the historically situated individual and of the collectively felt/accepted common features it shares with his/her fellow others.

Communitarians are thus wrong not because what they talk about does not exist or reality is different in any meaningful way from what they describe. What they force themselves to like, and what unfortunately even liberal thinkers share, as McCann (2004) proves, is actually there. It has many of the characteristics they recognize, and many more that it is not worth enumerating here because we have found the guiding principle. But what they describe is precisely the problem with capitalism: its anti-individual, anti-intellectual, illiberal dark core we have been exploring.

The communitarians, for all their good intentions, are thus right in many ways. But this is so because they are guilty for the very same reasons. Like the fascists, they want us to explicitly acknowledge and enjoy that yoke we are bearing and that is the cause of all that is bad in our age. This is in common with what economists say, from the classicals onward. Take Mill, for instance.

> The opinions and feelings of mankind, doubtless, are not a matter of chance. They are consequences of the fundamental laws of human nature, combined with the existing state of knowledge and experience, and the existing conditions of social institutions and intellectual and moral culture. But the laws of the generation of human opinions are not within our present subject. (Mill 1998, 6)

But

> in considering the institution of property as a question in social philosophy, we must leave out of consideration its actual origin. . . . We may suppose a community . . . bringing nothing with them but what belonged to them in common . . . for the adoption of the institutions and polity which they judged most expedient. (Mill 1998, 7–8)

In fact,

> history bear witness to the success which large bodies of human beings may be trained to feel the public interest their own . . . every member of the association would be amenable to the most universal, and one of the strongest, of personal motives, that of public opinion. (Mill 1998, 12)

While in the preceding quotation Mill was considering private property and capitalist institutions, in this last he is analyzing communism. The result, the method, and the tools used are the same. This is so because the point at stake (always rendered as a multiplicity of points, but this needs not detain us, for we have grasped the intellectually univocal nature of the problem) can be defined in practical, material terms, or left to the community: there is no difference.

Plan and market can overlap, like Napoleoni (1976) said. The main goal is not prosperity or welfare, but the institution and imposition of the idea of community.

The free cities of Italy, Flanders, and the Hanseatic League, were habitually in a state of such internal turbulence . . . yet during several centuries they increased rapidly in wealth and prosperity, brought many of the industrial arts to a high degree of advancement . . . and could defend themselves against the sovereigns of Europe. (257)

Nations have acquired some wealth, and made some progress in improvement, in states of social union as imperfect as to border on anarchy. (258)

Mill on the same page continues warning against the dangers of "arbitrary exactions" from the government, which brings us back to the known ground of liberal theorization.

Mill operated in a doomsday context conditioned by his fear that a stationary state was the inevitable end state of capitalism (Mill 1998, 124). Yet, as repeatedly argued, what he says above is evident in all the classical economists, in Adam Smith first of all, and thence in mainstream economics.

Having (inevitably) a degree of change in its material subject matter, despite one of the aims of the metaphysics being that of limiting the intrusion of nature's unpredictability to the strictly indispensable, capitalism as we know it allows an internal degree of change together with a discipline to which this must submit by iterating its own operations. Iterations are the rule at all levels of capitalism as we know it: we saw the presence of a big and a small iterativeness.

But iterations are also the mode of apprehension of capitalist reality itself. Before attempting a more general and precise definition, we should then take a careful look at the meaning, in the framework of capitalism as an intellectual mode, of novelty, change, and innovation. Novelty, we saw already, exists only as a possibility in capitalism. It survives in the rhetoric of the market or in the boasting typical of the vulgarity of common, everyday lingos. It is worth spending a few more words on it, as an introduction to the discussion of innovation and change.

Let us start from the question of art and literature. In the capitalist context of total intellectual limitation, art might well constitute the key to a return of creativity—that is, a tool for revolution/emancipation, potentially constituting the light at the end of the tunnel.

One in fact might want to argue that art is less constrained by the fetters of the dominant intellectuality, by choice or by the Bohemian way of life that is usually associated with practicing it. There is no denying that when alone in front of a white sheet of paper, or a blank canvas, one feels potentially able to chase the purely abstract, without conceding anything to culture and the other habits and needs of life. An artist of whatever kind might be the bearer of the flag of individual emancipation, it seems. There are, unfortunately, two orders of problems.

The first is to do with the big question of whether art is natural to mankind or just a reaction to the repression that comes from the impositions of organized societies. Will we all be artists under communism as anarchism, or, rather, no need for art will be felt at all?

I faced this question in a paper on the Russian nihilists (Chernishevsky, Dobrolyubov, Pisarev) written with Nino Pardjanadze (2000). The hypothesis we came up with was that society brings about, as a matter of fact, the need for the peculiar beauty and the abstract embodied in works of art. But unless communism as anarchism opens up new sensual and intellectual potentialities of expression in human beings, the very practice of art might well decline, due to the total physical and intellectual freedom enjoyed by the individual.

The second interrogative is linked to the first and to the general argument pursued in this book. In fact, the emancipative action that art undeniably exercises could well be a fundamental aid to the general awareness of the repression enforced by the system. But this would resolve itself in a number of punctual acts of Aristotelian catharsis, both on the part of the artist and on that of the enjoyer. These might even be enough in number and momentum to locally overturn the institutional setup. But we would be back to square one once that is done.

The only way to break out of capitalism as we know it is by creating a true rupture: everybody's simultaneous emancipation. But emancipation is much more than a momentaneous glimpse into the beauty of freedom of the type assured by Aristotelian catharsis.

All this goes to show once more the perfect uselessness of novelty even when and where novelty is possible under capitalism. The segregation of art to those in the know, and the segregation within that segregation of the great liberatory artists, who are known only by those in the know within those in the know, is easily explained by the incapacity of the general intellectual frame to acknowledge novelty. Such incapacity takes the form of an actual reception of the novelty—that is, its dialectical reabsorption into normality. A landing of the Martians or the appearance of God would be easily led back to one or the other of the known categories.

We are thus left with the more prosaic ideas of innovation and change. Given the great importance attributed to their role in capitalism by the economists, the other social scientists and the laymen, and even by Marx himself and by the classics, it is better to start with the question of innovation. Here there is a sort of tautology in mainstream economics, born out of a basic approximation in the use of the term. Innovation is taken to be the motor of capitalist dynamics, hence of the development of capitalism and of the capitalist development of not-yet-capitalist (underdeveloped) countries.

Yet, mainstream economists set no limits in practice to what can be passed as innovation. Therefore, the most diverse things (from a new production process to a new product, to new tools for peasant farmers, to the normal, unavoidable scrapping of plants) are attributed the ennobling title of innovation, according to the need and the environment.[13]

Schumpeter himself, the most famous name among economists when innovation is talked about, was very vague and incoherent. On the one hand he talked of a "cultural" role of the innovator, whom he straightforwardly identified with the entrepreneur. The entrepreneur's

> characteristic task . . . consists precisely in breaking up the old, and creating new tradition. Although this applies primarily to his economic action, it also extends to the moral, cultural and social consequences of it. (1934, 91)

But Schumpeter meant by cultural the limited environment of what goes on at the level of the entrepreneur.[14] A change in the role of the entrepreneur would surely bring about a change in the whole of capitalism. This was a way to exorcise his pessimism about capitalism, completely displayed in Schumpeter (1987). This opens up a whole new field of Schumpeterian studies that cannot be pursued here on whether he meant that capitalism necessarily brings about its own doomsday by the gradual hegemony gained by institutionalization and the consequent routinization.

He is clear in (1987):

> The fundamental impulse that sets and keeps the capitalist engine in motion comes from the new consumer goods, the new methods of production or transportation, the new markets, the new forms of industrial organization that capitalist enterprise creates. (1987, 83)

In fact, this completes his (1934) statement that

> the entrepreneur is merely the bearer of the mechanism of change. (footnote to page 60)

The kind of change Schumpeter was interested in was essentially the kind he needed to move from one *Kreislauf* to the next: the economic dynamism he was desperate to add to Walras's general equilibrium.[15]

The interesting result for our discussion is that innovation is only at the level of production. There are for Schumpeter five possibilities: the introduction of a new commodity, of a new method of production, the opening of a new market, a new source supplying raw materials, or a new kind of industry (the creation, or the destruction, of a monopoly, for instance). The point is to keep capitalism going, i.e., as "dynamic" as possible. All the other "cultural" meanings that economists (and the Marxists too) attach to innovation are just sweet dreams or empty rhetoric.

Such a strictly technical meaning of innovation has gained dominance in capitalism and is nowadays taken to be "innovation" in general. And, terrible as this is, it is not wrong. In a cultural frame that is incapable of recognizing novelty as such, where any novelty (in itself only a theoretical hypothesis, we argued) that might crop up is dialectically consociated (not associated, mind you) to what is known and to the present institutional situation, where else can one innovate? Innovations in fields other than production are bound to go unnoticed or are incapable of affecting, let alone revolutionizing, the whole.

All this is complicated, and as a consequence impoverished, by the working of the market: the big and the small iterativeness operate one after the other, with the latter further twisting the former toward aridity and repetition. The periodical, and not entirely predictable[16] slippages come in a recurrent way that makes it possible to notice that, for a sad instance, there are phases (like the second Iraq massacre) in which international politics gets closer to the ancient imperial conquests or straightforward devastations rather than to capitalist expansion. But what use is this in practice, other than contributing to a taxonomy of capitalist forms along time?

The painful question we have to face is that everything we have been describing in this section points to the absolute impotence of the individual vis-à-vis the big iterativeness. No individual and no mass struggle can affect it. I can, however, see a powerful way to dispose of the whole thing: to emancipate the individual from the tyranny of this mechanism, by means of the recovery of intellectual and sensual openness.

This consideration goes toward explaining the fact that the two types of iterativeness do seem one to the persons who undergo them. In fact, small iterativeness, operating second and on the items we all are bombarded with every day, makes of the market-determined iterativeness the only visible and "touchable" one. The intrinsic tendency of capitalist intellectuality to hypostatize everything, reducing everything in life to a trivial thing, gets reinforced by the consequences of small (market) iterativeness. If taken by the dominant mentality one is bound to see in the consequences of market iterativeness just one more empirical proof of this point.

Thus we should not wonder why even economists as eminent and iconoclastic as Schumpeter use innovation in several meanings, all of which converge to the vague idea of "innovation as the motor of capitalism." We should not wonder, either, at orthodox Marxists making the same mistake. Obviously, we should not be amazed that common people buy this misunderstanding of reality wholeheartedly.

The sad truth is that if we mean by reality the working and institutions of capitalism, with all the material entities linked to them, then that is indeed reality, in a sense: in a capitalist sense. It disregards the material as a whole with its natural laws to concentrate on itself instead, finding out its inner (logically faulty) laws of behavior and transcending them into pseudonatural laws, as capitalism is pretended (hypostatized) to be homogeneous to the whole of reality.

Innovations do change capitalist reality: computers have entered our houses, compelling us to adapt to their absurd working logic. They create new employment by multiplying former tasks and stimulating the growth of a whole army of supposed experts that are forever incompetent to solve software and hardware problems, for these are due to the evident imperfection, and imperfectibility, of the basic technology. We all patiently queue at public offices to get the same services we used to get before computers (using less paper), because systems are "down" often enough for us to get used to this type of inefficiency and to forget that before computers such queues were unthinkable.

Computers have also changed the proletariat, transforming the few who can still boast a wage into the virtual slaves of capillary job control, and moving the others (both those who have lost their jobs and have become "flexible" and those who, like the incompetent computer experts, hold "autonomous" jobs) into a form of insecure and disguised waged labor.[17] Many industrial workers pretend to themselves to be white-collar keyboard wizards.

Yet, the problem with computers is not this tragicomic set of troubles. The truly alarming thing is that computers are the product of a kind of scientific intellectual attitude that, by inventing them, has spread itself to all the sciences that use such devices. This is not just a problem with doing bad, or limited, science: we are imposing a limiting understanding of logic and mathematics on logicians and mathematicians themselves (and to statisticians, but this is less tragic). The "innovation" of computers is changing capitalism, for the worse, but only until the next slippage sets the next iteration on slightly different bases, recovering to science some degree of intellectual freedom.

We have reached the question of change. Again, we are faced by a problem of perspective. Innovations do produce changes: automobiles are no horses, just like horses are no mules. A ragged array of Luddites is a different thing from a well-groomed gathering of no-global or "no war for oil" protesters (though both of them are united by their willingness to be beaten by the government's lackeys). Is this change? Negri would say so.

With his characteristic erudition (Negri 2002; Negri/Hardt 2001), Negri sums up much of the Marxist and non-Marxist left's acceptance of the rules dictated by iteration. I dare say he sees, especially in Negri (2002), the big iteration, and adapts to it the recurrent capacity of his Spinozian "multitude" to intervene on the system to impose improvements. That this is the apotheosis of the alienation brought about by capitalist intellectuality, and the sufferings it brings about, is cunningly masked by the idea of multitude and its supposed past "achievements." Its coral longing brings us back to the rhetoric well epitomized by the paintings of Delacroix and Pellizza da Volpedo, muffling and transcending the actual inhumanity of the whole thing.[18]

Sylos Labini is well aware of this, which he called the "Luciferian" aspect of Marx and Marxism.[19] His innovation is intelligently limited to what economics calls so—that is, to what he plots in the graphics of Labini (2004, 106–9). His five "great" innovations (railroads, electricity, automobiles, airplanes, computers/transistors) are expressed in their variously measured growth in quantity and in technical efficiency. This, and it is no surprise with Sylos Labini, brings us back to Schumpeter and the relationship between innovation and capitalist economic dynamism in theory and in practice. Lacking Negri's cynicism, he has no room for mixing up big and small iterativeness and for accepting the noneconomic problems of reality and trying to like them.

In this general framework of iterative repetitiveness, the driving force of everybody's daily life is routinization. Not only do we undergo the routine that is intrinsic to any institutional setting, not only do we add to it the necessary routinization of our daily chores: we get, everywhere, the imposition of nothing else than routinization. We all know that the best antidote to routinization is routinization. The more we mechanically perform our compulsory chores, the more chance we have to be left in peace by that repetitiveness we cannot fight. But here capitalism plays its dirty trick.

The two iterative processes are in fact inserted, consociated, explained, and accepted by means of and within the hypostatizing dominant mentality. They are given a dignity and a necessity: "innovations are the motor of capitalism" becomes a programmatic manifesto, the summary of all the technical, political, and moral characters of capitalism. Here, we have descended so far into the hell of capitalism that we find that, to give the finishing touches to innovation and change, we must momentaneously leave behind our guide, philosophy. Philosophy has helped us lay reality bare, and now we are staring at its barrenness. So bare is reality that it needs no understanding, only description, and a stout heart to bear the sight.

Innovation being what we saw, change can only be defined in a negative way. If reality is the jumble of routinized behaviors we have been describing, then change is nothing but the effort of moving from one routinization to the next: the fatigue and the challenge lie in the painful move from a learned set of mechanical reactions and behaviors to a new, slightly different set. For an economist it might mean to move from strictly neoclassical views to, say, new classical macroeconomics, and for a worker it might consist in moving from the few switches he was operating to the many he can pompously call a "keyboard."

Adam Smith was well aware of the alienating consequences of capitalism. In book I of Smith (1999) he sees the difference between the rural worker, who preserves a degree of individuality due to his being detached from the goings-on of the Industrial Revolution, and the urban man.

> The common ploughman . . . is less accustomed, indeed, to social intercourse than the mechanic who lives in town. . . . His understanding, however, being accustomed to consider a greater variety of objects, is generally superior to that of the other, whose whole attention from morning till night is commonly occupied in performing one or two very simple operations. (vol. I, 231)

SIDE EFFECTS OF ITERATIVENESS

Capitalism as we know it has a high degree of predictability: one can always figure out the structure of reality and its inner logic as well as the inner logic of what comes next. What is impossible to predict is the where and when of "change." While there is little one can do about the structure and inner logic of the whole and of its iterative repetitiveness, the where and when of the changes matters terribly. The knowledge of the coming of a problem makes the incapacity to exactly predict it more worrying.

In fact, a society in which everything is similar, and which cannot even imagine anything "other," what is a problem in the limited and unchangeable set of iterating variables is bound to remain a problem forever. Here the image of the maieutics is perfect. As in almost every birth, the midwife is to cope with two contrasting expectations: the pain of the labor and the expected joy ensuing. It is worth emphasizing the word *expected*, which in capitalism is inevitably the most important thing. Nothing is unexpected; but some features of what is coming can be negative.

This makes problems unsolvable obsessions. The dominant intellectuality mixes up the problems with the imperfections, adjustments, and entailed discomfort of nonproblems. If nobody can leave the game, problems must exist but must not give the impression of being not solvable, lest they look like ruptures.

Thus problems are there, together with plenty of well-intentioned people ready to do anything that is possible[20] to solve them. The logical similarity between capitalist reality and capitalist intellectuality is fundamental here. Problems cannot just be solved: they are an integral part of the whole that not only cannot get rid of them but also cannot even see and investigate their causes: the metaphysics cannot look outside itself, nor see its own nature. Despite being an integral constituent of the whole, problems can, to capitalist perception and analysis, only be removed. But this amounts, obviously, to a piece of wishful thinking. If you want capitalism you must take its problems also, with no hope of a change. If you do not want the problems, then you have to denature capitalism.

If you do not want the problems, you have to make do with an amputated capitalism. You must excise whole parts of it, doing without the general, dominant logic and mentality on those issues only. You can only do that by acknowledging the dominance of the whole, cutting for yourself a niche in an opposition role vis-à-vis the whole in its very conception and practice and keep dealing with capitalism like a handicapped part of it.

Being built on a limited and limiting logic, capitalism abhors a vacuum (the threatened cracks). Nothing can be taken away from it without being replaced. The system does not bear disappearances and enforces this curse even onto the smallest and apparently useless of its subjects. If we want to deprive capitalism of one of its component parts, we must create a vacuum by force. One of the main ways to do so is to refer to mythical precapitalist concepts.

We have been reviewing in chapter 2 the consequences on famous liberal thinkers and free-market economists of the intrinsic faults of their way to formalize their utopias, which denatures the abstract character of the utopia itself to produce a metaphysics. Bridges are attached to whatever entities can be used to preserve in practice the empty utopian shell around the metaphysics.

Now that aspect can be seen in full light. The need to erect bridges is not just an inconsistent move by a scholar who is passionate about his subject and resorts to a lick below the belt of his perceived adversaries to defend the idea he cherishes. Seen in the light of the big and small iterativeness of capitalism, it is part of a structure geared to produce nothing else.

The inherent and implicit acknowledgement of the flawed intellectual structure of capitalism is a fundamental part of its iterative functioning. The very causes of the iteration of the big kind, the slippages, are a global instance of a problem that is part and parcel of the whole of capitalism: its flawed, unresolved relation with nature and history, even its own history, what we have so far called the whole of reality, the material, or nature in general.[21] Small iterativeness reinforces the process, at least in that its daily bombardment of repetitions helps the minds and bodies of individuals tame themselves and follow the tide.

To charge Hayek, or Mill, or anybody from the set of recognized masters of liberal and free-market theory of lack of consistency is therefore simply unfair. The particular type of contamination between pure thought and reality that we have been describing and calling bridges is a constant in the thought of capitalist times. This is not to detract from the capacity and independence of those famous thinkers.

We need to define now the set of common qualifying categories for those attempts to amend capitalism of its faults that history has witnessed so far. Let us start from the fact that the structure of capitalism that has been described so far not only is imperfect. Its local and more blatant imperfections bring about the birth of reforming and perfecting attempts. The whole history of capitalism has been haunted by the specter of reform and adaptation. A telling illustration is the passage from Adam Smith, the admirer of the market, to John Stuart Mill, the reformer and prophet of doom.

What are the common characteristics of the various attempts to reform capitalism? Let us start by grouping them. In fact, the dialectical, hypostatizing nature of capitalism makes all dialectical attempts at revolution a game within the game, a Negri-like hiccup of masses/leaders who feel they are acting for the whole. Capitalism's dialectics, geared as it is to consociate itself with anything that appears on its dialectical horizon, can only welcome those dialectical revolutionary attempts. This poses no difficulty, for such attempts are built upon the same dialectical logic and can only reproduce a similar setup.

In other words, even successful revolutions are capitalist manifestations. No wonder that most of them have gone back full circle: their capitalist nature was there, explicit, since their pseudodisruptive inception.

Solving problems by harnessing politics, economics, and the social to community needs is a well-known feature of the twentieth century, and an even more common occurrence in the twenty-first. It has variously been called according to places and circumstances, but as we need an umbrella term we might well anticipate, appealing to European history, the most comprehensive term we can use (we shall give the details of the definition later): fascism. Of course there are variations on this theme, mainly to do with the relative weight of politics, economics, and actual dictatorial power.

Let us outline the salient features of a possible, general, dialectical alternative to capitalism. We shall see that the name fascism anticipated here fits it like a glove. Let us begin by imagining why a need for alternatives should be felt. Considering that no author who has studied capitalism could deny it, and no movement against capitalism has done without it, we can take the idea of justice as our core question.

The injustice of the capitalist setup is the more glaring and stark because this is a system that has come out of the protest against the birth privileges of *ancienne regimes*, promising fairness through the market and democratic representation but keeping the tool of private property and hence the possibility of man being exploited by man. Plus, in practice capitalism has developed into a set of oligopolies rather than a market, and a privileged class looks down upon the efforts of the least lucky in monetary and power terms.

In a few strokes, we have captured what all movements of reform have been arguing, from different ideological positions. I would like to point out that if we were not concerned with producing a dialectical set of ideas, we would already have more than enough for a political action against capitalism. But dialectics, to work properly (without arising doubts, that is), must have many variables and many levels of action, and above all it must muddle the simplicity of the categories used. Let us see the main items anticapitalist movements have been adding.

First of all, our reformist alternative cannot do without a "community." However this meaningless concept is defined and articulated, we have seen that no dialectical thought of capitalist time has been able to do without it, from liberals to communists to fascists. We should not be detained, nor misled, by the wide variety of usages of this term. It is precisely the wideness of the interpretation that needs no discussion: "community" has no degree of intensity and application. The discussion concerning the great thinkers of the preceding chapter suffices in this respect. For an illustration from empirical evidence, it is sufficient to look at how easily capitalist democracies slip from liberal attitudes to nationalism and back.

All the other items of the possible list are just iterations, in the sense just explained, of what was said so far. For the sake of completeness we have to rehearse the most important (others could be added: here we stick to those that have proved more common). Also, we have to go through them in order for our general features to come out more forcefully. Thus we will fully justify the collective name fascism we have chosen for it.

Having started with community, nation is the most obvious consequence. Capitalism has marked itself in history by accompanying its growth with that of the nation-state. The Marxist movements have answered by means of their supposed internationalism, a collective name for the same thing. Capitalist development as well as decolonization have signified the same thing, whether successfully or unsuccessfully. Like community, of which it is a particular case, nationalism is a nonmeasurable entity: either you have it or it can be "dormant." The "intensity" of nationalism refers to the degree of violence brought about. This last is, obviously, a mass condition.

The market and its extension is another apparent issue. We have seen its intimate connection with community and how neither of the two can exist without the other since Smith and Mill. Anticapitalist movements do not question the presence of the market but only the extension of its prerogatives. The orthodox Marxists themselves, by their incapacity to think other than dialectically, have been unable to think of a true alternative, in theory as well as in practice. We have also discussed, in the preceding chapter, the lack of difference between market and plan. Many second-order items can be rubricated under the heading of market, from fairness to distribution to justice. No discussion of any of them is required here.

Private property is the next big issue. Without wasting words, for the same reason as for the other items above, it suffices to point out here that what has bothered the anticapitalist movements so far has been its distribution and not its abolition. The infantile Marxist progression from socialism to communism, as well as eurocommunism and the other brands of socialist reformism, have been devised to that purpose. Neither the USSR (by instituting state property and leaving precarious forms of private property in fields such as small holdings, housing, and even private initiative and cooperatives) nor Mexico (by nominally abolishing the private property of land in its constitution) has taken any step in this direction.

Redistribution follows logically, involving that variegated bunch of people who have been variously calling themselves Keynesians, socialists, labor, reformists, populists, fascists, and nationalists. This particular item has given birth to a huge and ornate literature, which has maintained to life an endless army of economists.

Banks and money follow suit. Here capitalism has been undergoing a remarkable change in the last few years, predicted by Marx: more and more, at the international level, financial issues are taking the lion's share of capital activity. Capitalists are becoming true plutocrats. The ignorance of the metaphysical features of the process of valorization described in the preceding chapters explains the amazement of scholars at this phenomenon. More than ever, banks and money are felt to be in need of "control."

The question of development and growth, and their supposed difference, also exerts the minds of anticapitalist reformers. Here the case is simply distraction on the part of the economists who philosophize about the difference: they have forgotten their economics.

Last, a metaphysics produced by a dialectical method must have a relationship with science and technology. There is no movement against capitalism that can do without dipping into science and technology. Alternative tools and appropriate technology mark the space race between the USA and the USSR as well as the inane efforts in the third world of development adepts.

In this framework, and above all within the (chosen) dialectical relationship with capitalism and within its iterative mode of movement, opposition to capitalism can only proceed in a step-by-step fashion: a "moderate" way. A moderate way concerned with the welfare of the community on behalf of the community, which identifies itself with a nation, is concerned with justice, dislikes the plutocrats, controls (or wishes to do so) banks and money, can shift from market to plan and vice versa, is willing to develop its own alternative technology, is able to take into its own hands its economic growth in the name of a determined path to development, has no other objection to private property but justice and class peace (class peace is also what Marxist dialectical class struggle boils down to), and has no major objection to the market but the good of the community, I call fascism (see also Micocci 2002b).

Some might want to take issue with my use of the term fascism, but I cannot see on which ground, other than the relative amount of this or that variable. But the answer to that is clear-cut: the questions dealt with matter in the framework of capitalism as we know it only in that they exist, regardless of their apparent extension. This is one of the main results of the metaphysics, and we should carefully ponder it in our daily activities and the delusions ensuing.

Two consequences of what has so far been discussed have a frightening momentum. One is the analogy between capitalism as we have described it so far, with its characteristic incompleteness and limitations, and the movements against it. We should have known it from the beginning, and in fact it is no surprise that in an intellectual environment that only can conceive of what it is made of, the opposition mirrors what is opposed. The frightening aspect is that also the opposition is fascist in general terms.[22]

The question now is therefore how far capitalism as we know it is fascist and, more importantly, if it could ever develop as capitalism, or if it will forever hang in this quasi-fascist form. The next chapter will take up a last important issue, that of the political institutions of capitalism as we know it. The choice of the "provocative" word fascism will be then further justified. The real loser here is not capitalism or the opposition to it but the individuals who have not found a mention yet.

The terrifying part is the inherent moderatism of this whole affair. Whatever we have been describing is moderate in that it derives from dialectical modes of thought with maieutical purposes. The very frenzies that make repetition bearable are moderate thoughts whipped up to a foam. The dominant, dialectical, and hypostatizing mentality is a moderate mentality. Capitalism can be identified with moderation. When capitalism brings along fascism, moderation is the game that is being played. Fascists are moderate, and the distinction that is usually made between extremism and moderation is one more case of capitalist wishful thinking.

It is easy to conclude, then, that the cause of the brutality of capitalism and the massification that it brings in its wake are the result of its structural moderatism.[23] What has been called revolution was just bouts of intense moderatism: hence the violence and suffering they unleashed and their invariably fascist outcomes.

THE FIRM AND THE MARKET

The present section discusses the question of firm management, with reference to our present-day situation. This last aspect is accessory in that the main structural characteristics of the whole are the timeless ones (relatively to the capitalist era) so far described. We look at the behavior of firms, entrepreneurs, and managers in order to explain what they do and how they do it and to also explain why such elementary schematizations as firm management, efficiency indices, and marketing come to hold a relevant role in a supposedly complex set of processes.

The management of firms should afford us a glimpse at what happens in practice in all the main aspects of the political economy of capitalism. Let us now illustrate the role, meaning, and function of the entrepreneur, grouping under this umbrella term the capitalist, the manager, and minority subtypes.

Markets, we saw, are a different thing from what the theory says, and a different thing according to the historical period. This, coupled with their metaphysical character, lends to them an almost infinite possibility to constitute the center of economic and political discourses. The core of the meaning of firm management is constituted by the apprehension, by the manager/entrepreneur, of the external "market" situation.

The recent changes in the shape and function of production and markets have been made much of, especially because of the globalization catchword. A huge literature has sprung up in all fields of the social sciences, and opinions are so strong that in several countries they have even taken the shape of street demonstrations. Although some changes have been going on, whose most evident effect is the creation of a new poverty in the countries of advanced capitalism, capitalism has in fact remained pretty much the same. This is so evident that the literature itself converges[24] on the basic facts. I shall take as instances of such convergence the writings of the liberal Paolo Sylos Labini and those of the Marxist-Leninist Luciano Vasapollo.

The premises of Sylos Labini (2004) are very apt to our purposes. Sylos Labini in fact says that

> it is not true that market is a natural phenomenon: it is the product of an evolution of centuries, which has undergone profound changes with time. Before it appeared as an economic phenomenon, the market presents itself as a juridical structure. . . . It is the law that creates the banks within which the water of the economy flows . . . laws are necessary. (2004, 80, translation mine)

We are fully within the framework described so far, and such a statement would be surely endorsed by any Marxist-Leninist.

The rest of the landscape is easily sketched:

> It seems to me that oligopoly is a form of market that takes different forms and it is the rule in the markets of industrial products and of services. (2004, 25, translation mine)
>
> In order to evaluate the role that in the process of development the different forms of market—free competition, monopoly, oligopoly—play, we must give fundamental importance neither to the number nor to the dimension of enterprises, like neoclassical economists do, but to the possibility for enterprises to enter the market that is being considered or to start the creation of a new market. . . . From this perspective Schumpeter is right—also monopoly can be judged positively, at least temporarily. (2004, 81, translation mine)

We are in the best possible environment to pursue our investigation: despite knowing that reality is sadly routinized, we are in Sylos Labini's "classical" environment where room for creativity potentially exists, or can be created. Sylos Labini himself generously tries to convince the reader (we have already discussed this in "The Philosophical Explanation") that a succession of phases has taken place, hinged on technological breakthroughs. Unfortunately, his technological innovations are the same old things (cars, railways, computers) whose actual working has contributed to capitalism as we know it, the metaphysics with an iterative working we have been discovering. Yet, let us imagine, in what comes next, the possibility that the new, at least in the economy, might show up any minute, in order to test our theory in the most difficult conditions.

To Sylos Labini in our days we are facing, in our oligopoly type of markets, a number of peculiar difficulties: the flexibilization of labor, with the entailed poverty and insecurity of several social classes (and the connected diminished demand at the macroeconomic level, which determines a vicious circle of recessive further flexibilization of the workforce at all levels of skill), globalization in the form of free movement of capitals and homogenization of production processes, the overprofits of the oligopolies themselves, changes in the production processes (prices depend on costs now, and not on demand, determining the widespread diffusion of "just in time" production processes, which depend on the flexibilization of the workforce), the development of underdevelopment due to the uneven international economic relations, the straightforward "imperialistic expansion" of the USA, the incompatibility between the logic of profit and the environmental problems, and the ignorance of peasants that makes them an unsuitable replacement for the senseless greed of ravenous multinational corporations.

Sylos Labini notices that these are phases in the development of capitalism, whose overall unfolding is not in danger. What this brings about, however, is the jeopardizing of democracies in the West and in particular in Italy. All this should not surprise us, given what so far has been said. What is a bit surprising is the convergence between all this and the work of the international orthodox Marxist-Leninist network best exemplified by the names of James Petras and Luciano Vasapollo[25] and of the Marxist Dumenil and Levy (2004).

Vasapollo and his collaborators, despite their announced Marxism-Leninism, do not make Lenin's mistakes about the obsolescence of capitalism, thus getting close to Sylos Labini (2004), whose points above listed they completely uphold, enriching them with plenty of empirical material. They are very clear:

> Even though nowadays capitalism takes new forms, the capitalist mode of production itself has not changed. . . . The relationships of exploitation within this mode of production have not changed. (Vasapollo, Casadio, Petras, Veltmeyer 2004, 55, translation mine)

They add to Sylos Labini a further point, kept unexplicited by Sylos Labini himself:

> The structure of global dominance by large capital . . . is based on poles within which nation-states coordinate their actions. (113, translation mine)

This nicely dovetails with Sylos Labini's emphasis on the legal framework.[26]

All the economically and politically unsettling items in the list by Sylos Labini shared by Vasapollo can take place as long as states insure the institutional and cultural environment needed to make them homogeneous to the moderate character of capitalist culture. This is the crucial requirement: the system needs a general cultural (intellectually maieutical) frame of reference. The state, whatever the term used for it, necessarily plays such a role despite in our present time being often referred to in a negative way (as a hindrance to the working of market forces) or as the war-mongering justification of international intercourses.

The second question to face is that in this situation of oligopoly big firms watch the costs rather than prices, and—this is the absolutely important aspect—make huge overprofits. A situation of lagging consumer demand worsened by the flexibilization of labor ensues, whose evolution is further delayed by the need to keep watching the costs in a situation of stagnating and diminishing demand. This involves all the other kinds of firms, who see themselves compelled to adopt similar strategies, even when their size is small and their management and workforce is a family business.

Profits necessarily go for reinvestment to the only sector of the economy that is bound to offer returns that move dynamically: the financial sector. Investments and plant modernization are postponed or avoided, fostering plant closures. Research and development are abandoned or, when coming from the public sector or the universities, compelled to meretriciously survive, devoting themselves to "practical" purposes and needs.

When a powerful workers' movement does not exist (a situation fairly common in our days), inevitably the issues of political debate are transported from the economy to the polity. Crime, war, nationalism are bound to become the important items on the agenda and to be expressed and dealt with in those moderate terms whose perfidious consequences we saw. Precisely because of this kind of environment, with oligopolistic firms ruled by managers rather than by "capitalists" and small firms that must copy their ruthless style of management and their ravenous appetite for increasing profits to take away to financial deals, the need for regulation becomes overwhelming. What we have called fascism in the preceding section can, and indeed must, operate without problems, because it has to be conducted closely following the rules of the moderate game.

This changes the social and political prerogatives of the entrepreneurs (not their technical role). The new routines that are being established, mainly to do with sleepy markets and scarce innovation (in all possible senses) and with the chance to be able to make huge profits, give the entrepreneurs a new, anti-Schumpeterian importance.

While in Schumpeter's idealized liberal environment the entrepreneur had the role of making social and economic life lively and dynamic, in the present-day environment of fascist structures played with moderate rules the entrepreneur (or the manager) is both the executioner and the savior of the system. Without him there is little or no economic activity, but with him recession is bound to darken the economic skies.[27]

When capitalism is formally delivered with the language of moderation, fascism as described in "Side Effects of Iterativeness" is more at ease than usual in supplying its eternal solution to the problem of routinization: this is transformed into "responsibility." It is easy to figure out how this concept can arouse enthusiasms in the moderate right and the moderate left and bland acceptance as a temporary situation (a "phase") in the free market, liberal ranks, and the "reasonable" extreme left.

The managers and entrepreneurs, being capable of ruining the economy and (potentially) of keeping it alive and well,[28] become the center of political activity. Whether they directly enter politics or leave it to professional politicians, it is their presence that politics is about, despite the empty talks about crime, nationalism, and so on, that serve only to enact the strict, repressive laws that insure the implementation of economic regulation. The others are there only to negotiate their share of the sacrifices to keep the entrepreneur. Now we are equipped to study the functioning of firm management in the iterative working of capitalism.

We have already seen that for firms we are talking of a "smaller" iterativeness within the more general iterativeness of capitalist intellectuality. We should not forget either the issue of the predictability of the inner logic of what is to come and the possibility to live with areas of amputated capitalism (an oligopoly situation is an amputation of market functioning). We must now add to the description above the irresistible drive to transport capitalist entrepreneurship from industrial production to the tertiary sector.

The tertiary sector is the heaven of the two types of iterativeness we have been describing. Indeed, it is made of nothing but iterativeness. It is the sector of the economy where multiplication comes from pure replication: it is in fact composed of a limited, legally enclosed, and regulated set of mechanisms, made obscure, imprecise, and imperfect by its nature of a compromise between different needs and drives (and ideologies).

Plus, the tertiary sector is a pervasive presence in modern capitalism, which everybody from firms to tramps must reckon with: hence, it is not strictly necessary that your "service firm" does anything particularly original. The very multiplicative character of this sector makes it so that the unfortunate customer finds himself in need to resort to the help of a service firm at once and immediately. Any of such firms he finds on his/her/its path could do, for such a limited and rule-bound intercourse.

Looked at from the side of the firm in the service sector this is nothing but an invitation to look at your own costs rather than market prices, reduce inventiveness to the formal presentation and actual presence of your "product" in the market, and use a workforce as flexible as possible, even involving it in the actual risk-sharing of the firm itself. There is no end to the conservative power of this situation: the participant is part of the game in which he must volunteer in order to not only bring home his bread and butter but also to help the game going, helping the others do the same, and hoping that this will suffice to keep everybody in business.

The inevitable pervasiveness of the tertiary sector, and its close ties with the financial sector at all levels, makes for a homogenization within the limited turmoil induced by the changes within capitalism described by Sylos Labini and Vasapollo. The outcome is that the (fascist) resolution of routinization into "responsibility" comes both from above and from below. The capitalist/entrepreneur/manager is responsible at all levels to the polity and to himself. The old, trite truth that in capitalism the capitalist has a positive social role is proved, just like it always is if you look at things with capitalist eyes (as explained in "Side Effects of Iterativeness").

We find all the items described in the section mentioned above at work, even though in different settings and with various degrees of haziness. A world like that described so far is absolutely predictable in its inner logic, for the movement toward the tertiary sector is helping a remarkable closeness between actual institutions, enterprises, and even single citizens, all compelled by the need to resort to services.

The imperfections of the system, which in general are seen as chances to participate both if you are in favor or against capitalism, in this framework perform this role to a degree of capillary diffusion never matched before. The growth of the "social economy" sector and the evil work pursued by the NGOs on behalf of governments, international organizations, and multinational corporations is a particularly heartbreaking reminder.

This brings us to the volunteering aspect of capitalism, the enforced necessity to have an "engagement," be it to the tasks of your job or to that of getting beaten by the police at demonstrations. Plus, and most importantly, volunteering does not need, and hence it loses, an ideological character. New and old entrepreneurs feel like they are volunteering their contributions to society (community), and so do the army of flexible blue- and white-collar slaves, especially those whose flexibilization has taken "autonomous" forms.

Capitalism has been amputated of true markets in all sectors. Plus, a resistance to the working of market forces has been inbuilt in the system with the spread of the tertiary sector. This, as seen, has rules of its own that impinge, limiting, on the very market forces it should be a service to. Community, nation-state, market, private property, redistribution, banks and money, development and economic growth, even science and technology are elementarized, trivialized, and homogenized by the all-encompassing action of the tertiary sector. This is the new "heavy artillery" that tears down all Chinese walls.

There is no need to expand on the possibility for what we have been calling the bridges to explain from within anything that takes place. Democracy can be exported with bombs, flexibilization can bring about more employment and is good welfarewise, admitting China to the WTO is as necessary as putting up barriers to its commodities' reach, and so on and so forth. The path is broken to all types of reformist intervention and to all types of crackpots and smarty-pant hypotheses. This very "transformation" of present-day capitalism, soberly seen by Sylos Labini and Vasapollo as a phase within the same old thing, is hailed as a revolution.

This was entirely predictable given the reasoning so far unfolded. The pointless mixing up of the observation of problems and imperfections, the reform attempts ensuing (or, equally and conversely, the perfect satisfaction with the changes), are part of that "intense moderation" all capitalist revolutions and reforms come down to. Intensity being by definition a term that comes in degrees and whose evaluation is left to the moment it is done, we find ourselves in a succession of revolutions. Post-Fordism is considered to be one, along with the last model of family car and the last program for navigating the Internet. This bears tremendously upon the role and function of the entrepreneur, making it much easier than it should be.

Just imagine how much easier it is, in a framework that already has the entrepreneur in the grip of small and institutional iterativeness and of their cyclical movement (which carries you in its wake), to manage your firm when there is such vast (and yet limited) degree for "revolution." You can surf the cyclical movement of the various iterations (all three types), always and unfailingly claiming originality for what you do as a manager. You can also claim the same originality for what you represent as an entrepreneur, giving a (hollow) meaning to your "responsibility" as above defined.

It is precisely this massification of originality (i.e., of individuality) that gives you a chance to stand out. This standing out, however, amounts to nothing else than being just identical to the others: what you do to stand out is to openly acknowledge such identity in public, knowing that the ebb and tide of identity will require you to do so again in a minute (this concerns both the self and commodities).

The above is precisely the mechanism to keep everybody in the game that we have seen. The market, and its related institutions, abhor a vacuum and do not let anybody out, lest some empty room should be formed. There is a perverse and antimarket logic in this, for if the iterativeness is at work, then there is no reward for the innovator. Sylos Labini's (and the classical political economists') new entry with a novelty and the creation of new markets are reduced to the slippage points we have seen. If they constituted true novelties they would be incommunicable and unmarketable in the capitalist game. The "service sector" is no other thing than the privatized old thing; computers are just a vulgarization of a very old and very limited, well-known working logic.

In *Anti-Hegelian Reading* (2002a), I proposed that the functions of the firm are those of shielding themselves from the markets' incidents or structural faults, remaining within the market itself, and in this framework produce and enter the market with production, adapting to whatever logic (cost or price) dictates the choice of production processes. The firm organizes itself in multiple ways apparently determined by the indications of the markets, but (as we saw) in reality are compelled by the absolute and inescapable power of the dominant culture. The number of combinations possible with all the endowments of the firm easily yields a rather high number (combinatory calculation always yields high numbers of possible permutations), feeding the rhetoric of the infinite possibilities you get in the market. This aspect completes our argument.

Now we have all the elements discussed by the social sciences and the common citizen alike about the market and the functioning of the firm. Put together an organic discourse at the intellectual level with an apparently high/infinite number of combinations/permutations, and you have what a market in practice amounts to. This is an entrepreneur's (or manager's, or capitalist's, or citizen's, or customer's who believes in the system) application of a "mystical rationality."

The manager is a person aware of his or her own social and political role and aware of the fact that such a role changes with the political climate. What does not change is his or her indispensability, which keeps him or her going. Also, he or she is not particularly worried by the technical innovation business, unless by that it is meant what production is about. Everybody, from software producers to shoemakers and cheese makers, seeks to come out with a new product as often as the profit rate of the old starts to decline. Of course, one has to brand this normal production activity "innovation," and claim revolutions.[29] The manager's attention is caught by the need to conform to the market and the Marshallian task of the engineering of the production process.

Whether production declines or increases, whether it is material or immaterial, the only way to summarize its management in the framework delineated is by the need to make its presence conspicuous. The name of the game is "conspicuous production," by which everybody must understand the stated conformity to the iterative game that has been historically called capitalism.

The regulation of the whole enforced by the fascist and moderate environment described makes for the prevention of unfair behaviors of the immoral kind (from cartels to low-quality production), as long as the profit motive can be adduced to signify responsibility. This last is the true and only justification for what goes on. It justifies it for the believer, and, in a negative way, for the protester, giving him the chance to pine about it.

In this set of circumstances the use of efficiency indicators of firm performance makes perfect sense. There is a plethora of such types of indexes, mostly based on some simple arithmetical ratio. The rigidity of such ratios, which should make for an evident incapacity to account for the (supposed) elasticity and variability of "market" reality, is the very cause of their effectiveness. In a world that is limited and limiting, but infinitely elastic to usage and bending, simple arithmetical ratios are the solution to get the thing in motion.

The meaning of management, and the psychology of the entrepreneur, are summarized in this double perspective of infinite talking about, and sudden stops to actually do, material things.

MARKETING OF PRODUCTS

The question of sorting out the firm's production in order to keep it in the market—what in technical as well as in vulgar terms is called "marketing"— is a good illustrative instance of what we have been discussing. It involves the firm management as well as the vast group (the rest of society) called the (potential) consumer, and the theory and practice of exchange. In so doing it necessarily puts together all of those aspects we have been dealing with: logical, cultural, political, and economic. Let us look at it with the help of one of the most popular textbooks on the subject, Lambin (2000), and of a summary from Wikipedia, just for a bit of Internet frivolity very much in tone with this subject.

Lambin (2000) (I had to make do with the Italian edition here) is adamant about the importance of looking at the subject, having made clear that market relations have at last established themselves worldwide. He gets this idea from the fall of the Soviet Union and of its sphere of influence, the widespread adoption of policies of deregulation and privatization (especially of formerly public services), the stabilization (at least, what he believes to be a stabilization) of the former socialist economies in a market routine, the globalization of the economy, the internationalization of the food sector, the role of the Internet, and the achieved "professionality" of consumers coupled with a new social and environmental awareness on all sides, brought into the picture by ecologist movements.[30]

Marketing is no longer an internal function of the firm: it is oriented to and by the market. The market orientation is too important to be limited to the sole function of marketing. It must be present at all levels and in all the functions of the firm (XV). The Wikipedia description of the subject is perfectly consonant.

This coincides with the way entrepreneurs and managers describe "new" economic environments.[31] Marketing acts here as a proxy for the more general functioning of all the rest.

Lambin's book and Wikipedia have a few salient characteristics in common. In the first place, in defining their subject matter they appeal to its relationship with, or even in some cases actual dependency from, other social sciences (mainly economics, the various branches of psychology, communication, and cognitive studies). Yet, a discussion of such relationships and of such sciences is not to be found. No theoretical systemation is offered. This does not prevent the practitioners, and here Lambin is faultless, from being precise with their references to single studies in these various sciences and in marketing itself. Bibliographic references are punctual (not so Wikipedia, for obvious reasons).

We do not know what we are doing, but our academic apparatus is immaculate: like the "nowhere man" in the "Yellow Submarine" cartoon, the marketing expert refers to a huge literature he does not understand to back his (lack of) decision.

Secondly, most of what they deal with consists in lists and classifications. Such lists and classifications are either borrowed from the various reference disciplines or less often taken from empirical material, especially about the functioning of the firm. This last is, obviously, mostly codified by economics and management disciplines from which the actual lists and classifications are taken (duly quoting the source). Lists and classifications are tremendously important, for they permit the organization of the otherwise infinite material that (iteratively repeating itself) would overwhelm the practitioner.

All this does not prevent marketing from having "scientific" ambitions. The methodology to do empirical research must be rigorous. Its characteristics must be: objectivity, confutability on empirical grounds, analytical character (they must originate in the scientific method of the actual science used), method and precision (the conditions of data gathering must be well stated), a critical stance ("the scientific doubts"), and communicability (to other analysts) must be sought (Lambin 2000, 126). In fact, marketing research must produce "certified" knowledge without which no good decisions can be taken. The market analyst must discover "objective truths." This means the use of the "scientific method," which only can validate results (Lambin 2000, 125).

We can now give the definition of what marketing is. A first definition, general and somehow linked to classical political economy, is given on page 4 of Lambin's book. Marketing is based on the theory of individual choices (the purchaser's sovereignty). Curiously, to Lambin (2000), marketing is "nothing but the social expression of the principles of the classical political economists."

But the true definition comes on page 7. Marketing is the social process that tends to satisfy the needs and wishes of individuals and organizations, interacting with the creation and voluntary exchange, based on competition, of products and services that produce utility for whomever purchases them.

If we subtract from the first definition the bullshit appended, we obtain the second. We can turn to the matter itself.

The question of the plethora of information (which, we saw last section, is a matter of fact in numerical but not in variety terms) is more than the cause of the lists and classifications: it is the very point of the whole business, not just of marketing but of the whole of economic activity. Marketing itself is presented as, and actually is, the solution of problems (especially strategic marketing, Lambin 9). Products themselves are, and should be passed as, solutions to problems. This deserves a few words, for it is more to do with the concept of need in economic theory than with what your toothpaste, shampoo, or washing machine does for you (and for which you are never grateful enough).

If we take economic theory in the approximate sense Lambin uses for Adam Smith and put it together with the postconsumerist world we live in described in "The Firm and the Market" and broadly accepted in marketing, we see that needs are not anymore basic. We, however poor in relative terms, do not just eat bread: when faced by hunger we "choose" between carbohydrates or protein-rich food. We do this even when our poverty compels us to choose the first rather than the second. If it is winter we might also want vitamins, just to keep colds off. And if in a hurry we might want to buy precooked food or go to a fast food restaurant, thus "choosing" which brand will satisfy our problem, and how. We are in the presence of a conception of a "problem" that overlaps with our conceptualization of capitalism as "problems."

This conceptualization of the product must be put together with another defining trait: product and market are in practice the same thing. Having defined a product, you automatically have defined a market, and the sorting out of that product is the market of that product—that is, the market in general. Thus in a market-oriented firm the choice of the target market is decided from the point of view of the purchaser referring to the "solution to the problem" and not from a technological perspective (Lambin 2000, 266).

In fact, the secret to sort out production is to catch, or create, the right "segment" of the market. It is easy to see that segmentation is something we can create out of the blue. Here marketing supplies an endless anthology of anecdotes that have been feeding the profession, literature, and cinema. A door and gate producer, in case his dominance of the market is threatened, recycles himself as a maker of "devices to control access," toothpaste becomes an oral hygiene program, and so on. We witness in action everything concerning the changes that are currently taking place in capitalism.

These days firms do not pursue any longer mass production, rather operating with a just-in-time logic. This depends on the flexibility of the workforce both in technical terms and because it reduces the burden of labor cost and reduces market activity to figuring out the life cycle of the product and to directly dealing with the consumer. Both activities are the realm of the marketing practitioner, and both involve a degree of prevision. We have already seen that capitalism is predictable, but it is very enlightening to see how marketing practitioners render this.

Coming to forecasting, the expert's judgement is based on experience, an explicative model, intuition, and statistical extrapolation (Lambin 2000, 301).

That is, given the facility to manipulate all of these things to one's purposes, and given the necessity to be as banal as possible, decisions are taken proposing a mix of all of these factors, as long as it looks feasible and/or it identifies a proper "segment" of the market (a consumer problem). The experts are managers, salespersons, and similar—those with the pulse of the market. The claim to scientificity discussed above can be invoked any time doubts surface from "external" people.

Previsions are possible, even necessary, or one would not even start producing. But this brings in the problem of innovation. In a world that is predictable in general (but this the marketing experts do not know, for they have not read this book) and where previsions are possible and likely to be right, the new is banned. The new is in fact by definition unpredictable. What is needed is innovation, new products—but that means new markets, or segments, and that, again by definition, is a variation or even a replication of what we already have. The new, as already shown, is anathema to capitalist production, which is what marketing is about.

Lambin is as vague and queer as he can be, therefore, on the issue of innovation. Fundamental innovations are for instance new medicines, and a wide degree is left for what one can mean by innovation, just like in economics. On page 431 he states that "not always a novelty is an innovation." In fact, there are in marketing four criteria of classification for innovation: with respect to the firm, to the intrinsic basic idea of the innovation, the origin of it, and the degree of novelty of the concept. In the end "basic research," the one that produces true novelties, is unpredictable (436).

The standardization of market and the end of Fordism and Taylorism under the names of globalization and post-Fordism are invoked by Lambin as the final stabilization of world capitalism. Here the importance of the new responsibility of the consumer, repeatedly emphasized by Lambin, is fundamental, and completes the picture we have been drawing of the cultural limitations of capitalist mentality and their fascist outcomes. The consumer is socially responsible: he associates with his likes to ask of the firm what is its duty to supply (quality, fairness, etc.) without polluting the environment or depleting the world's resources, in a truly fascist style of corporativism.

Consumers are getting "professional": they are getting to know the technicalities, using their knowledge to ensure the functioning of the system. This, insidiously for the faulty and elementary logic of capitalism, amounts precisely to that "fairness" that the free market in practice cannot deliver unless it is institutionally (corporatism is the word we need here) compelled to do so (by the consumer, in this case).

What the consumers, and with them the various ecologist organizations, the antiglobalization protesters, and the other self-appointed defenders of our liberties want is, to use Lambin's words, the full application of the marketing logic and methods (42). They, Lambin says, do not oppose the market (capitalism): on the contrary. In this framework, with a market that can never be, with oligopolies dictating their rules, with the consumer who wants the full application of the impossible but is contented to get some practical results, we are fully within the limits described by the theoretical treatment we have been unfolding so far.

The outcome should be the production of a series of statements that, claiming to represent the actual intercourses of capitalist society and its economy, are emptily repetitive to the casual observer, iterative for us. This is precisely what happens in marketing.

Marketing has a lot to say on "how to deliver the message." The whole point, as summarized on page 607, is that the message is geared to the receiver (Lambin 2000). It can only say what the receiver expects, with the language and the logic expected. Within the limits set by the institutional and juridical construction, the target of the message gets a tentative solution to a problem he is due to have that respects his responsibility and invites him to operate a choice, sporting as a mark of distinction the fact that all the others have done, do, or should do, also the firm that seeks to sell its product is behaving responsibly.

In full fascist style, we are moderate in logic and language, and being so we are part of an organic whole that is unattainable in practice and exists only because of the will of the body politics to substitute for its ideal features the chains of the "possible in practice," corporatist mass individual volunteering.

No wonder then that the core of research on marketing is the concrete and ideal symbol of man's (the fascist man) individuality and sociality: the family as a social nucleus. No wonder that even homosexuals want to get married under capitalism. No wonder that the moderate left backs all this. They are just being practical. They are doing their bit for the reform of society, its step-by-step improvement.

While few words are needed to comment in technical terms on what has been discussed, we must single out a couple of aspects that help us move to the next chapter. The first is the issue of the so-called service sector. Given what we have been saying about marketing, it is easy to see that service firms are a true godsend for marketing practitioners. Services and their commercial practice come more and more to actually represent the "regulations" themselves, the institutions.[32]

A second aspect is to do with the importance of words as concepts and of representation in words. Capitalist categories exist and look like things as long as they exist in words, from which they can be thought of as concepts. Instead of worrying about recovering what belongs to prolepsis, the capitalist person solves the problem by applying the working logic of capitalist intellectuality at the micro, personal level, and letting the general, faulty logic (the metaphysics) work itself out at the level of the whole.

This poses profound institutional problems. It is therefore to such study that we must turn now. The question, however, is not about institutions (even in the sense I have given to them in Micocci 2002a), but about them as related to capitalist state, society, community, market. It is precisely this archaic way to group them together that we are compelled to use that leads us to an archaic term, politeia, in its mistaken modern usage.

CONCLUSIONS

The conventional reader is bound to have abandoned the reading of this book long ago. Yet an author must believe that somebody will read his book to the end, and I figure that somebody, perhaps aided by a nice bottle or a broken heart, and hence more willing to overcome his/her inhibitions, could read this. Such a conventional reader must feel, at this point, that there is no hope.

It is time to stop identifying fascism with its extreme and horrifying consequences of the first half of the twentieth century and face it for what it is: a coherent part, a constituent part of what we imprecisely call capitalism. Besides, postfascist history has shown itself capable of such atrocities that one is led to think that the difference is just how such absurd deeds are publicized and connected.

All this, and the question left pending in this chapter of the "institutional" problem, make it imperative to turn to the capitalist politeia. Is it as capitalist as its economic structure? Or perhaps we have overestimated its historical coherence with what has come out of the Industrial Revolution? After all, if capitalism as we know it is iterative and abhors both a vacuum and novelty, and if its inception is driven by the economic forces, we might hypothesize that it has stifled rather than enhanced the evolution of its own political institutions.

There are some huge, disquieting phenomena that have been with capitalism throughout its entire life and are making their nth comeback while writing this. Imperialism and savage mass murder are one. Nationalism and blood ties are another, or more likely the same thing. Everybody still approves of the persecution of anarchists of all kinds, instead of seeing the anarchist roots of the liberal and communist utopias. War keeps being a word with meaning.

If capitalism existed all, this would not take place, for we would have a situation close to anarchy if we had taken either the liberal and the communist path.[33] We have been studying the intellectual failures of capitalism as we know it. It is time to put such knowledge to work to explain the present success of the institutions we have, their archaic character, and their terrifying outcomes and unspeakable cruelty.

Emancipation is indeed possible, perhaps inevitable, precisely because there is no hope in capitalism. What we are doing here is like discovering sex in adolescence: there is no going back to the former ignorance, and innocence from now on consists in going along the knowledge path. Pleasure lies there. Let us lose our ignorance then, and let us go ahead, to emancipation and its delights.

NOTES

1. The language part inevitably tends to elementarization of structure and simplification of meaning. This affects the emotional sphere, which perhaps constitutes a cause for the revolutions we have known in history. See Micocci (2002a). The simplification I am talking about here resembles very much, inevitably, the ones Marcuse (1967) describes.

2. The supporters of globalization are among the staunchest supporters of the presence and intervention of the state, if only to insure the implementation of the rolling back of the welfare state or of the precarization of labor, which are erroneously given an exclusively economic meaning. Vasapollo et al. (2004) and Sylos Labini (2004), from opposite fronts, seem to have caught the complex meaning of hitting labor.

3. See Micocci (2005a, 2005c), and McCann, (2004).

4. See Micocci (2002b).

5. See Micocci (2002a, 2004a, 2005a, 2005c).

6. Hayek is a respectable case. Mussolini (see Micocci 2002c) is a nonrespectable case that nonetheless succeeded in drawing most Italian liberals (from Croce to Einaudi) to his cause, at least for a while. Berlusconi is another nonrespectable case, with Marx's proviso that history repeats itself as a farce. It took, for instance, Berlusconi's racist declarations to convince the Nobel laureate Modigliani of what was self-evident (see Micocci 2005f).

7. Take Schumpeter's (1951) view on the importance of remaining bits of feudal classes on imperialism, and Micocci (2005a). See also Micocci (2001c).

8. Continuity in the mathematical sense is a good approximation to the dialectical functioning of capitalist relations. For a treatment of mathematical noncontinuity and its insertion in dialectics see Micocci (2002a) and (2005d). We can anticipate here that the hypothesis of noncontinuity does not change the general framework, whether a dialectics is admitted or not.

9. Going to work every day is iterative rather than merely repetitive. Parliamentary democracy is iterative too, by definition. Even our morning shower, or breakfast, are iterative rather than repetitive, for little differences and needs to reset the operations crop up all the time. This is not, however, to do with the wider, cultural iterativeness of capitalism.

10. See Micocci (2002a, 2004a).

11. Keynes, the good English gentleman, was less concerned by technology and creativity. He was instead bothered by the issue of money and its use and by the issue of social classes and their cohabitation. His capitalism is redolent of Galsworthy's old Forsyte, or Defoe's hero Crusoe and heroines Lady Roxana and Moll Flanders.

12. To them innovations are one of the definitional categories of capitalism and must not be challenged.

13. There obviously is a racist component in this: a new type of seed or tool is the most Africans can expect by way of innovation, and they are highly praised when they get it, just as we do with children or handicapped people when they show they can perform simple tasks.

14. His entrepreneur was probably a respectable, art-loving book reader who found it morally rewarding to enter politics by means of entrepreneurship, conscious to be contributing to his country's welfare, a sort of *pater familias* that Cicero would have loved but that never had a counterpart in reality.

15. See Micocci (2001c), and Orati (1981).

16. Here the question is to be taken with as much care as possible: the fact that one can predict the coming of the various possible slippages does not mean that these can be predicted or prevented. Too many variables, and the concurrence of the natural, make any form of statistical and probability treatment impossible, or too vague. Vice versa, there is a high degree of predictability in the working of all those matters of capitalism that are mainly determined by "capitalist" variables. See Micocci (2005d).

17. I owe this point to many conversations with Luciano Vasapollo and to his books. He is of course not responsible for what I made of our conversations and my readings.

18. For the conservative contents of this type of argument which, I want to emphasize, is perfectly traditional in the left, both extremist and moderate, see Micocci (2004f).

19. In a private exchange with me in 2004.

20. We are surrounded by revolutionaries, reformists, and conservatives who go at any length to do what is "possible." The fact that this is totally meaningless (possible is whatever you end up doing, even if it looks impossible before you do it), does not deter their single-minded infantilism.

21. Time and history are part of nature, in which men have the delusion to play a role. Whether they build or destroy, even when they destroy nature itself, human beings are just serving the flow of time exactly like the rest.

22. Naturally many in the opposition are not fascist in fact. But this only increases the tragic sadness of the situation and the need to put an end to it as soon as possible.

23. See Micocci (2002a). Such moderatism is not new in history and is typical of those transition periods in history when something new might seem to be brewing. In "The Perfidy of Moderatism", (2007a) I have shown its characteristic traits in Ovid's *Metamorphoses* and Lucretius's *De Rerum Natura* (1992), associating its perfidy to the delinking from nature as we have been defining it so far.

24. Attempts to say the opposite are there nonetheless and are also very successful saleswise. Rifkin and Negri are the most obvious names that come to mind. The lit-

erature that disproves their opinions is so vast and convincing that there is no point discussing it here.

25. See, among others, Vasapollo (2003a, 2003b); Casadio, Petras, Vasapollo (2003); Vasapollo, Casadio, Petras, Veltmeyer (2004); Arriola, Vasapollo (2004).

26. It is worth repeating that this was clear in the classical political economists, implicit in the neoclassicals, and strongly emphasized in the Austrians and of course in the Marxists. The consequences of this acknowledgement, whether explicit or silently taken for granted, cannot be overemphasized. See also Micocci (2004b, 2005a, and 2005c).

27. Capitalism is unanimously recognized to be characterized by recurrent crises.

28. In oligopoly situations there are barriers to the entry of new firms: the actual entrepreneurs you have are something you must therefore keep and even please.

29. These days some lines of production are just let die. This is not bad management, and even less substitution of products by innovation. It is simply a corollary of the peculiarities of competition already described.

30. He also indulges in some Adam Smith extravaganza to ennoble his chosen subject that we can mercifully leave out.

31. In the parlance of economists, politicians, and entrepreneurs/managers, the economic circumstances, whenever they must be talked about, are always "new." The logic behind this has been discussed; the minor and contingent motives can be easily guessed.

32. For a more thorough treatment of institutions see Micocci (2002).

33. I have tried hard all my life to identify a third way besides those two, but could not find any with the same utopian revolutionary potential. So I stick to them as my reference.

Chapter Five

Capitalism's Politeia

History cannot escape re-elaboration. It is only natural that capitalism comes to be conceived as a continuation, and indeed an evolution, of the preceding modes of production. The very word democracy is supposed to openly recall an ancient Greek ancestry that is, obviously, completely invented. Capitalism hangs between the claim to descend from a millenary evolution that cuts across different (and how different!) modes of production[1] and the equally strong claim that it is a mode of production by itself, a novelty on the world stage.

Capitalism thus claims to have perfected the oligarchic institutes of the Greek and Roman politeia. This process has taken a theoretical form, named "Classical Political Philosophy," whose practical (not material) outcome is modern institutions and their representative democracies. This is obvious nonsense that looks apparent to anybody who has an understanding of the flow of time and of the difference between ancient Greece and present-day reality. This, however, poses no problem to metaphysics: it is precisely the field in which its generalizing, homogenizing, and moderation-enforcing means operate without obstacles.

Hypostatizations (the evolution of the social systems, the presence and use of money, the law of value, commerce, and so on) frantically perform their *danse macabre* that we call capitalism. Their ghosts can appear to capitalism but can also be appeared to by capitalism. It is to these ghosts, to use Adam Smith's words, that we owe our meat and our beer, and the poor their poverty.

Yet, the analogies to ancient times and to instincts are there: like in any good *danse macabre* we have on stage the skeletons and ghosts of what has been, or more likely could have been, however disguised they are and however frantic and varied the choreography. The main theme of the dance is the

149

politeia, the avatar of capitalism and its logic, that imprecise word that in classical political philosophy is pretended to mean constitution.

Politeia is what the Greek *poleis* used to have, what gave them their distinctiveness: what made their communities separated nucleuses, vivacious amoebas in the dirty water of the world imagined by metaphysics. Capitalism is, in this sense, a politeia. Its metaphysics is made of all the things that made up the Greek polis, whether the correspondence is true or invented. The basic analogy is summarized in the nucleus idea. This last is a recurring image, a pseudoconcept that capitalism endows everything with. Cells in biology, atoms in physics, truth itself are conceived as nucleuses around which life develops. The whole of social life is a repetition of differently sized nucleuses: family, country, community, politeia.

We shall argue here that capitalism is a nonfully developed and autonomous mode of production, which has not completely broken materially with what came before, despite its economic traits having started the rupture already in Adam Smith's times. Its hybrid nature is held together as a metaphysics, making up that quasi-capitalist monster we all can witness. I shall discuss this topic by means of presenting some relevant features of capitalism as we know it, which prove the incompleteness of the development in the direction of an autonomous mode of production.

CAPITALISM'S INSTITUTIONS

Everybody seems to agree that capitalism is a distinctive social and economic formation: a mode of production, in Marxist jargon. As for the characteristics that define it, we find ourselves lost in a confused and confusing maze of proposals. Almost at every step we find assertions of "capitalism is . . .," "capitalism is characterized by . . .," "the defining feature of capitalism is . . ." type. Such assertions come from the Marxist as well as the mainstream camps. The usually guarded mainstream attitudes toward general statements in fact are here slack. The main difference between the mainstream and the Marxist camps is that in the former statements are just thrown there, isolated from one another, as pieces of a supposedly well-known and shared truth not worth mentioning, let alone explaining.

In the Marxist camp instead it seems very important to give general definitions of capitalism. Here the difference between the Young and the later, apparently Hegelian and/or dialectical, Marx is solved by appealing to the former to initiate the argument (the usual, grand theory *incipit*—modes of production are first introduced in the "unreliable" *German Ideology*) and then working through the subtleties of the latter, especially using *Capital*, Vol. III.

Given all that has been built up in chapters 2, 3, and 4, we can instead safely work our way to the definition of mode of production, and of capitalist mode of production, backwards, from *Capital*, Vol. III, to the "Introduction" to a *Critique of Political Economy* to the *German Ideology*.

In Part VII of Vol. III of *Capital* (1978), chapter XLVIII ("The Trinity Formula") Marx says,

> [We have seen] that the capitalist process of production is a historically determined form of the social process of production in general. The latter is as much a production process of material conditions of human life as a process taking place under specific historical and economic production relations, producing and reproducing those relations themselves, and thereby also the bearers of this process, their material conditions of existence and their mutual relations, i.e., their particular socio-economic form. For the aggregate of these relations, in which the agents of this production stand with respect to Nature and to one another and in which they produce, is precisely society, considered from the standpoint of its economic structure. Like all its predecessors the capitalist process of production proceeds under definite material conditions . . . the bearers of definite social relations entered into by individuals. . . . Those conditions, like these relations, are on the one hand pre-requisites, on the other hand results and creations of the capitalist process. (818–19)

Marx goes on spelling out the role of capital (personified by the capitalist) and of surplus value, labor, and all the usual rest. Despite not mentioning the expression "mode of production," we can take this as a definition of the capitalist mode of production, because Marx uses these expressions interchangeably when dealing with technicalities and because it comes as the culmination of his lifelong work, and with large bits of Engels's intrusion.

The ground has been prepared through the whole of the three volumes, and Part VI (especially ch. XXXVIII) has spelled out how the prerequisites of capitalism get transformed into capitalist objects (Marx starts from land and its ownership). We are, it seems, in a fully conventional kind of treatment, which all social scientists, Marxist and mainstream, could accept. But let us go on exploring the issue.

In Part II, chapter X (on the equalization of the rate of profit, market prices, market values, surplus profit), in discussing the equalization, Marx makes the general observation that much depends upon "the extent of capitalist development in a given nation."

> With the progress of capitalist production, it also develops its own conditions and subordinates to its specific character and its immanent laws all the social prerequisites on which the process of production is based. (196)

Given the existing conditions—that is, the degree of accomplishment of capitalism's characteristics, capitalism's "immanent" laws subordinate the "prerequisites," and so on. This is completely different from saying that capitalism just imposes its predetermined laws concerning production on the material world at hand, like in the propaganda of the *Manifesto*. Precapitalist relationships are given a treatment in chapter XXXVI; that, however, is mainly concentrated on capital (usury) and banks. The interesting part is still in the treatment of the Trinity Formula.

> [The Trinity] [as put by the vulgar economists] corresponds to the interests of the ruling classes by proclaiming the physical necessity and eternal justification of their sources of revenue and elevating them to a dogma.
>
> In our description of how production relations are converted into entities and rendered independent in relation to the agents of production, we leave aside the manner in which the interrelations, due to the world market, its conjunctures, movements of market prices, periods of credit, industrial and commercial cycles, alternations of prosperity and crises, appear to them as overwhelming natural laws that irresistibly enforce their will over them, and confront them as a blind necessity. We leave this aside because . . . we need present only the inner organization of the capitalist mode of production, in its ideal average, as it were.
>
> In preceding forms of society this economic mystification arose principally with respect to money and interest-bearing capital. (830–31)

Marx continues expanding on how in the Middle Ages

> the domination of producers by the conditions of production is concealed by the relations of domination and servitude. The same applies in communal societies, whose reproduction appeared as its ultimate purpose. Similarly in the medieval guild. Only when the capitalist mode of production. . . [The manuscript breaks off here.] (831)

Tantalizing as this may be, the question is that Marx is introducing a fundamental aspect, and the psychological relation to it and to the very structures of the mode of production. Marx is driving along the direction of what is argued so far in the present book, though we do not know how and with what results.

We can now see in a different light what was stated on page 26, at the beginning of chapter I ("Cost-Price and Profit").

> The grouping of the various value portions of a commodity which only replace the value of the capital expended in its production under the head of cost-price expresses, on the one hand, the specific character of capitalist production. The capitalist cost of the commodity is measured by the expenditure of capital, while

the actual cost of the commodity is measured by the expenditure of labor. (emphasis in the original) (Capital, vol. III, 1978)

Marx goes on about the fact that the capitalist cost-price of the commodity differs in quantity from its value, but this need not concern us yet. What counts is that we are witnessing metaphysics in action.[2]

In Vol. II, in dealing with the metamorphoses of capital and their circuits, Marx says (ch. IV, "The Three Formulas of the Circuit") that

in the relationship of capitalist and wage laborer, the money-relation, the relation between the buyer and the seller, becomes a relation inherent in production. But this relation has its foundation in the social character of production, not in the mode of exchange. The latter conversely emanates from the former. It is, however, quite in keeping with the bourgeois horizon, everyone being engrossed in the transaction of shady business, not to see in the character of the mode of production the bases of the mode of exchange corresponding to it, and vice versa. (1978, 120)

This quotation is crucial and is just one of many similar statements in Marx.

All sorts of confusions can arise, when immersed in the haze of capitalist affairs. The ones we are especially interested in are those concerning the understanding of the character, the mode of operation, the internal connections and causal relationships, of the mode of production.

Earlier on within the same discussion (ch. 1, "The Circuit of Money-Capital"), Marx notices that

generally M-L is regarded as characteristic of the capitalist mode of production . . . it is so regarded because of its form, since *money* in the form of wages buys labor, and this is the characteristic mark of the money system.

Nor is it the irrationality of the form which is taken as characteristic. On the contrary, one overlooks the irrational. (29–30, emphasis in the original)

The irrationality consists in the fact that labor as a value-creating element cannot have any value: wages are a "disguised form," which expresses the value of the operation of labor power.

The characteristic thing is not that the commodity labor-power appears as a commodity. (29–30)

All this brings us back to the process of valorization and its importance as the source and example for all the other deals taking place in metaphysics. This constitutes the capitalist mode of production. But let us go further backward to finish our search for the meaning of mode of production, and of capitalist mode of production, for Marx and for us.

In the *German Ideology*, in the part on Feuerbach, Marx says that

the production of life, both of one's own labor and of fresh life in procreation, now appears as a double relationship: on the one hand as natural, on the other as a social relationship. By social we understand the co-operation of several individuals, no matter under what conditions, in what manner and to what ends. It follows from this that a certain mode of production, or industrial stage, is always combined with a certain mode of co-operation, or social stage, and this mode of co-operation is itself a "productive force." Further, that the multitude of productive forces accessible to men determines the nature of society; hence, that the "history of humanity" must always be studied and treated in relation with the history of industry and exchange. . . . Thus it is quite obvious from the start that there exists a materialistic connection of men with one another, which is determined by their needs and their mode of production, and which is as old as men themselves. This connection is ever taking on new forms, and thus presents a "history" independently of the existence of any political or religious nonsense which in addition may hold men together. (1985, 50)[3]

This statement is a condensation of the reasoning proposed in this book. The distinction between natural and social hints at the hypostatization/metaphysics question pursued here, which, as shown in chapter 2, comes directly from the so-called Young Marx.

I do not wish to push this point too far, for no other reason but the absolute boredom of getting trapped in arid, erudite diatribes with the dialectical majority of Marxists. Simply, this is a possible reading of Marx. What I am saying is well within the materialistic/conflictive tradition. The proof of its relevance must not be sought in its adherence to Marx but in its capacity to produce a revolutionary vision without the "human waste" that has characterized Marxist dialectical paths to "revolution."

We can now quote Marx once more on an important aspect, discussed in the justly famous *Introduction to a Critique of Political Economy*:

Laws may perpetuate a particular means of production, e.g., land, in certain families. These laws acquire economic significance only if large-scale property is in keeping with the social mode of production. . . . The influence exercised by laws on the preservation of existing conditions of distribution, and the effect they thereby exert on production has to be examined separately. (1985, 138)

We shall not do that, however. We have already moved beyond economics/political economy earlier on.

The bourgeois economists have merely in view that production proceeds more smoothly with modern police than, e.g., under club-law. They forget, however, that club-law too is law, and that the law of the stronger, only in a different form, still survives in their "constitutional State." . . . To recapitulate: there are categories which are common to all stages of production and are established by reasoning as general categories; the so-called general conditions of all and any production, however, are nothing but abstract aspects which do not define any of the actual historical stages of production. (1985, 128, 129)

These words, again from the *Introduction to a Critique of Political Economy*, summarize what has so far been discussed and helps us move on to explore capitalism as a mode of production. A mode of production is marked by the kind of legal repressive apparatus it has ended up having. We must therefore look at the intellectual/cultural justifications for the presence, and the keeping, of such apparatus. The law of the strongest is in every "constitutional State," regardless of the bonhomie they put in their arguments.[4]

So, what are the defining features of capitalism, those characters that mark it as a distinct mode of production? Listing the most important ones does not help much: division of labor, mass production, monetized exchange economy, power subtracted from the aristocrats and managed by the bourgeoisie, commodification in general, commodification of labor, are all derivative aspects of something more general.[5] However we twist and turn these aspects, and all the others we can add, we find ourselves staring at something that has a general, in the taxonomic sense of genus, similarity.

We have identified capitalism by describing it as a dominant mentality that unifies all of the actual material transactions. The capitalist mode of production has isolated itself from the variable and rupture-prone free flow of reality to build a dialectically functioning bubble. Things being this way,

1. It can never be sure to manage and make last its self-inflicted isolation from nature.
2. It cannot break with former modes of production, for its only way of proceeding is by way of dialectical contradictions, pseudocontinuities (and pseudorevolutions) that are but intellectual artifacts. These can be true or invented.

Thus its qualifying main entities—the process of valorization, the illusion of the "market," and the similarly boasted delusion of democracy—can work both when they are true and when they are invented. They are intellectually built upon a hypostatized continuity with the past that denies any distinctiveness to the mode of production itself. The distinctiveness itself, the rupture-cum-disappearance with the past, is ruled out. To put it in the words of Gramsci, to capitalism the future (and hence the present relation to the past) is in the womb of the present.

This death sentence for capitalist distinctiveness in economic and political terms is valid both for what is actually conceivable as continuous with preceding epochs[6] and for what is conceivable as brand new. The process of valorization can (even for thinkers as great as Adam Smith and John Maynard Keynes, as we saw) be thought as harking back to activities that were going on in the preceding modes of production. Like Wood (1997, 1994, 1991) intuitively puts it, capitalism is seen as "the liberation of an opportunity rather than the imposition of an imperative" (1997, 5).[7]

The free-market utopia envisaged by Adam Smith, the world of fairness where "alone rule Freedom, Equality, Property and Bentham" (Marx 1978, Vol. I, ch. VI, 172), that could and should have led to the complete freedom of trade and to civil liberties, has never taken off. The tragic mistake of dialectical Marxism is evident. The Marxists in fact have been talking about the variables of capitalism as if the distinctiveness of capitalism were a *fait accompli*. This mistake has mortgaged the future, too.

On the one hand, as repeatedly said, the most important result is that the dialectical vision has blinded Marxists to the very meaning of revolution. On the other, "revolution" has become a far away, impossible reference to cover up for a moderate (dialectical and evolutionary) monster: that of "progressive" ideas and attitudes. The twentieth century has been indelibly marked by this surreptitious substitution. Marxists could thus mix up with the Keynesians, and even the fascists (whether it was just for their joint strikes with the Nazis before these latter took power or to concoct the Argentinian mixture of Peronismo and Marxism), in the self-righteous compulsion to do the "progressive" thing.

To date, the frowning, self-righteous, highbrow, pretentious progressives have kept to the same strategy: some of them have (progressively) joined the ranks of the neoliberals (take Blair and the Italian DS party), some others stick to their pseudotrade-unionism past, some others have engaged in the frivolity of postmodernism, whether it be the Spinozian infantilism of Negri and Hardt's empire or the fancy-dressed issues of the Greens. While true liberals agonize over the incompleteness of capitalism as a mode of production (take Sylos Labini 2004), the progressives thrive and flourish out of this very situation: they, in other words, contribute to its preservation.

But this tragic outcome should not deceive us into inferring that it is the polity, politics as it is practiced, that blocks the evolution of the economy. Politics and the economy are not the only metaphysical players here: there is also the "community," that shadows powerful enough to destroy the utopian dreams and intuitions of Adam Smith, John Stuart Mill, Hayek, and Schumpeter and to constitute the never-mentioned deus ex machina of Marxist dialectics. We must explore in more depth these three elements.

First, concerning the economy, there is little discussion that some changes we can tentatively identify as ruptures have taken place here. The workers have regressed from serfs to commodity, changing taxonomic genus. The idea of "economic growth"[8] has replaced that of production for a living.

But economic activity is never conceived as disjointed from a "community," be it a state, nation, or nation-state, an ethnicity, or any other kind of collective entity that can be thought about as a nucleus. And here, with the nucleus, as it is easy to see, ends the rupture chance. Once in a nucleus ruptures are ruled out and even forbidden.

If we think about the political structures and the political features of capitalism, we notice that they directly descend from preceding, even fully medieval, ideas and actual institutions. The republics of Venice and of the Dutch are the examples to follow, and Hobbes and similar nightmares the looming dangers to defuse and exorcise.

There is a straight line that leads, through classical political philosophy, from the ancient to the modern to the present (see Micocci 2004f, 2004b). Second, and as important, the widely celebrated passage of power from the hands of the privileged classes their religious excuses to those of the bourgeoisie with their secular ("mystical rational") motives is a typical case not of rupture but, as most Marxists say, of dialectical contradiction. Privileged classes and religion make periodical comebacks.

The community thus comes to play a truly structural role. By its nature of being an intellectual (flawed) artifact with potential bridges to erect toward material entities (nation-state, ethnicity, raw materials production, for three obvious instances), and by being an outcome of both, community holds the whole thing together. Not being tied directly to material entities, it is the falsely dynamic source of the movement of the system. It also is its intellectual source, as we saw, since Adam Smith himself. Most importantly, it is by definition a nucleus.

Community, or any of its substitute concepts, does not have a form of its own: it takes, like gas, the form of the container in which it is put. When the container is big, it expands, when it is small it shrinks, in the former process acquiring weakness and in the latter power to detonate. Community is the driving feature of capitalism because it can be secular with its secular part and religious with religion. Community is also the root of fascism.

Finally, community is an impassable barrier to the development of revolutionary, rupture- and oblivion-dependent, changes: free market and communism, to mention the usual two. With this last observation we have gone back to the general point: despite an initial set of ruptures, capitalism has taken over a dialectical functioning that, by its capacity to cover everything material and abstract, has prevented and will always prevent change, condemning it to the stasis of its iterative mechanisms.

We have no difficulty now in accepting that capitalism is a politeia. Such a thing exists only in the imagination of those who conform to the dominant maieutics, and the fact that it has nothing to do with what the ancient meant by the word and by the actual thing helps rather than obstructs the identification. Capitalism's politeia is the "constitution" of capitalism, whose imagined ancestry is just the projection of the nucleus idea in the history of the past.

It can only be added that we are facing a clear case of lack of imagination. That, for a system based, as repeatedly shown, on a limited and limiting mentality, could be easily foreseen.

THE NATION-STATE

The confusion around the concept of mode of production and the actual, historical trajectory of the capitalist mode of production obscure what points to clear ruptures, which become dialectical relationships. The social sciences produce endless chicken-and-egg problems to this purpose. Particularly interesting are the related questions of "primitive accumulation" and of the "rights of man."

The chicken-and-egg question of the relationship between "primitive accumulation" and human legal rights within the development of capitalism (bracketed by Marx in the quotations of the preceding section from Marx 1985) are among the causes, and defining features, of the coming, and staying, of capitalism. They are taken as emblematic of capitalism's historical dialectical progression. We are before a case of infantile, fairytalelike description, geared to the needs of starting from, and returning to, the nucleus image.

Let us see the matter through the anti-Hegelian eyes of John Rosenthal.

> Practical concepts of economic activity which explicitly designate things while covertly alluding to relations obtaining among the individuals who own them are, then, the symptomatic expressions of a sort of social formation in which social relations are in general "mediated by things." (1998, 60)

This, Rosenthal continues, marks the difference between the capitalist age and the preceding ones.

> In a society based upon generalized commodity production . . . each given individual appears in the first instance as a legal person pure and simple [and] . . . the relations of dependence which obtain among these legal persons are realized and reproduced only *indirectly* via the exchange of material goods. (61, emphasis in the original)
>
> This is, if you like, the irony of exchange relation: that through it each of the exchanging subjects is constituted by a person, but only in order then to be per-

sonally indifferent to one another. The mutual acknowledgement of personhood
. . . built into the relation between exchanges of commodities amounts in effect
to—is indeed exhausted by—the mutual acknowledgement of their status as
owners . . . their equal rights with respect to the use and alienation of what belongs to them. (65, emphasis in the original)

What came first, in the making of capitalism, the individual legal person,
the law apparatus that helps sustain that, or the primitive accumulation of
wealth by the individual?

None of these questions are as important as the fact that all the above is
possible because, unlike in other ages and places, where individuals retained
their general material personhood even when bound by laws or godly dictates
and involved in exchanges and alienation of property, in capitalism man has
lost its material personhood and counts only as the bearer of the rights to, and
alienation of, property (which accumulation is about). This is a true historical
rupture, to which there is no remedy but another rupture.

Precisely such rupture is the aspect of the whole story that it is impossible
to situate. It has come unnoticed, and unnoticed it remains with us: we just
see its effects. Meanwhile primitive accumulation, the Industrial Revolution,
Fordism, and post-Fordism have come and gone. The very invisibility, or conversely the apparent inevitability of these ruptures, is easy to erroneously interpret as dialectical processes.

It is fairly obvious that laws and rights are just the most trivial expressions
of the "general will," the community with its institutions. To these we turn.

The preceding chapters have shown the intrusion of the general will into
the thought of liberal thinkers (and of Marxist thinkers alike: only, to them it
came via the Idealistic, dialectical route). In Hayek and the Austrians the confusion reaches its peak: as the idea of community has a rather collectivist af-
tertaste, emphasis is given to the "rule of law." This contains that "abstinence" aspect that is typical of the dominant intellectuality of capitalism:
abstinence from the free flow of instincts and sentiments, whose petty outcome is abstinence from consumption (i.e., accumulation).

Laws/rights (in that they are meant to distill the limited and limiting mentality of capitalism/the community into precise sets of prohibitions, recom-
mendations, and applications of a "shared morality") are there to be obeyed,
because they are to be believed in and respected as values in themselves.
They are transcended into the symbol of that hypostatizing mentality that has
produced them. Laws and rights, in their arid and schematic sentimental
poverty, are the bone that capitalist supporters and capitalist "revolutionaries"
contend to each other. With laws and rights, Marx's expression "mystical rationality" is used at its most exact effectiveness.

The counterpart to Menger, Mises, and Hayek within the orthodox Marxist field are Lenin, Gramsci, and the leaders of "Marxist" parties who talked about revolution when meaning mechanical continuity with capitalism. The whole history of the USSR has been an attempt to enforce a "socialist" legality, culminated in theory with the rather democratic and unapplied 1977 constitution, and in practice in the nationalist breakup following 1989.

All this is not surprising. If we look at the present state of things in the developed countries in institutional terms, we notice that we are in the presence of a Hegelian setup. Marx's nightmare has come true. The Idea is getting materialized, and it is even getting close to God, in the USA and in Europe. One can only hope that part of this folly is due to the intellectual inadequacy of some leaders and of their advisers, from Huntington on.

As a consequence the literature[9] has been bombarding us with the connection between capitalistic development and the nation-state. The problem is what a nation-state is. If we look at European history, we see that nation-states with capitalist success stories like France and Great Britain, or even Germany, in fact are no nation-states: they host different, and turbulent, nationalities that claim to be oppressed, and their borders, which means the extent of their "national" character, have been significantly changing with time. The same can be told for other developed European countries, like Italy and Spain, while the USA, Canada, and Australia present, in a different form, the same problem: assimilation is the name of the game, there.

The last twenty years have given us a return to virulent manifestations of nationalism.[10] "New" states are formed at the drop of a hat. They are much smaller than the preceding entities and yet contain one or more minuscule enclaves with alternative, and equally argued, claims to be states. Yet, contrarywise to the overwhelming tendency, some of the oppressed minorities who have been trying to have their own state to at least stop oppression, like the Palestinians, see their struggle denied, refused, and even opposed by a general framework that should instead be sympathetic to it.

This game of calling things by a name with a meaning in the dominant intellectuality, making them appear as if they had a claim to actual existence, is the working way of the dominant intellectuality of capitalism. The legitimacy supplied by the agreement of all the social scientists and the general public in the name of capitalistic evolution is automatically and immediately transferred to whatever is being talked about. But here the process can grind to a halt, like for the case of the Palestinians. In fact, some claims might look, when seen from the dialectical, dominant point of view, unfeasible.[11] They lack some requirements.

The importance of the nucleus image within the dominant mentality, and the power of law and rights, explain this. It is the presence of these two features that makes for the legitimacy of a nation-state. If a nucleuslike structure is present (take France, which could boast a nucleuslike character much earlier than many European nation-states, despite the various internal divisions that have succeeded each other through the ages) we can talk about a nation-state: but only as long as such nucleus-centered structure has, or can easily have, the appropriate laws and rights framework in relation to primitive capitalist accumulation.

Without these minimal requirements, the metaphysics is simply unable to identify/recognize the aspiring nation-state. But nobody can exit the game. A collocation must be, despite the unidentifiability, found: among precapitalist formations/cultures, or underdeveloped (i.e., yet to develop the inevitable capitalist way) situations.

Let us take the most difficult cases: the nation-states of populations that have been marked by a significant diaspora. The cases of the Jews and the Palestinians illustrate the point above made.[12]

Israel is a perfect case of capitalist legitimacy: the diaspora started to settle in the chosen area, buying land from the owners and seeking international legal and political recognition (the rights) that arrived and was extended to cover up for the following illegalities and injustices. The nucleus analogy here could be applied because of the presence of the law, rights, and state variables, which made up for the actual dispersion on all continents of the diaspora, that outnumbered the settlers at the beginning.

On the contrary, the Palestinians' legal rights were shaky from a capitalist point of view: they were settlers from precapitalist times, without a prior nation-state claim in the capitalist sense, and their diaspora is politically weak and even financially tied to accusations of terrorism. The whole Middle East area was being reorganized (see Hourani 1998) by the French and the British since the beginning of the twentieth century on lines that had little or no sensitivity for a Palestinian "state" in the capitalist sense.

It was the Israeli attack on their land that led to the creation of a claim to a state. When the closest thing to the formal fulfillment of such a claim came, with the Oslo agreements, the nucleus requirement was unredeemably shattered, and the laws and rights part undermined. There was, and there is, no nation-state way out for the Palestinians.

Like for the market, which can claim the presence of its Idea, or the process of valorization in the glory of its metaphysical nature, the nation-state has a number of metaphysical processes at work that can be claimed to be furthering its quasi-Hegelian progression. Let us see them.

In the first place, the nation-state, in order to join the ranks of the recognized institutions of the dominant mentality, must be a market-oriented entity. In the heydays of socialist projects a would-be nation-state could have declared itself a "socialist state," obtaining the same result while sporting an aura of defiant bravery.

The market orientation can take, without changing the final result, ridiculous forms. Take the neoliberal essence and jargon of the European constitutional project (now disguised as the Lisbon Treaty, fortunately rejected in the Irish referendum), that not only shows the ignorance of those who drafted it but also does so years after neoliberalism has shown its fallimentary record. Its defeat in the French and Dutch referendums is due to the motivated fear people have that things could be worse than they are now.

Second, a legal system and its international, and also diplomatic, counterpart must be in place. The value of this aspect is mainly at the level of appearance and communication: it is a passport for international deals to take place. Trade or colonization by capital needs it, and so does war: to declare war you must have an enemy to declare it to, even if such enemy, like Afghanistan and Iraq, means little in military as well as in political terms.

Unfortunately this does not mean that a nonstate is a way to avoid war. Organized evil has always been able to work a way around this: note the carpet bombings that by now routinely precede military invasion (witness Yugoslavia, Afghanistan, and the two Iraq massacres). Once the equanimous leveling justice of explosives has been administered, there is nothing left in the way of a state even when that "community" used to be one.

The third requirement, which almost goes without saying, is the existence of a certain level of economic activity in terms of exchange—in those very terms that grant, and are granted by, the presence of metaphysics and law and rights.

The fourth condition, the most momentous in terms of practical outcomes and human sufferings, is the habituation of individuals to the organic connections between all the above: the uprooting of humanity from the body and mind of the individuals, the actual enforcing of the metaphysics. When dealing with this aspect it is impossible not to start from everybody's Aristotle, for all the subsequent tractations of these problems have not substantially departed from what he is deemed to have said in the *Politics*.

This fact in itself should give an idea of the problems with this fourth condition. It is not Aristotle we are dealing with, but the common wisdom about him. It is no major sin then to resort to an English translation without crosschecking with the Greek original: we need to know what everybody's Aristotle had to say. In (1981) we read,

> It is clear therefore that the state is not an association of people dwelling in the same place, established to prevent its members from committing injustice against each other, and to promote transactions. . . . The state is an association intended to enable its members, in their household and the kinship, to live *well*;

its purpose is a perfect self-sufficient life. (1981, 197–98, emphasis in the original)

I could have quoted this when introducing the idea of nucleus, had I not needed to introduce all of the other critical discussions. In any case, I would like to point out how even a person with a scanty notion of Greek history could see the inapplicability to our own times.

Let us stick to Aristotle, however:

> It is useless to have the most beneficial laws, fully agreed upon by all who are members of the constitution, if they are not going to be trained and have their habits formed in the spirit of that constitution—in a democratic spirit, that is, if the laws are democratic, but oligarchically if they are oligarchic; for as one individual may be morally incapable [reference to akrasia], so may a whole state.[13] . . . It ought not to be regarded as slavery to live according to the constitution, but rather as self-preservation. (1981, 331–32)

Now look at this, and behold:

> next we must ask whether education should first proceed by means of reason or by the formation of habits. Certainly these must chime in perfect unison. (1981, 438)

Not only do we find ourselves within the cozy, nucleus-based atmosphere of presumed Greek—and modern—politeia. Not only do we find nothing in modern authors concerning these subjects that everybody's Aristotle had not said, coming to the same, or similar, conclusions (witness the preceding discussion of Adam Smith, J. S. Mill, Hayek, McCann's sample of liberal thinkers, or all the contemporary authors each of us can quote). Without what Arthur would call the "inculcation of appropriate values" (by reasoning and habit), the whole thing would not stand up.

What we have here is "a combination or adaptation of parts, elements or related things, so as to form a consistent and orderly whole; agreement, congruity. . . . Agreement of feeling or sentiments; peacebleness, concord"[14]: a harmony.[15] Whatever we do, wherever we go, however we look at things, we find ourselves staring at Hegelian, dialectical images that show capitalism for what it is: a nightmare from which there is no exit if one plays with the rules of the dominant maieutics.

Aristotle justly notices that the kind of institutions we have makes little difference: as long as the game is played at the level of the metaphysics, all we have to do is be virtuous. And virtuosity is not what is morally just, or beautiful, and obviously not what our instincts would dictate. Virtuous is what the system allows.

Virtuous are the capitalists who exploit the working class. Virtuous are the leaders who export democracy by military force. Virtuous is he who acts in accordance with the metaphysics; virtuous are thus all those elements that hold the politeia in its metaphysical nuclear appearance together. Nationalism, militarism, authoritarianism, state socialism, and free market where free markets and socialism do not exist are virtuous.

Two political ideas make of harmony the inculcation of habits, the reference to the nuclear image, the complete reliance on the discursive dialectical dominant maieutics, the cozy communitarianism of metaphysics, their *raison d'etre*: fascism and nationalism. This connects us to the two main modalities of international intercourses: war and trade, from which the corollary of imperialism ensues. These things must be explored in order to fill the bones of the metaphysics, to give, that is, a description of capitalism's politeia.

INTERNATIONAL DEALS: TRADE AND WAR

Harmony is not sufficient to render what we mean here. While it surely is a constituent part of the intellectuality, and even more so of its institutional outcomes, and while the very rendition of antiharmonic things such as the free market and socialism is converted into harmonies, it cannot be used in general. Harmonies are connected to the nucleus idea in that they are themselves the results of something more general, the limited and limiting logic of capitalism. They cannot summarize its inner logic. The more general concept we are after is the already introduced one of moderation. This is the glue that binds all the evils we have dealt with, and all of the others we are about to consider.

The structure of thought that characterizes capitalism as we explained it so far is an inevitably moderate one. It is structured so as to produce only moderate outcomes. It is worth dwelling a bit on the ancestry of the moderate attitude. Once again in fact, capitalist categories in theory and practice are expressed by means of concepts that are claimed to come from the depths of antiquity.

Classical political philosophy, with its acritical mixing up (and misunderstanding) of the ancient, the old, and the new is to be blamed for this. For many centuries the *est modus in rebus* maxim has been cultivated, and it is fair to hypothesize that this has misled the understanding of what was meant by moderation in ancient societies. But the *gravitas* of the Roman *pater familias* was not lack of passions, but their external domination. A man was able to burn his own hand, like Scevola, and to hold his emotions without renouncing them: these not only exist but also determine behaviors in practice, only without unmanly manifestations. The same can be said for the Roman understanding of Stoic philosophy.

Cicero praises Archyta of Taranto who, having found his farm overseer at fault, said *"A te infelicem"* . . . *"quem necassem iam verberibus, nisi iratus essem"* (1992, XXXVIII, 56).

Moderation in human individuals had no place in antiquity (Aristotle's moderation, as shown, is a result of conditioning), at least in the capitalist sense of abandoning instinct, nature and the rest—the material itself—and substituting it with discourses about it expressed by means of the dominant, limited/limiting maieutics. The most telling outcome of such moderation is respect for the law and the rights. These are not, like in Cicero's own times, the expression of a venerable past in which morality was practiced fully and emotions used as they must. To the capitalist, the Webers as well as the Hayeks, laws and rights are an expedient to hold the nucleus together. If they can be referred back to the past, and they can in the surreptitious way we repeatedly saw, it is even better—but it is not indispensable.

The intrinsic moderation of capitalism that makes everything look continuous and slowly evolving, that transforms revolutions into evolution and secondary scientific breakthroughs into "revolutions," that tames the economic ruptures that could have given birth to a free-market society producing capitalism as we know it instead, contribute to that exercise in self-explanation and self-justification that capitalism as we know it, and its social sciences, continuously perform.

Such argument is very hard to discuss with those within the dominant mentality, even when they are aware of the limits it enforces. The encroachment of the logic of the system with the reasonings that are produced by it makes any attempt to come to terms with the material as such, and to reasoning about it, a painful and frustrating exercise in reciprocal deafness. Add to this that emotions are aroused, and you have a true communication problem.

Such a communication problem does not take place when two individuals within the metaphysics communicate. This is the root of the birth, and eventual dominance, of what I have called fascist management of capitalist intercourses. Fascism keeps haunting capitalism as we know it, whether it is by the presence of all or some of its traits in a disjointed form or in a structured and developed form. There is not even the need to be conscious of reproducing it. Fascism in capitalism as we know it means moderation: fascism's barbaric nature and outcomes have, paradoxical as it may seem, a moderate origin.

After these general and necessary premises we can delve into the theme of international deals already introduced in chapter 3. The history and economics of capitalism as we know it has provided us with two main international ways to connect (or disconnect, in many cases) nations: war and commerce.

The fact that these two are the main possibilities and that the rest (diplomacy, international rights, issues of disagreement, etc.) are just choreography was no news since Hobbes and Grotius. With capitalism the issue is narrowed down to its bare essentials.

Adam Smith himself had it clear:

> The wealth of a neighbouring nation, however, though dangerous in war and politics, is certainly advantageous in trade. In a state of hostility it may enable our enemies to maintain fleets and armies superior to our own; but in a state of peace and commerce it must likewise enable them to exchange with us to a greater value, and to afford a better market, either for the immediate produce of our own industry, or for whatever is purchased with that produce. As a rich man . . . so is likewise a rich nation. . . . A nation that would enrich itself by foreign trade is certainly most likely to do so when its neighbours are all rich, industrious, and commercial nations. (1999, Book IV, 73)
>
> The first duty of the sovereign, that of protecting the society from the violence and invasion of other independent societies, can be performed only by means of military force. But the expense both of preparing this military force in time of peace, and of employing it in time of war, is very different in the different states of society, in the different periods of improvement. (1999, Book V, 279)

Society must be protected, Adam Smith says, from other "independent societies," that might perpetrate "violence and invasion." There are several themes for meditation here. Firstly, Smith talks about, with his characteristic effectiveness, independent societies. He beautifully summarizes the conceptually cumbersome (limited and limiting, deriving from the above mentioned encroachment of the general logic and the practical issues) nation-state. All the various uncertainties of the meaning of this term are inglobated by Smith in this concise, economistic term.

Second, Smith's independent societies inflict "violence and invasion." Here we must take the two words to mean exactly what they mean, for we have just praised Smith's precision. Violence and invasion are to our days the two main warlike activities of nations and communities. Violence, obviously, can take verbal and compulsion forms, too. Like in Aesop's fable of the wolf and the lamb, the wolves exert verbal violence until they want to then attack in practice. Neither of them makes sense, other than by the law of the strongest.

Verbal and diplomatic violence is, and only can be, the application of the moderate mind and language of capitalist intellectuality. The atrocities and unspeakable bellic cruelties ensuing (like the second Iraqi massacre) are the inevitable result.

What is obscured by this set of structural characteristics is the evident failure of capitalism in delivering its own promised evolution. This is not a failure to fulfill a promise: it is a case of unexplicited promise. Smith himself is completely unable to think of anything but the nation-state as the nucleus of what he was observing while it unfolded its potentialities. The central question: what is the market? How far should it reach, and with what results for the existing institutions, that come straight from precapitalist times, as we saw, in theory and practice, have simply not been rightly posed.

There is in fact an unexplicable hiatus in the economic theories that explain and/or criticize the market. On the one hand, one is allowed to glimpse at a social mechanism that has enormous revolutionary potentials. Commodities could just sweep away all of the existing routines and institutions ("all Chinese walls," in Marx's evocative rendition). There obviously are powerful question marks as to its efficiency compared to communism, but why should one be put off by this and not by the daunting task of believing that the world could turn into a set of free markets?

Despite most social scientists ignoring this, there is no denying the evident fact that the market can, and must, do without state institutions as we know them. But the situation deriving from the absence of the state and the effective presence of the market is nebulous, especially because nobody has even thought about it.[16]

Perhaps we would see a world divided into areas of specialization in the primary sector, which is directly linked to geography and climate, and a homogeneous distribution of the other activities. Something to shake equilibriums could always happen—say, technological breakthroughs, cataclysms, or sheer aesthetical needs. But the thing will not be able to stand time, for the type of intellectuality that has produced the market in the first place will show its limited nature and produce its own nemesis: the new.

Here we are, facing the same old thing. Here were those, like Adam Smith, who saw the tremendous potential of capitalism unfold. Here was Karl Marx, who being braver than the others, saw the process and saw the potential succession of the modes of production. That potential stopped unfolding. The intellectual liberation that was in what was materially taking place, and that Feuerbach, perhaps helped by his interest in theology, saw, was thwarted by a comeback of the old, perfectly tolerated by the general metaphysics we have been discussing.

We cannot, and should not, hold Adam Smith responsible for the comeback of the nation-state with the pseudoarchaic arrangement of democracy.[17] He saw so many other things that we can forgive his missing this: but we should look critically at J .S. Mill and everything thereby coming. We witness with Mill a side of the culture of capitalism: its refusal to indulge in positive utopias and its shameless capacity to think out as many lesser (and evil) nonutopian substitutes as possible.

Adam Smith's treatment (see especially 1999, Book IV, ch. 3) has been the foundation of the comparative advantages approach to international trade, started by David Ricardo and known in our days as the Heckscher-Ohlin-Samuelson approach. With an unargued and consequently undemonstrated logical leap, the "market" is reproduced at the international level. It is not, however, reproduced in a clear-cut way.

We have a generalized market condition in which nation-states play a role. A market, that is, where the participants are individuals as dictated by the theoretical rules, but respond, and belong, to groupings based on nationality. A set of complicated theoretical measures is thus devised to demonstrate the advantage a nation would get from specializing as a consequence of trading internationally.

The market of the theory is there, but so are the national institutions of the practice. A contamination has taken place between two realms in the suspended intellectual world of metaphysics. This directly and materially challenges neither of the two main actors. The theory can continue pretending to be abstract, and the practical deals among nations go on as if nothing were the matter.

Yet, a communication has been started. The national leader who takes a decision can give it a recognized name (say, opening or protectionism). While the material goes on, while trade is opened or protected, endless discussions can go on "in the wilderness of speculation," fuelled by the "mystical rationality" of the Heckscher-Ohlin-Samuelson method[18] already introduced in chapter 3, to exemplify the bridges. Those who should be critical of the method in practice use it, as discussed also in chapter 3.

There is also the question of what would be the outcome of the unfettered working of comparative advantages at the global level.[19] But perhaps we should not worry about that, for the unfettered operation of comparative advantages has not yet moved from its safe seat in the "rational mysticism" heaven. Not that this deters in any way the political leaders or the leading economists from pontificating about the good of opening to international trade and the giant strides that have been taken in this direction. All this, but we should by now expect it, is accompanied by pleas to at last start all of it in practice.

The eminent Professor Fischer, in his *Ely Lecture* (2003, 27) can candidly say that the promarket, proglobalization approach is the worst economic policy, except for all the others that have been tried. Promarket and proglobalization policies have never been tried! This is, as usual, both true and false. Most third-world countries have in fact been brought to their knees by promarket and proglobalization policies, and even compelled to virtually disappear for a while, like Argentina.

International trade is the moderate, dialectical adaptation to what is found in the world. Those who deal with trade questions, be them theoreticians, politicians, actual traders, or the amateur, make do with what they have. The only condition to do so is the use of the dominant mode of thought. Like Professor Fischer, they make their variables take that life in between the abstract and the concrete we have called a metaphysics.

In such an environment things interact, and they do so because they are reduced to what can interact. Sometimes it is sheer simulacra, like the "pro-market, pro-globalization policies" of Stanley Fischer. They exist, and yet they do not. In fact they are both inadequate, tremendously far from the target set of "pro-market, pro-globalization policies" that have brought Latin America and Africa and part of Asia to their knees, and from the ideal, and simultaneously idealized, set of true "pro-market, pro-globalization policies" that Professor Fischer means without meaning them.

Nowhere in the writings of these people do we find a clear statement to the effect that "these are the true, complete and perfect policies." Nor can we, or the game would not be moderate and dialectical.

As theoretically demonstrated earlier, capitalism cannot produce true abstractions. It cannot conceive of utopias, despite protestations that it is this very type of thought that hampers its smooth functioning. Any time a utopian concept is to be mentioned, it has to be brought down from its (abstract) pedestal and reduced to the same nature as the "oral hygiene program" that your toothpaste has become in marketing (see "Marketing of Products," chapter 4).

Economic theory is beheaded and betrayed in the process, as explained in chapters 2 and 3. People, actual people, are reduced like the rest, like toothpaste and economic theory. They die, and suffer, and their deaths and sufferings can only be registered in numerical terms, accompanied (I hope this is just a temporary fashion) by gruesome photographs and films.

International trade is defined and designed with the market pencil. This is no scandal after all, for if economics can be called "good housekeeping," like many economists are fond to say, then the abuse of the word market can be perpetrated. Economists and politicians are assimilated to your corner grocer, who complains about "the market" when his potatoes do not fetch a good price.

Trade then consists in taking what is metaphysically there and fixing it, following the rules of the game. For economic variables, dialectical by definition, this can and must be done. But not all things are like that. In that case, things can be a priori decreed to be moderately, dialectically reconcilable. There are many instances of this second approach, but none is more telling than our second way to practice international intercourses: war.

War is a way to solve—to reconcile—conflicts by means of organized violence. War is the only way conflicts can be solved at the international level (embargoes and blockades being highly ineffectual and falling more properly within the realm of international trade). But why should we solve conflicts in the first place?[20]

Here there are three possibilities: conflicts can be dialectically reconciled; they are true oppositions, so, they cannot be reconciled (one must dislodge the other, creating a rupture and sometimes an oblivion, or they must keep away from each other); or simply there is no conflict but "otherness."

The last case is the most interesting in international relations, for it is very common. The Romans were different from the general category of the Barbarians, and these days anarchists and, in spite of Huntington (2000), Perle and acolytes, Muslims, and Americans are different from each other: they are cases of "distinction" (see Traversa 2004). Distinction—otherness—entails no conflict, unless external causes intervene (for instance, the pressure from Asia on the Barbarians at the borders of the Roman Empire) or unless they are misconceived as dialectically reconcilable. Then war is the option.

Modern wars[21] have been conceived as an *extrema ratio* for cases in which no negotiations could do. A second feature of such wars is the fact that the more we get close to our own days the more they involve the civilian population, in a sort of extreme application of the nucleus vision of society. So far as this practice has gone, whole civilian populations are bombed in order to relieve them from undergoing the cruelties of some dictatorship (take Yugoslavia, Afghanistan, the two Iraq massacres).

We can draw only one conclusion: modern times have been operating on the a priori, universal assumption that conflicts can and must be reconciled. Hence, the resort to war whenever the conditions require it.

The situation is similar and opposite to the case of trade: while there the actual was molded to follow the dictates of the dominant intellectuality—that is, a degree of mental elasticity was allowed—here an a priori condition of moderation is imposed. Wars are a possibility in that conflicts exist, and they can, and are, to be solved, at all costs.

Therefore even cases of actual distinction take a conflictive nature, despite the fact that otherness is a normal condition that not only does not need to entail conflict but also could even mean lack of relation, separation, peace, and mutual recognition and respect. So radicated is the capitalist vision that not only wars are waged but also those who oppose them have to grope in the darkness of finding moral, economic, or political reasons for their position.

Even the "war is wrong" position is compelled to rely on arguments that are not only shaky and vary with cultures and fashions but are also easy to reject on grounds of political emergency, *raison d'etat*, and the like. The interaction between the "war" and "no war" factions in capitalism are yet another instance of the iterativeness of capitalist intercourses and ideas.

Like for all of the other arguments concerning capitalism as a mode of production, here we are in the presence of the usual pseudohistorical mystification. Wars bear the same name as ancient clashes, and they are associated with their namesakes for no other reason than this. I suppose, however, that no ancient army commander would find any honor in the way wars are fought in our days.

The important question is that we find ourselves dealing with the usual mixture of the old and the capitalist that makes us wonder whether capitalism is an accomplished mode of production. Put this together with moderation and the nucleus feature, and you find imperialism.

IMPERIALISM

For the purposes of the present section we can separate the process of acquisition of colonies and the phenomenon of imperialism. Imperialism is not so much the actual process of military conquering and/or imposing one's economic might. This is what present-day imperialism has in common with the imperialism of other, ancient modes of production.

It is fair to hypothesize that conquest of areas that are perceived of as empty, or populated by irrelevant human settlements, but that are or might be important in the future for geographic, strategic, and economic purposes, would take place whenever nation-states or empires, or even organized societies of settlers, are present. The very variability of the meaning of strategic, geographic, and economic (for instance, control of oil-producing areas became a blessing only after oil became important) makes conquest an absolute need, even when no direct advantage can be seen for the time being.

We can thus separate capitalist (as we know it) imperialism from its aspects that are just the vestigial remnants of former ages, the inevitable outcome of military and economic inequalities, or simply a casual analogy. What we must look at in terms of atavistic behavior is linked with the nation-state constitutional setup: the idea of war as the resolution of a conflict, connected with the obsolete elements intrinsic to the management apparatus of capitalism as we know it. We must also look at what happens in the upper echelons of the state administration and in those areas of capital that more directly interfere with their action.

The history of reasoning about imperialism is characterized by a remarkable homogeneity among those who participate in it. We start from Hobson (1968), a British moderate and a socialist, we pass through Lenin (1972), we

reach a period when structuralism characteristically muddled the issue, transforming it into the unequal exchange and development of underdevelopment
complications, to then make a slow and painful comeback to proper mainstream theorization by means of the "dependency" detour and its "underconsumptionist" attitude à la Luxembourg. In our present days imperialism is either mixed up with the globalization literature, entrusted to postmodern
"empire" treatments à la Negri/Hardt or reproposed in the Marxist-Leninist
way.

None of these approaches is satisfactory for our purposes, for they use the
items and the overall logic of the mainstream and dialectical Marxist social
sciences. In the literature the characters in the game of imperialism are always
the same. Hobson[22] identifies them easily.

> Thus the triumph of nationalism seems to have crushed the rising hope of inter-
> nationalism. Yet it would appear that there is no essential antagonism between
> them. A true strong internationalism in form or spirit would rather imply the ex-
> istence of powerful self-respecting nationalities which seek union on the basis
> of common national needs and interests. . . . Nationalism is a plain highway to
> internationalism, and if it manifests divergence we may well suspect a perver-
> sion of its nature and its purpose. Such a perversion is imperialism. (1968, 10,
> 11)

Whether the issue has been tackled from an economic or political point of
view, Marxist or bourgeois, the terms of the problems have not changed since
Hobson wrote this. Hobson had clear ideas on a number of other momentous
issues, unlike some of his present-day epigones.

On page 46 he writes, after pointing out (27) that the areas of imperialism
are tropical, where white families are unlikely to settle, and populated by
lower races,

> Although the new imperialism has been bad business for the nation, it has been
> good business for certain classes and certain trades within the nation. The vast
> expenditure on armaments, the costly wars, the grave risks and embarrassments
> of foreign policy, the checks upon political and social reforms within Great
> Britain, though fraught with great injury to the nation, have served well the pres-
> ent business interests of certain industries and professions. (1968)

This was very prophetic.
Also, Hobson notices that,

> a completely socialist State . . . would soon discard imperialism; an intelligent
> laissez faire democracy . . . would do the same. (1968, 47)

In fact,

> Imperialism repudiates Free Trade, and rests upon an economic basis of protection. Just in so far as an Imperialist is logical, does he become an open and avowed Protectionist. (1968, 67)

But let us allow him to conclude his anti-imperialist tirade.

> Imperialism is a depraved choice of national life, imposed by self-seeking interests which appeal to the lusts of quantitative acquisitiveness and of forceful domination surviving in a nation from early centuries of animal struggle for existence. Its adoption as a policy implies a deliberate renunciation of that cultivation of the higher inner qualities which for a nation as for an individual constitute the ascendancy of reason over brute impulse. It is the besetting sin of all successful States and its penalty is unalterable in the order of nature. (1968, 368)

A lot of right things, in the wrong order, are included and bent to the capitalist metaphysics.

We need not waste time on the absurd comparison of state and individual morality so dear to capitalist mentality, nor on the sad difference between reason and impulse already discussed. What matters here is that we are facing international relations as a set of opposing alternatives: nations versus nation, nationalism versus internationalism, economic opening versus self-sufficiency, expansion versus its economic shortcomings, diplomatic choice between the risk of embarrassment and standstill, the profit rate trend versus innovation, even the laissez-faire and socialism versus nationalism question and the role of cartels and big capital in general.

Lenin put a heavy accent upon the role of big capital combines, the banks and financial capital. Unfortunately, his work was undermined by his unreasonable belief that capitalism was past its maturity phase.[23] Vasapollo and collaborators (2004) adapt this concentration on big capital to the present-day situation: big capital means more and more financial capital free to move at the international level, linked to the practices of privatization and deregulation. These greatly need the direct intervention of international organizations (the United Nations (UN), the World Bank Group (WBG), the International Monetary Fund (IMF) and of Western armies and political and economic influence to fix and arrest what disasters have been wreaked on single countries.

The consequences of all this lie in the continuous squeezing of the lower classes in welfare and wage terms to pay for the skyrocketing overprofits that are being made and to insure the needed political stability in the Western countries, and that lesser thing that is given to lesser countries: governance.

Vasapollo, Casadio, Petras and Veltmeyer (2004) are concerned with welfare and the poor and with preserving Marxist praxis along the lines of what
it used to be in the twentieth century. Plus, they gather together what I have
split: to them, the modern era since the discovery of America and the Treaty
of Westphalia has been the history of the imperialist age. Military and territorial conquest, with the human sufferings and genocides entailed, are assimilated to imperialism *tout court*. Instead, the only thing that the two have in
common is the unperturbed cruelty, which makes them akin, in their approach, to Hitler's conquest of "vital space" for Germany.

Vasapollo and his associates (2004) also bring back an almost forgotten discipline—geopolitics. This last move is very intriguing. On the one hand, if you
use it to the limited purpose of explaining recent American imperialism, it
makes a lot of sense. The Americans in fact do seem to have in mind an overall plan to reshape the political world to the needs of American geopolitical requirements (the infamous document on the "American century" that is waved
under our noses by all opposers of recent American international misdeeds).

On the other hand, geopolitics, even in the new and more elastic sense proposed by Vasapollo and collaborators, supplies a set of functionalisms that
cannot account for a most important item in present-day international relations: the role of ideology. I mean by this the often unexplicited neoliberal
ideology that any internationally respectable politician must embrace in
deeds. The project of the European Constitutional Treaty, for instance, presented marked neoliberal features. Straightforward pieces of imbecility were
proposed in it, the most resounding one being "the right of citizens to have
access to the labor market."

Neoliberal ideology fits so well with whatever has nothing to do with, or
even against, free market and democracy, that it prominently figures in the
Iraq and Afghanistan massacres. Geopolitics, as well as economic and political analyses, helps understand the logic of imperialism. But it is very unfortunate that it is the illogic of it that predominates.

Vasapollo, Jaffe, and the others share in the absolute consensus, among
scholars of imperialism and learned observers of the ways of the world, that
the USA is the most powerful, and above all the most determinate and
unswerving, imperialist actor of the post-WWII period. Liberals such as Sylos Labini (2004, 131) (already discussed) agree with them on the fact that
important firms, being oligopolies, operate in an industrial and trade environment in which prices depend on the variation of costs and not of demand
(121). In the opposition of true socialists and true liberals to imperialism,
Hobson is proved right.

Alex Callinicos is a good companion to the above writers. Despite the inevitable brevity of *An Anti-Capitalist Manifesto* (2003), he manages to refer the source of poverty, social injustice, economic instability, environmental destruction, and war to

> the capitalist system: the solution to these problems must, accordingly, be a radical one. (2003, 66)

He seems to take a different position from the other writers on the issue of financial markets:

> Although the financial markets provide the most visible evidence of the irrationality and inhumanity of liberal capitalism, they are more a symptom than the fundamental source of the problem [of world crisis and inequality]. (2003, 65)

He thinks like Vasapollo and collaborators (2004) on the role of geopolitical variables in capitalism:

> The US is at once general guardian of the capitalist system and a fierce participant in global economic and geopolitical competition. (2003, 64)

The USA also fear the "have-nots," "whose members are swelled by neoliberal policies" (2003, 64).

> These anxieties reflect the logic of capital, a system that, as I have tried to show, is based on exploitation and driven by a blind process of competitive accumulation. . . . Capitalism is thus also imperialism: it comes armed to the teeth against external rivals and domestic rivals. (2003, 64–65)

Liberals and Marxists agree. We have our villain: the US and its simultaneous role of guardian of, and participant in, the blind game of capitalist valorization.

But we know that we do not have "capitalism" but capitalism as we know it, the accomplished metaphysics without the market. If only we could see this, the "radical solution" advocated by Callinicos as well as Vasapollo and his group would gain truly radical features.

Instead, so far Marxism has been able to propose only[24] nucleuslike answers. Marxists have variously supported national self-sufficiency, import-substitution industrialization, the nonaligned movement, and the like in the 1950s, 1960s and 1970s, and for part of the 1980s. Those were the days of nationalism disguised as socialism, with the various major and minor Guevaras who acritically reproduced the Stalinist—that is, czarist (see Lewin 2005)— path to nationhood worldwide. The Heckscher-Ohlin-Samuelson method fits like a glove such an approach.

Structuralism, dependency theory, unequal development are still with us, whether it is in the flesh and bones of neoliberal Brazilian presidents (Cardoso as well as Lula), in the work of the system theoretician Wallerstein, or in the anti-imperialistic tirades of Samir Amin (2005, for a telling instance).

Disguised nationalism is in the ranks of the no-global, whether they take it in the self-regretful way of the Anglo-Saxons with their tearful "we did it to you," or in the multicolored no-global and go-native celebration of peasants by environmentalists, who have no idea what it means in terms of hardship to be a small peasant, and the burden of necessary ignorance it entails.

Few remember that it was Schumpeter who got closer than anybody to the question when (in 1951) he argued that imperialism was a legacy of the past, a medieval remnant. His mistake was to indulge in the sociological mistake of attributing its presence to quasi-Gramscian "fractions of classes," thus confining it to the role of a shadow from the past. In this, Schumpeter was making the same mistake as Lenin: he thought (1987) that capitalism was not only mature but also well on its way to slide into socialism.

We have learned in this discussion of old and new literature on imperialism that some feel that there is a contamination in act between the archaic and the modern. Most of the authors attribute the evils of imperialism, however, to the blind needs of oligopoly and the importance of keeping a hold on the Earth's resources. Thus, each generation of writers has sought to blame one of the two aspects more than the other. Nobody has been able to transcend the dominant logic and to look at the material in its bare baseness. Let us see an indicative tractation in what follows, aimed at just setting the problem of the fascist management of capitalism as we know it.[25]

What we have is a stunted mode of production, in which the material changes that had started to unfold have brought themselves to a halt by breeding a discourse-based general intellectuality that has transformed everything into a metaphysics. I am not saying that capitalism could have developed any other way: all that has been said so far seems to point to what has happened as the inevitable outcome of an economic process based on the absurdity of the question of valorization.

In any case, the result we have is that the management of international relations is left to a nucleus-based, harmonious relationship of dialectically reconcilable conflicts: trade and war are the only means to solve such conflicts, for moderation is the rule. The market delusion cannot and does not kick anybody out of the game, and each must be reinserted. Instead of the needed *homo homini lupus* we have an organic functioning, with social roles given to any category that is perceived to be part of the organic, nuclear whole.

The state administration must choose between these two main options. They must justify their choice with a reasoning that is completely determined by the iterativeness of the metaphysics. To give it strength and originality they can only resort to ideology and moral crusades, and the flexing of muscles. This takes us straight to the USA illustrative case.

While I am writing violence continues in what used to be called Iraq. The resistance keeps attacking with guerrilla as well as suicide bombing; the Americans with their lackeys and their puppet government's troops and police periodically devastate some areas to clean them of "terrorists." A huge American contingent is occupying the area, as well as Afghanistan, and the US federal budget is running a huge deficit due to the military expenditures. The dollar is kept low in an attempt to help the situation, and all sorts of other financial and economic pressures are exerted on friendly countries (mainly Japan and Europe) to finance the US deficit.

Meanwhile, oil prices are soaring to unheard-of heights (prices have been high in preceding crises, when one considers the changes in the value of money; what matters here is that China and the other big consumers are challenging the productive capacity of the system, and not vice versa like during the oil crises. Also an important role is played by the artificially low dollar). Nobody is gaining, if we exclude the highly provisional gains of those firms that deal in privatized services to the US administration, whose dishonest profits coming from the advantages of insider trading are about to be challenged by the judiciary.[26]

Choirs of unanimous voices have qualified the Iraq massacre wreaked by Bush Jr., Blair, and their acolytes as imperialist. Nobody believed for a second that the local dictator owned weapons of mass destruction or had links with terrorist organizations. Millions have instead bought the story that the Americans have done all this for oil. Some plausible yet ineffective reasons are given for this, of the economic sort that the dominant capitalist culture can process.

So powerful is the consonance of such reasonings with the dominant mentality of capitalism that few dared check it with the facts or dared think that not even a Bush Jr. could believe he could militarily occupy Iraq holding, and operating, the oil fields and pipelines. That was simply unthinkable, so unthinkable that not even the Americans must have thought about it. Only the opposers desperately hung onto that conviction, and lost their battle.

This sad comedy could have been predicted down to its smallest details. In our days, it is the left that plays the conservative watchdog for all those items that capitalism has thrown up in its history (nation-state, economic interest, big capital collusion with governments, military conquest for economic purposes, rights of self-determination, and so on and so forth) and that the Bush clique with their Blair/Berlusconi appendices are merrily ignoring. It is these last who rule the dance and come up with "new" ideas and behaviors along the iterative logic of capitalism. The sooner we see this, the better.

Petras (2005) gets closer to the point than many of his left-wing colleagues when he indicates on the one hand the pointlessness of the oil straw man and on the other the high relevance of the neo-con and theo-con presence. He argues that the neo-cons have made the typical Israeli paranoid style of politics their own, adding to it the religious (both Jewish and Protestant) messianic attitudes of the Bush administration. If we add to this the well-assimilated lesson taught to them over the past 40 years by Huntington, Almond, Coleman, Fukuyama, and friends, we see the picture of a group of people who have a Middle East of their dreams in mind and ruthlessly work to militarily impose it. The budget problems entailed by the purely military strategy seem not to concern them much.

Petras points to important aspects, despite doing so for the wrong, Marxist reasons. The Iraq massacre is the most evident and pure epitomization of the delusions caused by the dominant culture of capitalism. The intrinsic moderation of this last compels the rulers to resort to war and trade to compose conflicts, and to recompose countries that are felt not to be the way they should be. What drives the security of these people, their insouciance in paying no mind to budgetary constraints and to economic variables in general, is the absolute and justified faith that the nucleus structure of what they call capitalism, and the incapacity of what they call the market system to throw anybody out of the game, will play to their advantage.

Once the smoke and debris of war have settled, the economy will have to go back to "normality." In normality, those within the game need not fear. It is those out of it—that is, those who erroneously feel to be out of it (we saw nobody is) that are bound to panic and make mistakes. Hence the constant tendency of the left toward the safe heaven of purely capitalist concepts.

But let us call things with their name: the management of a market system where nobody loses other than relatively,[27] where militarism is rife and necessary, where everybody seems engaged in furthering the issues of their own corporation, in which nation-states clash, or are wished to exist, where the economy is closely coordinated with government's and big capital's wishes, where the death of enormous masses of people is not considered a political or economic problem worth paying any mind to is a fascist enterprise.

FASCISM AGAIN

Petras (2005) accuses the Zionist and Protestant neoliberal extremism of Bush Jr.'s working group. The phenomenon of terrorism is a case of extremism. So fascism is claimed to have been. In a world that cannot conceive of anything but moderation and harmony, why don't they go? Why are they not confined to the fringes of society? How can it be that the US administration is run by a bunch of extremists and has been behaving just like those extremists it purports to oppose?

Capitalism hosts "extreme" individual behaviors: sudden episodes of violence that are thoroughly disproportionate to their cause. There is no problem with this, as long as we understand it as the nonmediated, nonintellectually constrained outcome of a loss of control. Such episodes happen despite the all-encompassing rationalization we have proved so far: they are the outcome of the emotional strain ensuing from social life. But they are confined to episodes by definition and left to individually isolated action. They are of marginal interest to our examination of the political economy of capitalism that must be concentrated upon general lines, in general and institutional terms.[28]

On the other hand we have the moderate intellectuality of capitalism as we know it, with its enforcement of itself over all aspects of life in the metaphysics. The cruel and disproportionate behaviors of this respectable side of capitalism go well beyond, in terms of disproportion, whatever an individual can do in a moment of unguarded rage. Millions of Americans heartily hate the Iraqis because of the totally unrelated massacre of September 11. Millions of Italians hate the Romanians and the Gypsies and would go to any length to hurt them.

This takes place despite the absurdity of it all, and even, in the case of Gypsies, despite fascination for their way of life and the magic ensuing. Millions of Germans who had no grudge against the Jews tolerated and even helped Nazi actions against them. Examples could fill volumes. We have recently witnessed the destruction of Yugoslavia, backed by the Europeans, to punish the Yugoslavs for the supposed misdeeds of their dictator—that is, for what was by definition beyond their control.

This originates in the fact that the homogeneity that the shared intellectuality enforced on people makes individual deaths and pains irrelevant. They count only after, when appalling figures can be waved triumphantly by the perpetrators and enragedly by the opposers.

Hatred becomes a shared doctrine of normality that is used to justify, on the basis of a common feeling, collective action, "violence and invasion." What matters is that the nucleus does it: identical actions perpetrated by individuals are criminal.

The moderate rationality within the metaphysics is the cause of the cruelty and violence of the system. Let us, for the time being, leave aside the violence it enforces by emotionally limiting individuals (the hysteria and the other various kinds of frenzies), and concentrate on the politeia. This is a body that has placed itself between the material and the abstract, keeping to itself the right to appeal to one or the other, or both, as suits the situation.

Like McCann (2004) correctly notices, we have no liberals in theory. We do not, and cannot, have them in practice either, due to the metaphysical position of the politeia. We are left with a communitarian (not necessarily in the sense proposed by communitarian thinkers, even though this does not make much difference) attitude. This is the actual glue that holds everything together, the hypostatizing source of capitalist discourse. Above all, this is what serves to connect actual policies with their ideal origin, the market, and the rest.

This is the framework for emotions and rationality to share in the same nature and be hard to distinguish. In fact, the politeia cannot rid itself of emotions. Capitalist rationality itself is not disjointed from emotions: on the contrary, it seeks to understand them and transform them into something politically usable. If societies are natural to man, as they are supposed to be by their hypostatizing logic, than all of man's qualities have to be considered by, and within, the politeia. As we have repeatedly pointed out, there is no escape for individuals: all of their capacities can (and must!) be dealt with by the politeia.

All of this takes place not in reality in general—within the realm of the material, but in the politeia. The maieutics whereby this process of (dialectical) reciprocal interaction takes place is the limited and limiting logic of capitalist (as we know it) intellectuality.

Emotions and rationality interact, and even interexchange, because they share in the same metaphysical nature. Emotions can become rational pieces of policy, and policies can slide into emotions without any crisis of the system. On the contrary, this is precisely what ensures the stability of the system, lubricating its capacity to move from the rational to the emotional, and vice versa, in no time and with no warning, and as a matter of routine. Hence the cruelty.

It is evident that the type of argument brought forward so far entails the need to question ideas on ethics and morality. This is inevitable, but premature here. We can therefore keep working on the understanding that what I have been calling cruelty and referring to as repugnant is, for the purposes of the present discussion, nonretaliatory violence meted out on the innocent with no regard for the individual. Let us also use, for the remainder of this chapter, a kind of "communist criterion," whereby we take any form of private property wrong and equal sharing of resources and labor time necessary.

In capitalism as we know it emotions and rationality stand in a sort of dialectical relationship. They are Rosenthal's Chamberlain and Maradona example (1998, 125): short and tall are "the incessant transition of the one into the other." This very mixture makes the iterativeness of capitalism bearable: it brings, with every piece of intercourse, some emotional strain. This can take a negative ("they did wrong") or positive ("we are doing right") feature, which by their alternance makes the whole thing go on dialectically. One of the necessary conditions for this to happen is institutional stability: hence the recourse, in the major Western democracies, to majoritarian methods of representation. These make the negative and positive features more pronounced and inexorable in their action.

There is also a more general historical way to look at it all. Before getting there, we must recall Marx's expression for all that has been described: "mystical rationality." What we have been reviewing, the very meaning, organization, and mechanisms of the politeia of capitalism as we know it, is spiritually allegorical or symbolic. It has that connection to a transcending entity that goes beyond human comprehension, when it strays into the fully moral or the *raison d'etat*, or the good of the community.[29]

The ideology that hinges on this very mystical rationality, and even bases itself in the community/organic society conception of the religious aspect, is fascism. Let us explain this last feature.

> Fascism is only the organized political expression of the structure of the average man's character, a structure that is confined neither to certain races or nations nor to certain parties, but is general and international. . . . *Fascism* is the basic emotional attitude of the suppressed man of our authoritarian machine civilization and its mechanistic-mystical conception of life. It is the mechanistic-mystical character of modern man that produces fascist parties, and not vice versa. (Reich 2000, XIII, emphasis in the original)

While correct on this score,[30] Reich inverts the poles of the reasoning:

> In its pure form fascism is the sum total of all the irrational reactions of the average human character. (XIV)

It is instead precisely its rational origin (in the dominant intellectuality of capitalism) that makes fascism the universal character of the capitalist man.

Reich also beautifully perceives the subtly emotional perversion of the emotion-rationality interchangeability:

> the sexual effect of a uniform, the erotically provocative effect of rhythmically executed goose-stepping, the exhibitionistic nature of militaristic procedures, have been more practically comprehended by a salesgirl or an average secretary than by our most erudite politician. (32)

The structure of fascism is characterized by metaphysical thinking, unorthodox faith, obsession with abstract ethical ideals, and belief in the divine predes-
tination of the fürher. (80)

Substitute fürher with society/community, and you have described capitalism as we know it.

Also sober and positive descriptions of fascism in the jargon of mainstream
economic theory are possible.[31] Einzig (1933) tried to do so. His times were
very similar to ours: a laissez-faire view was in crisis, and a need for a more
direct management of the economies by the governments was increasingly
felt. Unorthodox views of the management of capitalism were springing up,
in theory and in practice. The communist alternative, then just like now, was
a nightmare to the capitalists rather than an actual threat to their power. Let
us see.

Einzig starts by stating that

instead of leaving the Fascist movement to the mercy of demagogues—as is at
present the case in most countries—if its economic ideas were to be taken up seriously by responsible people, mankind would only gain by it. (1933, 9)

There are unmistakable signs that the present trend of evolution is towards an
economic system which, in substance if not in form, is likely to be very near that
of Fascism. (1933, 4)

Others . . . become Fascists merely to give vent to their anti-Semitic prejudices, little realizing that, far from trying to stir up new conflict, Fascism in the
real sense of the term aims at conciliating the existing ones. (1933, 7)

Let us go on, with discourses that might make quite a few feel uncomfortable.

[Fascism] endeavours to eradicate the selfishness ingrained into the minds of
mankind by nineteenth-century individualism . . . with its slogan of "the survival
of the fittest." . . . The philosophy of *laissez faire* is nothing but the apologia and
glorification of the mentality that disregards public interest. (1933, 9, emphasis
in the original)

Fascism in fact is

a new kind of democracy.
In fact, it need. not necessarily be based upon dictatorship. (1933, 25)

After arguing that the capital-labor conflict has been "grossly exaggerated"
by socialist literature, he produces a veritable treasure of capitalist (as we
know it) talking, well worth quoting at full length:

In spite of the existence of the elements of a conflict between labor and capital,
to a very great extent their interests are identical. Fascism is based on the real-

ization of this principle. Instead of trying to accentuate the differences, it has endeavoured to bring forward the points in which the interests of the two groups are identical. The aim of terminating class warfare could not possibly have been attained if the two parties had been allowed to fight out their differences. (1933, 62)

This is truly astonishing in its modernity. It is a piece of lucid, candid, and open-minded capitalist self-awareness. But there is material for the no-global too.

Under a system of laissez faire, the commercial interdependence of nations tends to strengthen the factors towards the inevitable periodic crises. In fact, the increase of interdependence has been largely responsible for rendering the world's economic system more and more vulnerable. . . . After all, the basic principles of fascism, co-operation between conflicting interests for the common good, need not be confined within the borders of any particular country [but] . . . it should be relatively easy to apply the same principles in international relations. (Einzig 1933, 105–6)

But this is not all.

[In Great Britain] [w]ithout any spectacular change in the political regime, an economic system approaching Fascism may then be introduced, if not in form, at any rate in substance [and] . . . much of the Italian system could be transplanted to this country without coming in conflict with the special characteristics of the British nation. (1933, 122)

It is even conceivable that from the economic turmoil in the United States a system will emerge which economically will not be very far from Fascism. The firm hand with which President Roosevelt deals with "big business" seems to point in that direction. (emphasis in the original)

We might dislike his preference for fascism, but the various aspects he points out are beyond doubt the very same we have seen in the dominant culture of capitalism.

The turning point, the no-return point in fact, has been the abandonment of laissez-faire in actual, historical terms, while keeping its rhetoric at the theoretical and practical level. That, we saw, can be traced back to the pioneering times of Adam Smith and John Stuart Mill. The question remains of whether capitalism will ever make those breaks with the past that are needed to make it into a compute mode of production, finally liberating its revolutionary forces, both in the liberal and communist sense.

There is a flip side to this coin: the similarities between fascism and the socialist movements. Einzig points them out as often as he can, in order to mark the difference he needs between fascism and Nazism as they actually were and the "Fascism" he has in mind. Yet, there is no denying the similarities between socialist, and in general progressive, movements and ideas, and fascism. This continues to our days.[32]

Another disturbing empirical proof of the homogeneity and communicability between fascism and socialist and progressive ideas lies in the Argentinian case. In this country the contamination between socialist ideas and Peronismo has reached levels that are as unthinkable as they are unknown in the West. This mixture is still there, and proudly so. Helman (2005) explicitly and strongly states this simple truth, claiming that his Marxist socialism is a "Peronist" ideology. In this, he is simply stating the obvious for most Argentinian left-wingers.

The present discussion does not aim at giving a historical, economic, and political definition of capitalism and fascism, but rather at identifying as fascist the fundamental aspects of capitalism as we know it. Yet it is worth glancing at a far more frightening empirical instance of the reciprocal communication between capitalism as we know it and actual (let me emphasize it: actual) fascism in its most rabid, racist form (the one Einzig was disgusted by). Scarpari (2004) in a paper that not surprisingly has passed unnoticed in Italy, despite its publication in the locally prestigious *Il Ponte*, has studied the short-lived journal *Il Diritto Razzista* (*The Racist Law*).

This was a journal devoted to give juridical bases to racial relations in Italy and the colonies. It was helped by the German Nazis, even because of a lack of interest on Mussolini's part. The first issue saw the light in 1939.

The truly astonishing thing was that despite the fact that the founder, Stefano M. Cutrelli, was no academician, all sorts of old as well as young academicians took part in the initiative, despite there being for them, for opposite reasons, no career rationale. They were those very same legal experts who, just three years later (the last issue came out in 1942) went to form the upper echelons of the Italian democratic republic and helped shape its juridical system from an antifascist perspective. This is too much even by the standards of Italian *trasformismo* and should make us all meditate.

We have finished this philosophical description of the nature and structure of the political economy of capitalism as we know it. We see an unaccomplished mode of production that has "gone astray" and drifts in a metaphysical realm where everything is harmony, moderation, and conciliation of conflicts.

The free market is a far-away dream, the economy is managed (sometimes to increase, other times to roll back, the role of the state), oligopoly is rife, democracy precarious and based upon majoritarian fictions, and emotions and rationality end up coinciding. The whole thing thinks of itself as a politeia, and acts accordingly. The politeia itself is but an invention of the system, conceived with its dialectical hypostatizing means.

The ranks of the reformers of capitalism as we know it comprise all of the possible philosophical and ideological positions, from the strongest to the silliest, from the most angelic to the most evil-minded, from free market dreamers to socialist reformers. The outcome, the actual management of capitalism as we know it, is that concoction that is prepared in the metaphysics, out of the logically flawed mixture of the concrete and the abstract that continuously seems to change, while in practice iteratively repeating itself, with the necessary occasional slips.

Such iterative concoction without ruptures and oblivion, homogeneous through time and willing to reconcile conflicts at the cost of war, I call fascism. Fascism is a moderate way to manage capitalism concerned with the community's welfare, that identifies itself with that community, concerns itself with justice and the problems of the uneven distribution and management of wealth, that can shift from market to plan and vice versa, that cares about technology development, has a (true or presumed) path to development, is in favor of private property, and that needs no individual.

Fascism is, therefore, capitalism as we know it, a mode of production that merrily mixes up archaic and modern institutions, in an embrace tightened, and made unbreakable, by the refusal of real oppositions. The true liberals who are backing the "system" in order to see it improve toward perfection are serving their own delusions. They are serving, in practice, a fascism without a way out.

It is time that liberals and communists regained their capacity to see, and use, ruptures and oblivions. That means, for the communists, to accept the inevitable anarchist outcome of the communist stance. At stake here is the idea of revolution that is still awaiting a definition (and a practice!) that severs it from the dialectical fetters we have seen. It is time we see the failures behind us and learn from them. It is time we emancipate ourselves—our individualities. It is time to tear ourselves away from the dominant culture, its mass homogenization and its inevitable proselytism.

I could have referred to the degeneracy of capitalism in another way, perhaps inventing a new term, like many social scientists are wont to do. But the protean nature of fascism makes it an unbeatable term to our purposes here. Some, myself for the first, acknowledge that many actors on this lugubrious stage are not fascist. That is true, and if on the one hand it raises some hopes, on the other hand it makes the scene even more heartrending. What a huge "human waste," to use Marx's own expression!

CONCLUSIONS

Capitalism is an intellectually based situation, and a faulty one at that: there lies its strength and resilience. Its boredom from the intellectual point of view is counteracted by means of the interchangeability of the rational and the emotional and by the astonishingly powerful effects, in terms of human destruction, of both.

Its structural moderation causes so much physical and psychological damage that it can conceal its intrinsic iterativeness. But the source of its evil, the dialectical harmony that enforces itself at all levels, structural and individual, is moderation.

The core of the political economy of capitalism as we know it consists in the process of valorization and its absurdity. All the rest just descends from the application of such flawed logic. Imperialism, fascism, and the nonexistent choice between plan and laissez-faire, international trade and war, all belong to the same logic. We are faced in practice by the need to deal with the damage that they inflict as a matter of "praxis."

Perhaps this has helped mislead the orthodox Marxist movements in the direction of dialectics. But it is obvious that there can be only nondialectical answers to the solution of such dramas. This means that there cannot be a mass reply to capitalism in the sense so far pursued by proselytism. Each individual must be willing to act on his/her own.

We must abandon capitalist rationality. We must eliminate both its intellectual structure and its maieutical capacity, as well as its reference categories. Keeping one or the other would not help, for it would mar us, keeping the link to the capitalist logic-cum-emotions that cripple our lives. Thus, we must both think along different lines, reconquering to ourselves the abstract and the material, and produce a different taxonomy of the categories of capitalism as we know it.

Thinking about the themes we have been discussing in this chapter, it appears that there are, for the time being, quite a few "practical" things we can do. But to do so we must understand the logical flaws of capitalism and emancipate our individualities from them. We must gain a detachment from the grabbing power of capitalism. This is an operation to do with intellectuality and the emotions that must be practiced on those grounds.

It is important to point out here, however, that this does not mean that in the short run we must simply undergo the political and economic injustices of capitalism. Class struggle in fact, regardless of what many left-wingers seem to believe and have believed, is not a choice in capitalism as we know it, but a necessity. It is a matter of fact of capitalist intercourses. What we must do is take it away from the dialectical grounds where it has been confined by the orthodox Marxists as well as, let me emphasize this, by the owners and managers of capital. Fighting the day-by-day class struggle that is enforced on us by those in power is a different thing from fighting to eliminate capitalism.

We are back to the question of conflict and to the issues of reconciliation and distinctiveness. Both Marxist theory and liberal theory make room for conflicts; liberal theory in particular has plenty of room for nonreconcilable issues of diversity, and even for curbing self-aggrandizement and ambition.

It is, for obvious historical reasons, the liberals who have lost their battle, so far. It is time for revolution both for the Marxists and the liberals.

NOTES

1. To the dialectical Marxists and the economic mainstream the continuity in the supposed diversity is the key point.

2. That the whole process is but a "waste of human life" is stated by Marx on page 88 of the same volume, with emphasis.

3. The paramount importance of nature in Marx is evident from the following quotation about a "higher form of society": "Even a whole society, a nation, or even all simultaneously existing societies taken together, are not the owners of the globe. They are only its possessors, its usufructuaries, and, like *boni patres familias,* they must hand it down to succeeding generations in an improved condition" (Capital Vol. III, ch. XLVI 1978, 776). Those who claim that Marx is no use to ecological protest are not refuted by this telling quotation, however, but by the very separation Marx keeps between the natural and the social. Here lies the only chance we have not just to correct natural devastation, but to actually see, and study, nature.

4. Jurists themselves perceive this. Mounier was well aware of the inadequacy of the juridical apparatus to deal with the complication of the "human person." I thank Professor Limone for pointing that out and explicitly mentioning its subversive consequences, discharging him from any involvement in my argument.

5. That is why Marx uses the term *mode of production* only when talking about general historical cycles, referring to it with more economistic terms when involved in studying capitalism itself.

6. This, obviously, does not mean it is continuous in fact.

7. For a criticism of the limits of Wood's work, see Micocci (2004a).

8. With the privilege of hindsight we have in our post-Fordist times, it looks evident that mass production and consumerism and the emphasis on exchange as a natural human trait are not fundamental. In fact, they are just the consequence of the idea of the economy as an ever-growing process of wealth creation, whatever the meaning of that is. In turn, this is nothing but the apotheosis of the process of valorization. The two things are one and constitute the most egregiously dialectical, Hegelian part of the metaphysics of capitalism.

9. See Micocci (2002a) for a more detailed theoretical argument.

10. It is evident from the whole discourse so far displayed that nationalism and community are two aspects of the same thing. One should not therefore fake surprise at the return of jingoistic, chauvinistic, and nationalistic movements of all sorts. They are part of the dialectical functions of capitalism, which also explains why orthodox Marxists have never been able to free themselves from the very same temptations.

11. The habit of saying "unfeasible" rather than "difficult," or "lacking some requirements," is a typical secondary feature of the dominant mentality. It is indeed a logical consequence of the whole, for if reality must proceed dialectically, then breaks and leaps are conditions of unfeasibility.

12. We are pursuing the theoretical treatment of an intellectual mode: the burden of proof rests with the coherence of the argument, not with the strength of examples.

13. This sentence is not strictly indispensable for the purposes of the quotation, but I have left it, for it brings a ray of hope for those of us with subversive purposes in mind. It also hints at the intrinsic evil of the capitalist metaphysics.

14. *Oxford Universal Dictionary*.

15. The list of quotations in political science concerning harmony is endless. I limit myself to Cicero here, for he influenced rather heavily the debate until the oblivion the twentieth century condemned him to. "*et quae harmonia a musicis dicitur in cantu, ea est in civitate Concordia*" (XLII, 1992, 120).

16. Even those who dare a little bit, from Nozick to Rawls to Fukuyama, stop very short of where they have started, limiting themselves to envisage solutions to the problems we know (in the capitalist sense).

17. Especially considering his harmonic views of society displayed in *The Theory of Moral Sentiments*.

18. Orati (2003) proves that what happens in practice is that the stronger economy exports its crisis when opening its market. We all can see that by reading the newspapers.

19. See Micocci (2004b).

20. The following has got much clearer after a joint seminar on this theme Guido Traversa and I gave at the Seconda Università of Naples, S. Leucio, Caserta. He is to be discharged from any responsibility for what I say here, obviously. See also Traversa (2004).

21. I like to think ancient wars were different in nature. Such demonstration, however, is of no consequence here and can be left out.

22. Luciano Vasapollo pushed me to revise my Hobson. I thank him, discharging him from any involvement in my argument.

23. See Warren (1980) and Micocci (2005a).

24. I am here friendly provoking Vasapollo and Callinicos to come up with those radical answers that their hearts hold.

25. It is not my intention to propose a developed theory of imperialism here.

26. It must also be signaled that a minor industry is thriving: that of measuring the dead and maimed. Figures on the number of men and women, military and civilian, that have been killed or hurt, or displaced, or tortured, by the war effort (all of them highly unreliable) are produced with relish, as if the fact that they are 150,000 made it worse than 50,000, or better than 150,001. Left-wing scholars without scruples are

getting tenure for this, while charities, the true *deus ex machina* behind all this, are gathering funds ("with only x dollars a year you can make a third-world child study!"), and the NGOs rush at the service of the winning powers and of the international organizations, contributing to spread the neoliberal gospel.

27. Obviously, some do lose: their lives, their wages, their jobs, their limbs. But they enter the limbo of statistics, not the heaven of the dead or the hell of those who are alive.

28. Individual episodic resentfulness is in fact a very important psychological character of the individuals under capitalism. But we cannot understand it before we have completed the understanding of the rational part. The rational part in fact is the cause of it.

29. Many are complaining these days of the increasing religious contaminations of present-day capitalism (say, the "Christian roots" debate in the EU constitutional project, or the religious zeal in the Bush administration). This is part of the recurring bouts of religious mania that have been succeeding each other in Western history and that are in fact a necessary part of the secular establishment of the state.

30. See Micocci (2002a) for a discussion of Reich and Cassirer about fascism in connection to the anti-Hegelian argument.

31. See Micocci (2002b).

32. See Micocci (2005a, 2005c, 2007a).

Chapter Six

Capitalism versus Individuality

We have the problem (the forced, stultifying socialization imposed by capitalism within the limited set of actual options its intellectuality comes down to in practice) and the solution (philosophy as an individual project). The latter can destroy the former. We should find ourselves in a revolutionary set of circumstances. Why is there no sign of such revolution instead? Why do even those who call themselves anticapitalist revolutionaries keep within the intellectual logic of capitalism?

The argument unfolded so far has presented us with two main causes for this situation. The first is the fact that the intellectuality of capitalism is a moderate way of thinking. It can deal with conflicts and relationships of difference and distinction only by mediating the two sides (the dialectical attitude we have been criticizing).

The second cause is the complexity and iterativeness ensuing from the unfinished character of capitalism as a mode of production. Capitalism's main features show such an unfinished character, presenting us with a most complicated set of problems when we seek to describe and explain them with reference to capitalism as it could be in the theory.

The complex maze of activity determined by the unfinished character of everything under capitalism makes repression (of all types) and injustice the most salient and visible traits of normal life. Both the opposers and the supporters of capitalism find in the hyperactivity habit the reason, and the way, to fight for justice. The former want to stop the development of an inherently unjust system, laboring under the illusion we have dispelled in the course of the book. The latter, taken by the same illusion, operate so as to further capitalist development that will bring fairness for everybody (i.e., justice). The process keeps winding up, iteration after iteration, making the whole thing even tighter and more impermeable to the material.

For the past two centuries, the term revolution has been used to indicate this dialectical search for an impossible social justice. The damage wreaked by this move is incalculable. This betrayal of the meaning of revolution has blocked the development of Marxist thought, and of any thought that is set upon materialistic bases and is not measured and construed by the yardstick of present-day rationality. This is not to deny that injustice and liberties (I prefer this term to the capitalist-laden democracy) are terrible problems. But their solution is communist anarchist: a rupture with capitalism.

Capitalism, due to its iterative characteristics that mistake continuous self-amendment for development and/or revolution, might look endless. We might be facing the end of history, although not for the reasons put forward by Fukuyama. This is not very likely, however. Whatever contributes to the resilience of capitalism also contributes to the repression of human characters and prerogatives, physical and psychological. No system can survive repressing its individuals because repression must self-feed and must increase and spread all the time.

Capitalism as we know it might undergo fatal turmoils for reasons that are similar to the cycles of the politeia as described and discussed in Polybius and Livy.[1] Instead, one more conceptual mistake typical of capitalism is the widespread conception of cycles in the Vico way. Eras of human development are made up as similes to the "Hegelian" path of improvement that is desperately sought for in history.

Yet another moderate outcome is highly possible as a consequence. This will surely make the Marxist-Leninist and Spinozians of all kinds rejoice. But it is a horrifying possibility: we have already witnessed so many similar events, and we know what they mean in terms both of human losses and of the uselessness of the outcomes.

The apostles of revolution as derring-do are bound to get disappointed by what comes next in this chapter, if they have been at all able to withstand what has been said so far. In fact, the general discourse unfolded points to a rediscussion of the meaning of act/acting.

In capitalism as we know it, hyperactivity, and the profit motive, are benevolently looked upon and even encouraged, as well as their *alter ego* practiced by capitalist opposers, a "political struggle" of the Leninist and Spinoza kind.[2] They are acts of political (individual or multitudinous) will. They are strict relatives of "pure action," that fascist concept that stretches, explicated or not, from Sorel to Gramsci. They are "Reichian frenzies," the transcending of those human impulses that have already been distorted by repression. Most of all, they are acts in the capitalist metaphysical sense that in the human sense can be translated as abstinence or self-humiliation.

The thrifty capitalist who acts toward getting rich practices abstinence from consumption, humiliating himself and his family in the process.[3] The revolutionary who devotes his existence to the cause practices abstinence even more than the thrifty capitalist: he is ready to give up his/her own life, like Kirillov in Dostoyevsky's *The Devils*. The masses that rally to the call of the leaders and sacrifice themselves as cannon fodder without thinking twice are practicing abstinence and humiliation to a high degree. Of the fascist there is no need to talk: with their organic societies, true or dreamed, they epitomize the most egregious example of sexual repression and self-enforced humiliation.

Masochism never comes without sadism, however. The relationship between capitalism as metaphysics and its participants as a relationship of abstinence and hyperactivity is just like sado-maso encounters, from which, despite the gruesome display of instruments of torture, the participants come out unscathed. This last aspect makes for the addictiveness because the harmless results enhance the intellectually produced feelings, first of all the feeling of risk.

Thus, those very masses that have been murdered, beaten, and arrested find themselves unscathed after the event: masses they were, and masses they are. The dead are gone, the wounded are not: they are ready for another go. The thrifty capitalist emerges from his labors unscathed, and if he feels otherwise he can pick up a blond or brunette, pretend to have some fun, even marry one, and be ready to plunge back in the maelstrom of the market.

But the arresting aspect is that the most important thing that comes out of the process unharmed is capitalism as we know it. You can storm the Winter Palace, destroy thousands of human lives in Bhopal, have the 1929 crisis, carpet bomb Yugoslavia or Iraq, pass from fascism to democracy and back to fascism endless times, replace Fordism with post-Fordism and all that is entailed. Once the event has taken place, the metaphysics of capitalism is there, unscathed, to reassure you that you can have—or not have—another go at it. Some mistake that for the working of the "invisible hand." Nothing could be more wrong, of course.

But this is not the whole story, we saw. Acting is valid only when it can be expressed and understood with the limited and limiting means of "capitalist culture." Therefore nonacting can be both the fact of nonacting and an action, as long as either of them can be transformed by the unceasing maieutics of capitalism. The point then is not to devise anticapitalist, or even noncapitalist acts. The point is to devise an alternative intellectual frame to capitalism, a frame that cannot communicate with it, lest it is swallowed back by the dominant intellectuality.

Hence the need to build a naturalistic materialism based on the concrete. Here philosophy can actually "change the world" like Marx proposed, in that the very act of philosophizing, starting from the concrete, is a rupture with the existing state of things at the economic and social level. A materialist philosophy is a change of reality, and we have been awaiting its arrival for too long.

Nobody should expect a list of things to do. The task here is rather the negative one of detaching ourselves from the straitjacket of capitalist intellectuality, with its maieutical embrace, opening a whole new range of possibilities that cannot be prescribed and supplied but must be sought for by each of us. I think that there is infinitely more out there than an individual alone can hope to grasp. Individuality, once recovered, can constitute a new kind of social bond, based on the reciprocal dependence from the capacity of each of us to see a portion of the material. But detachment is the first task for now.

MATERIALISM IS A LONELY ENDEAVOR

Materialism as emancipation is a very lonely type of endeavor not because it is an individual task but because the need for "extraneous standards" and detachment take you out of the comfortable, continuous, and continuously pointless dialogue with the existent. Once you set off for this kind of journey, you have to face the consequent communication problem.

This in itself is not much of a discomfort. You still have your sentimental and sexual connections and your shared tasks that can be referred, à la Marx, to the necessary sociality of work. Plus, you have, open before you, the infinite field of nature, bare of social incrustations and silent in its existence. You do not even know where it starts, and this is an exciting perspective.

Your physical contact with your fellow human beings is still there: what you have lost is the obligation to interact with the metaphysics that pervades it. It is in this sense that materialism is a lonely enterprise. You also lose ties with your old comrades in the dialectical Marxist camp. This is not to say that you drop commitment to the need of defending social justice. Class struggle is a necessity—rather than a duty—enforced and compelled by capitalism (as we know it) itself.

Another form of loneliness is the fact that a materialistic attitude compels you to stop mediating. You cannot any longer follow the tide and pretend. You must call wrong what is actually wrong, capitalist what is capitalist, and boring what bores you. This is perhaps the heaviest consequence to bear of a materialist stand. The hardship does not consist so much in the scorn that "practical" persons pour on you, but in the fact that you cannot slack, and rest for a while, any longer. Being a materialist means to burn the bridges with much, very much, of capitalist culture: its general logic.

A last form of loneliness consists in the continuous discovery that authors that meant so much to you have to be discarded.[4] Precious pieces of intuition have to be abandoned or consigned to the role of historical signals of undisclosed truths. This would, on the other hand, relieve many ancient authors, from Spinoza to Smith to Hobbes to Locke, just to mention a few of the most obvious, from the burden of folk interpretation.

I am not pleading here for a return to the purity of exegetical analyses: I am simply signaling that we must read the ancient without making an asset of the burden of our capitalist culture (the hypostatizing mentality), a banal enough point. I am generalizing Marx's critique (see Chapter 2 and Micocci 2002a) of the classical political economists. From this perspective, emancipation from capitalism is the liberation of excitement and curiosity, the opening of infinite horizons, many of which might well be wrong. But they shall be so in a nonboring way.

Starting from the material we free ourselves from what Epicurus called "investigations about words." Silence will replace the useless syllogisms we are compelled to listen to in all fields, from our corner shop to the halls of famous universities to the slogans of the opposers of capitalism. It might be lonely from the capitalist point of view, but it makes everything fulfilling: intensity is its name. This last capitalism lacks, due to its being the practical application of moderation.

We can now set an example of materialistic practice, with the entailed loneliness, by considering Francis Bacon, for whom words are an obstruction to science, for discussions of rigorous language become discussions of word, while things, the given, get lost (see Rossi's "Preface" to Bacon 2005). The recurring importance of Bacon in capitalist times makes him generally relevant to our purposes.

Francis Bacon was looking for a way to study the material by sticking to its inner characteristics. His interest in what we would today call the method of science and the topics of the natural sciences had consequences in politics, too (all translations from Bacon's Latin are mine):

> And just like vulgar logic, which organizes everything by means of syllogisms, concerns not only natural sciences but all sciences, our science, which works by means of induction, must comprehend everything. (I, CXXVII, 2002, 230)

This quotation shows that Bacon's induction is something that cannot be endorsed here, especially because of the role of experiments in it. But let us see things progressively.

Given above, we can limit ourselves here to the study of the *Novum Organum*, the "great instauration" of science. Bacon starts by beautifully pointing out how most people rest contented with adding their little bit to science without challenging the whole, and even enjoy their pretended modesty. But this reinforces old opinions and traditions, damaging science.

> In this way men of such kind correct a few things but contribute little to science; they improve on it rather than expand it. (Praefatio 2002, 18)

A second, beautiful start is in his attacking dialectical modes of operating and the syllogisms ensuing.

> If in fact dialectics as it is generally accepted can be very correctly applied to politics and the arts that are based on discourse and opinion, it is, however, very far from the subtleness of nature; and by grasping what it cannot hold, it helps consolidate and stabilize errors rather than open the path to truth. (Bacon 2002, 20)

Bacon takes these questions back in I, LXXXII, where he claims to be amazed by the fact that no mortal has made usable for human intellect a road starting from *"sensu et experientia ordinata et bene condita (from sense and an ordered and well-founded experience)"* (152), to escape the fog of the received wisdom.

Yet we should not be deceived by this statement. Bacon is not a man who trusts senses to deal with material reality. A barrier, an interpretive apparatus, must be set between the material and the senses to give organization to what is being done, and because man is intrinsically fallible.

We should not trust our senses not just because philosophical arguments can be produced on the tautologies of a reckless use of the senses in human understanding. Bacon has, unfortunately, a religious argument:

> Senses in fact (similarly to the Sun) reveal the surface of the Earth while closing and sealing that of the Heaven. (*Praefatio* 2002, 26)

Man should not exceed the limits that the Heaven-Earth dichotomy sets to his role. There is no need to expand on the formidable potential of this kind of argument. Any fact, object, and situation is amenable to judgement from this terribly vague and yet all-encompassing perspective. Plus, the material is consigned to a creationist conception that is the most effective way to prevent direct observation of the material, whether from a sensual point of view or by means of a scientific method.[5]

Francis Bacon is after a methodology for scientific observations of a strictly "technical" kind. His mixture of experiments and induction has a limited purpose, therefore. It is not a form of philosophical materialism in the sense we have been pursuing in this volume and cannot be compared to that of the philosophers who belong to the "conflictive" stream of Western thought.

Yet there is no denying that Bacon's *Novum Organum* is laden with powerful intuitions. Some of the concepts that the conflictive thinkers and I myself have been putting forward can be found in his work, starting from the attack on dialectics. We shall keep to this for a while, to then pass to his interesting treatment of the misleading role of institutions and the market. The purpose here is to point out that not only in modern/contemporary times dialectical ways of thinking are perceived as intellectually limiting.

We can start from a most eloquent summary of the sterility of Bacon's attempt from our perspective:

> In this way we think we have been able to establish a for ever true and legitimate union between the empirical and the rational faculties (whose painful and undesirable divorce and repudiation had confused everything in the human family). (2002, 24)

Also, throughout this work Bacon repeats the argument that truth resides with God: a sense-based understanding and a culture-influenced rationality is not sufficient to contemplate it (see for instance I, CXXIV 2002, 226). This must be born in mind.

But Bacon is formidable on dialectics and on syllogisms, despite his reliance on induction and rationality, his lack of trust in the senses, and his religious perspective on the nature of the world and of truth. This makes him see a number of interesting things.

On pages 36 and 38 he explains how his logic is different from those logics that end with the practice of syllogism, and therefore make nature slip away (*naturam emittit e manibus*). Syllogisms are made of words, and words are labels and signs of notions (*tesserae et signae*). Yet, induction is the solution and we are back to what was said above.

It is intriguing to notice, however, that a little later Bacon admits that "thus the mind, when undergoing the impression of things through the senses, in making up and forming its own notions inserts and associates its own nature to the nature of things" (2002, 42).

In other words, the mind is obstructed in its activity by its own being immersed in a world that the senses alone cannot help interpret: the nature of things get mixed up with the nature of the mind.

The nature of the mind is determined by a most important set of limitations, the *idola*:

> The Idola which occupy mind are either acquired or innate. (2002, 42)

The former, the acquired ones, enter the mind by means of the theories of philosophers and of philosophical sects and also of flawed rules of demonstration. The latter are innate: the mind projects naturally (i.e., not in the sense of Feuerbach's hypostatizations) its own limitations on the things it sets itself to grasp by using the senses. The acquired faults are social in practice, in that they come from "nurture." They also are fully intellectual in nature. They constitute a set of problems very similar to those we have posed in this book.

In order to avoid overplaying the analogies, we should keep in mind the fundamental limits of Bacon's thought we mentioned before.

In the *Praefatio*, Bacon claims that even those who aimed at establishing dialectics as the mode of thought for science might have been looking for a way to help the limits of the senses alone in the perception of things (2002, 66). Yet their remedy is too late, for the situation is compromised by the presence of *idola* originating from daily life and corrupted doctrines. There is here, with the dialectics-*idola* connection and the need to emancipate our minds from it, a sort of anticipation of what has been discussed in modern terms from Marx onwards.

What is there argued is fixed in the form of formulas in the *Aphorisms*, in this case, aphorisms IX, X, XII, and XIV.

Towards the end of the *Praefatio*, Bacon insists on the value of acting directly (experiments and direct scientific observation) in the attempt to penetrate nature, a hint of an analogy with the idea of prolepsis we have discussed (2002, 71). Now the picture is quite complete, and we are ready to see the characteristics of the *idola*. This will bring to the surface some amazing observations Bacon was not capable, or willing, to develop.

Bacon states that there are four types of *idola* in I, XXXIX. His classification is very intriguing: *Idola Tribus*, *Idola Specus*, *Idola Fori*, and *Idola Theatri* (2002, 92). In XLI he explains that the

> Idola Tribus are founded on human nature and human tribes and stocks. In fact it is false to assert that sense is the measure of things human, for on the contrary all perceptions, both of the sense and of the mind, are conformant to what is human, not to the universe. And the human intellect is like an irregular mirror to the rays from things, which it mixes with its own nature, distorting and corrupting them. (92)

This is full of powerful intuitions and of undeveloped lessons for us.

In general, in this aphorism we find the very common fear that man's understanding of nature and reality in general is flawed. It might well be flawed: it probably always is, but this should not deter us from pursuing our observations.

A flawed understanding, if it is the result of using all the analytical possibilities of the human mind, is good enough for human purposes. Reality is not outside human beings: humans are a part of reality. Their understanding is therefore part of reality. There is no need to figure out a reality "out there" and (like in the capitalist case) to conjure up a self-contained bubble meant to make such a separation stable, defending that bit of understanding "man" has reached.

What counts most of all, Bacon intuited, is the social aspect of human limits. This is the part that should be cleared first of all, in order to deal with the most difficult and frustrating one, the intrinsic limits of our mind itself, even when free of cultural intellectual boundaries.

Bacon has taken some important steps in this direction by dividing his *idola* into four categories. The *Idola Tribus* (LII 2002, 104) find their origin in the homogeneity of the human spirit[6]—its prejudices, its limited boundaries, its aimless moving (*inquieto motus ejus*), its emotions, the incompetence of the senses, and the way impressions are received.

This means, with great clarity, a fundamental thing: Bacon mixes together the concerns of the human mind and the inadequacy of senses. These two, which we have linked in a causal relationship in this volume (capitalism's dominant culture impinges upon the use of the senses), are conceived instead as immutable. Senses, as we have already seen, are in fact intrinsically inadequate.

To this Bacon adds the historical and anthropologically peculiar worries of the human mind. What we have inferred instead from our perspective is that we do not know yet the potentialities of our senses.

Idola Specus instead are the *idola* of individual men (XLII 2002, 94). They originate in that mental framework each of us sets up for him/herself, to organize our thoughts and to defend ourselves from uncertainty and indecision. Such framework is powerfully determined in Bacon (we can only agree) by our readings and the things we have learned, both when we have understood them properly and when we have not.

The *Idola Fori* deserve a full-length quotation:

> There also are Idola that derive from a contract and from the reciprocal relations of humankind, which we called, because of man's traffics and societies, Idola Fori. Humankind in fact associates by means of discourses; but words are imposed by the understanding capacity of the people. Thus the intellect is ambushed all the time by a bad and incompetent attribution of words. The definitions and explanations about some things which erudite men are used to provide themselves with and to redefine, cannot put anything back in its proper place. Rather, words exert violence on the intellect, and bring confusion everywhere; and men are dragged into innumerable and empty controversies. (XLIII 2002, 94)

While we can deal with the *Idola Specus* with a bit of Marx's "extraneous standards" in a historical sense (LVIII 2002, 108), we find ourselves in serious troubles with the *Idola Fori*. These are dangerous because they depend on the institutions of society, but above all because they are made of words that are misleading. They in fact originate in a general, widespread approximation, and not just in occasional misunderstanding.

The social nature of the process makes them a hopeless set of concepts that not even the efforts of wise and knowledgeable scientists can change back to precision. Before going more deeply into this matter, let us see the last type of *idola*.

Idola Theatri (XLIV 2002, 94) are those *idola* that derive from "theatrical" philosophical doctrine. Here the danger is that of attributing to Bacon a much too subtle vision of intellectual relationships. I suppose he means those doctrines "*quae mundos effecerunt fictitios et scenicos*" (94)—that is, those that supply a ready-made, self-contained, and cozy construction that impresses for its analogy with the "bubble" (in the capitalist case). A typical example of this type of doctrines is Vico's *Scienza Nuova* (2004), as we shall see next section.

Bacon expands on *Idola Fori* in LIX (2002, 108), but we shall be careful in drawing conclusions similar to those proposed here. The similarity consists only in the fact that he identifies in economic and political life a set of word-based deviations from a straightforward, direct apprehension of reality. LIX and above all LX are very clear in this respect. Bacon blames the association of words and names, due to the erroneous human belief that reason can dominate words. On the contrary, he argues on LIX, words can strike back, distorting the intellect and transforming philosophy into sophistry and ineffective constructions in general (in LXIII he will attack Aristotle on this ground, and further on the Scholastics, although in a rather general way).

"Common opinion" is a danger for words: it transforms the dominant opinion into a truth, an existing concept with a name. Bacon, in LIX, states that definitions are needed, and it is from this that research should be started. Yet, he is quite pessimistic about this possibility ("*definitiones . . . malo mederi non possunt*"): the power of words consists in their capacity to produce more words, and the consequent impossibility for even wise scientists to extricate themselves from the ensuing maze of wrong and right definitions.

He takes refuge in scientific topics, giving up whatever reference to economic and social reality he has made in his classification of *idola*. Nor can he do otherwise, given the means he himself has put at his own disposal.

In any case, he is very clear on the existence of "*Idola quae per verba intellectui imponuntur,*" which are of two types. They either are names given to things that do not exist, or misleading names given to things that exist. The analogy with what has been said so far is there, but it cannot be overplayed in any way. Bacon is in a different set of problems.

Also, Bacon lacks the capacity to see the power of ruptures, despite having a clear idea of their presence and of the naturality of that presence

> because any violent movement is also natural, for it takes place when an external acting cause makes nature different from what it was before. (LXVII 2002, 124)

To the fixity and nonmendability of the limits to knowledge (individual, social, and innate to man's intrinsic limitation), Bacon does not oppose the possibility of rupture/disappearances that he sees in nature. Despite Bacon's materialistic attitude, an artificial separation between man and nature is kept (the religious argument shown at the beginning).

Little help then is his distinguishing between metaphysics and physics (2002, 260) and pointing out in various places (but see especially LXXXI 2002, 150) that science is meant to supply man with aids for the practical purposes of living. In fact, what this amounts to is an attempt to limit the scope of his attempt to put science on new bases. All his intuitions of a wider kind are thus compelled to become merely technical observations and serve the "scientific" attempt (induction, experiment, and that little bit of redefinition that is possible, plus the struggle against dialectical wastes of time and effort).

Bacon failed to propose a materialistic and naturalistic approach, for he failed to dare on the connection between a flawed grasp of the material and the social, cultural, and economic reasons for it. He takes refuge in a "scientific" focus that is not granted by his premises, which encompass a much wider subject matter.

Facing that would have brought him into the cold of the loneliness we said before. That cold was even more dangerous in his days, for it leads to an atheistic position, like in Epicurus (Epicurus's peculiar form of atheism was made of attributing a superior *ataraxia* to the gods) or in Marx (whose atheism is, however, more of an antireligious attitude than an atheistic philosophical argument), or in Feuerbach (potentially, this is the only philosophical argument that could lead to atheism).

Lonely we are too, alone with unusable intuitions and beautiful insights when we study materialistic authors. A fundamental lesson we have learned, however, is that Bacon has seen, before the dawn of capitalism, the role of economic and political arrangements in limiting human understanding: the *Idola Fori*. This nicely dovetails with the argument of the incompleteness of capitalism as a mode of production and the archaic components that remain in it.

Precisely because materialism, when rigorously pursued, leads to loneliness, plenty of thinkers, within materialism itself, adopt the typical compromises of those who fear being on their own. Bacon is not the most exemplary case: he has a number of reasons to be partly excused, first of all his being among the first to propose an experimental method based on empirical reality—that looked awesome at the time.

There are much more telling examples: Vico is one, for his work led him to say a number of things that later thinkers, and especially twentieth-century thinkers of the capitalist kind, wanted to hear.

CAPITALISM AS AN ANTICULTURE

Giambattista Vico's fame, unlike Bacon, has endured more evenly in the past couple of centuries. There is no place in the world where you do not find at least somebody who knows about him, and many of those can be counted among the "Vico said it first" believers.

Benedetto Croce produced a *Bibliografia Vichiana* and a *Philosophy of Vico*, and went so far as to make successful pressure on the Neapolitan authorities at a time when he was politically disgraced for a stone on Vico's house, whose text he anonymously authored. He famously said in his book on Vico that he "*egli fu né più né meno che il secolo decimonono in germe (represented the seeds of the nineteenth century)*." De Sanctis talks about Vico in his epoch-making history of Italian literature, and Carlo Cattaneo deals with Vico, too. Gramsci and Gentile highly considered him and saw the powerful, ideal connection with Hegel. Vico has crossed Italian culture transversally, in parallel with Idealism, Catholicism, and nationalism.

But what is it that Vico said that appeals so much both to the provincial issues of Italian culture and to a terribly heterogeneous set of international admirers? First, Vico poses himself among the continuators of Francis Bacon. On page 186 (2004) he warns that he is applying Verulam's method for natural sciences. He is transferring Bacon's scientific rigor to history.[7]

Vico has a more powerful role for the divine providence than Bacon: to him providence is the alpha and omega of history, the setter of conditions and the maker of the intellectual mechanisms whereby man both makes and understands his own history.

He insists on this argument throughout the *Scienza Nuova* (2004, see for instance 451, 706, 708) (in what follows I shall give the Bergin/Fisch translation, 1984, except when I find it distorting or when there are discrepancies with the Italian (2004) edition I base myself on, in which case I shall translate Vico myself).

> The design of divine providence is one of those things this new science principally concerns itself with [and] . . . as a consequence it represents a reasoned civil theology of divine providence. (2004, 87)
>
> Hence Epicurus, who believes in chance, is refuted by the facts, along with his followers Hobbes and Machiavelli; and so are Zeno and Spinoza. . . . The evidence clearly confirms the contrary position of the political philosophers, whose prince is the divine Plato, who shows that providence directs human institutions. (1984, 425; 2004, 706)[8]

The book's conclusion (2004, 708) is a paean to piety.

At the roots of this pious attitude of Vico are two powerful and limiting decisions. On the one hand, he bases his labors on the assumption, smuggled as a fact, that man has a common human nature, a homogeneous historical and anthropological development that proceeds in phases, and a language that develops with history and is the means history has to discover and organize the past.

On the other hand, and complementarily, in a way reminiscent of both Hegel and vulgar Hegelianism, to Vico history progresses. Providence has organized, and is supervising, the whole process of evolution and of the closing up to the divine will. Let us see these two aspects in more detail to then move on to see Vico's role as a precursor of the hypostatizations of capitalist times.

Paolo Rossi, in his rich "Introduction" to Vico's *La Scienza Nuova* (2004), properly and correctly emphasizes Vico's *verum-factum* theory, introduced in his *De Antiquissima Italorum Sapientia* (1710). What is true must be understood through the fact: the truth of a thing is in doing it.[9] Man can build knowledge of reality by means of constructing an intellectual method.

This poses him inside nature, because nature's and man's languages emanate from God/Providence (see also Vico 2004, 232). The superficial analogy with the argument of this book that could be made thus immediately evaporates. Also, senses are misleading in Vico.

To Vico man is naturally sociable, just like in the hypostatizations of the classical political economists and of those who followed them, up to our days. From the Fall due to the original sin that has thrown man into the temporary wild solitude of early ages (one wonders why, and also why such solitude is qualified as *"da fiere bestie—wild beast like,"* 2004, 87), from which utility makes the first forms of socialization emerge, man started "to live with justice and in society, thus celebrating their sociable nature; which, in this work will be proven to be the true nature of man" (2004, 87).

It is precisely the humanmade nature of society (directed from Providence) that makes a systematic study of history possible. This, however, needs a number of assumptions to be passed as undeniable matters of fact like in the philosophers, economists, and political economists we have been studying throughout this volume.

Man has a common language corresponding to a common intellectuality that derives from nature (i.e., Providence itself) and develops in phases associated with a progressive set of institutional and cultural facts (truths). That means that we move from the elementary to the complex, from the rough to the refined, from the beastly to the human.

Nature is neatly separated from man, who shares with it his material body as a consequence of original sin. Man, unlike nature, is destined to higher states. Social institutions and their progressive complications witness to this fact.

Vico says (what is astonishing is not that Vico said it but that it is in various degrees endorsed to these days) that language went through phases, of which the first was by gestures, the second by metaphors, descriptions, similitudes, and heroic tales, and the third was "the human language from voices agreed upon by the peoples, of which the peoples are absolute lords, typical of popular republics and of monarchies" (2004, 112–13).

There is no denying that we still find the basics of this vision in economics, history, and even anthropology. Primitive men were and are supposed to
be rough, and their society correspondingly rough and clumsy; but their language progressed with their institutions. Heroes were proper for ancient societies up to the Middle Ages, which Vico considered a lost era of a return to
barbarism.

Today instead free people democratically state to each other with syntactic
wealth the beauty of modern arrangements. The whole thing has progressed
without ruptures. Vico, indeed, said it first.

Yet Vico overplays his case. His arguments on the elementarity of primitive men, the *verum-factum* and that of the progression of language lead him
to posit that mythology must have a high degree of truth.

> The first men of gentility having been as simple-minded as children, who are by
> nature truthful, the early fables could only be truthful; hence they had necessar-
> ily to be . . . true stories. (2004, 287)

Consequently, Vico proceeds to systematically use mythological "facts" to
prove historical arguments and progressions. He even produces a *Tavola
Cronologica* (124–25) that in a chart form summarizes the history of the
world.[10]

Vico states that the primitive languages with their metaphysics created the
gods, logic created languages, morality heroes, "economics" (*iconomica*)
families, politics the cities (254). Man made man through the divine principles that are in him. Thus, his *Scienza Nuova* "comes to be at once a history
of the ideas, the customs, and the deeds of humankind," from which "the principles of the history of human nature which are the principles of universal history" will stand out (254).

No "extraneous standards" are possible despite man sharing a natural body
with the rest.

It is a pity then that the majority of Vico's references to ancient facts,
mythological and nonmythological, are plain wrong. I must praise here Paolo
Rossi's edition of *Scienza Nouva* (2004) that systematically points out such
mistakes and imprecisions, doing a job that would have been forbidding.

The question is that nonetheless erudites of the strength of Croce continued
to credit Vico with historical and philosophical soundness. The reason for
this, needless to say, is not in what he said but in how he framed it philosophically, which coincides with the most cherished prejudices and hypostatizations of capitalist culture.

There is more to the credit of Vico that proves the above point. We should
not underestimate in fact that Vico was a *sui generis* "reactionary" that was

defending from the influence of Spinoza and Hobbes whatever moralistic institutions were available. Let us turn to this most interesting aspect.

A first feature of Vico's reactionary attitude we have seen is his insistence on the role of providence. Indeed, that was part of his reaction to what he feared was taking place in European culture. A second aspect was the mentioned intention to refute Epicurus, Spinoza, and Hobbes.

But the most telling feature of Vico's reactionary aims lies in his very approach to that *Scienza Nuova* he wanted to create. The very idea of the progression toward development in intellectual terms was nothing but an attempt to show that the present times are the highest point of history and should be preserved and protected. In this respect, the history-language-intellect and rationality-culture mixtures are perfect tools to prove the point, especially when strengthened by the endorsement of the whole erudite apparatus of your culture, mythical and actually historical.

The *Degnità* from LIX (202) to LXXXIII (210) are meant to summarize this point in easy-to-learn aphorism form. Vico knowingly transformed the hypostatizations of his time (and, sadly, of capitalist times) into formulas that looked obvious, undeniable, and easy to absorb.

Another anticipation of capitalist common sense is the separation of the beastly from the (modern) human. Humans are beastly in their early historical ages, when they let themselves go at instinctive drives.

Among these last, the one that most seems to disgust Vico (Wilhelm Reich would see his whole life work vindicated here) is sex. Early ages men had free sex, and they did it without shame. The world did not progress until they started to fear shame, which put a brake to their mindless couplings and led to the institution of marriage. Fear of the gods (353) led early men to hide their sexual intercourses in caves. This brought about the habit/need to keep only to one companion as the "forever" sexual partner, and the sense of shame (*pudore*), which was "*il calore della virtù*" (353).

Virtù (it is hard to translate this word: it means virtue in the sense of the capacity not to do the things that would bring shame on you; in the old days it was used as a synonym of virginity, in fact), after religion, "is the other bond that keeps nations united, just like audacity and lack of piety are what ruins them" (353).

Institutions with their formal solemnity and their emanating from God (true or mistaken gods, it makes no difference, in that Providence is at work anyway) are the basis of modern, shame-pervaded societies that conceal what is natural and perform, in the secret of the alcove, only what is institutionally allowed. Again, Croce had it right: Vico saw it all.

From page 240 onward, in a further prescient effort that might have amazed Croce and Gramsci, Vico states (especially pages 240–41) that even when the religious motive and the cultural nature of man were not able to act with effectiveness and clarity, the same historical results would have been reached. Utility in fact is what man in the most diverse conditions—even in the early natural ones!—is after.

> We thereby establish the fact that man in the bestial state desires only his own welfare; having taken wife and begotten children, he desires his own welfare along with that of his family; having entered upon civil life, he desires his own welfare along with that of his city; when its rule is extended over several peoples, he desires his own welfare along with that of the nation; when the nations are united by wars, treaties of peace, alliances, and commerce, he desires his own welfare along with that of the entire human race. In all other circumstances man desires principally his own utility. (Book I, Section IV, 1984, 101; 2004, 240)

The prescient coincidence with capitalist common sense as stated implicitly and explicitly by the classical economists is there. What differs is the reason for it: while this whole thing is in fact natural to man (on which capitalist upholders would agree), in Vico we must not forget the action of Providence.

> That which regulates all human justice is therefore divine justice, which is administered by divine providence to preserve human society. (Book I, Section IV, 1984, 102; 2004, 241)

We might even argue that even in this mixture of religion and the social Vico was anticipating one of the main characteristics of capitalism as we know it, but this is of no consequence here. What matters is that Vico continues (241) by attacking on these religious grounds Epicurus and whosoever has dared figure out reality as *"ordine delle naturali cose"* (the order of things natural) in which chance and natural events have the upper hand. In a prescient vulgar Hegelian fashion, history must be a *"teologia civile ragionata della provvedenza divina"* (241) (rational civil theology of divine providence, 1984, 102).

Vico, continuing his argument, says that his history (*"questa Scienza"*) describes

> [...] an ideal eternal history traversed in time by the history of every nation in its rise, development, maturity, decline and fall (1984, 104; 2004, 245).

Man has certainly made this world of nations (a principle he poses as the basis of his whole book), and its proof is something to be sought for in the human mind (we saw the reasons for it, which are of a "materialistic" kind, somehow).

Così questa Scienza procede appunto come la geometria. (Thus this science works like geometry.) (1984; 2004, 245)

In geometry, Vico continues, we know our material because we have constructed it ourselves. Its perfection witnesses to God's power, which made us clever enough to make up such intellectual operations.

We are equipped now to consider the last important aspect of Vico's conception of historical development: the famous *corsi e ricorsi*, the possibility of historical recurrence. Vico does not see history as a linear development but admits of the possibility of a comeback of earlier phases. Not by chance, he identifies the Middle Ages as one of these comebacks (the *barbarie seconda*).

If history progresses and only provisional and temporary comebacks of barbarism are possible, then anything that does not look like what you want (e.g., the institutions based on shame we saw) can be opposed, fought, and refused on the ground of being a return to atavistic, long-lost, beastly barbarism.

Book V of the *Scienza Nuova* opens with the statement of the historical recurrences, which it inscribes within the working of the Divine Providence. Vico added some further thoughts in the later editions, among which are two *ragionamenti*. We could finish our treatment of his quasi-materialistic approach to history with a quotation from the second of these:

> civil liberty being preserved by the laws, for that golden statement by Cicero: *"ideo legum servi sumus, ut liberi esse possumus."* (2004, 743)

But it is worth finishing by noticing with Croce instead, *"Si potrebbe presentare la storia ulteriore del pensiero come un ricorso delle idee del Vico"* ("we could present the history of thought after Vico as a coming back of Vico's ideas").[11] Indeed, Vico's arguments are the very arguments of modern social philosophers/scientists we have been confuting in the preceding chapters.

The first lesson we can draw, that is valid for Bacon too, is that materialism cannot stand without a complete openness to the "beastly" side of man. Such openness can only be granted by an acceptance of ruptures and disappearances and something similar to a "sane" (in the Reichian sense) relationship with the natural, bodily drives of man; these must be heeded.

The conception of "historical recurrences" is not useless in itself: in practice recurrences might well happen. It is wrong when it is posited as a mechanical rule, natural to the historical progression itself. In such cases it brings about all the various consequences we have been studying in this book. The most unbearable of all is the boredom of observing the same items repeating themselves over time.

Vico's arguments can be transported, *mutatis mutandis*, to our own capitalistic times, which Croce and Gramsci hoped. But this is precisely what is wrong with them. This leads us to notice once again that capitalism as a mode of production has not operated a complete rupture with its past. The presence, and undeclining strength, of these types of arguments in capitalism is widespread and accepted. The two sides of the same argument—the suppression of instincts and naturality and the openness to the comeback of the atavistic (the refusal of the possibility of ruptures and oblivion)—go hand in hand, and their conservative power usually goes unnoticed.

All this further contributes to show that capitalism is an incomplete mode of production with an arrested development and a dominant intellectual logic, passed by the participants in the game as a culture that strives to keep the passages with the past open. Barbarism is kept alive only to keep its exorcisms going and to forbid actual dialogue with it.

It is worth going back to the economists discussed in chapter 3, who held that man emerges from his prehuman existence already as a social being, the evolution of reason, language, and cooperation being the outcome of the very same process.

Marshall (1910), at the opening of his chapter 4 ("Income, Capital") goes on discussing the well-known relationship between primitive community and modern society in the same way as everybody else. His Appendix A seems, apart from the disgusting racism that pervades it,[12] built around the same conception of anthropology as Vico's and everybody else's among his colleagues. The savage's common and impulsive behavior is tamed by civilization by means of compulsion (moral compulsion). Man's evolution and the mastering of nature go hand in hand.

We have seen John Stuart Mill's reliance on community in chapter 3 as well, and there is no need to go over that again. In Hayek we find the most powerful similarities to Vico's approach.

In chapter 1 of his 1978 work, Hayek says that society does not originate in a conscious decision but is a collective collection of (supposedly homogeneous and converging) acts. Language and culture grow with the development of civilization. Civilization equals elimination of instincts. Needless to say, the highest point of civilization is capitalism with the rule of law, which implicates the need to keep off the possible return of barbarism.

The above derives from a point Hayek had been making throughout his life, well expressed in *Individualism and Economic Order* (1948), part III. There he states, echoing Vico, that we look at nature from outside (this implicates that senses are insufficient, or even misleading) and at society from inside. What we can call "facts" are things we have built with language and intelligence. They depend on theory, then, so historical facts depend on historical theory.

Social sciences

> do not pretend to discover by empirical observation laws of behavior or change of these wholes [social wholes]. Their task is rather, if I may so call it, to *constitute* such wholes, to provide schemes of structural relationships. (72, emphasis in the original)

Empirical evidence cannot disprove a theory but only show its consistency.
All this reminds us of Von Mises's statement that with praxeology cognition of human cooperation is attained and "social action is treated as a special category of the more universal category of human action as such."

> All the praxeological categories are eternal and unchangeable as they are uniquely determined by the logical structure of the human mind and by the natural conditions of man's existence. (1949, 199)

This is not to say that there is a "Vichian" mortgage on capitalism as we know it. All I am saying is that there are undisputable similarities between Vico's arguments and those who write within the intellectual frame of capitalism as we know it. Vico's case is relevant in that, in the steps of Bacon, he intended to build a human-centered account of the material variables of history. His insistence upon the role of providence does not detract from his (failed) attempt to remain within the material. It just shows that any attempt to concoct a materialistic explanation of the material without accepting the role of ruptures and oblivions is doomed to fold and come back to "investigations about words" and to supporting the existence of the gods.

The difference we want to consider now is between a moderate and an extremist reading of materialism. The first can give up pursuing the inner logic of a materialistic argument when it strays too far from shared, accepted, and conventional views of society and of human beings with their development. From a moderate point of view, we cannot and must not conceive of ruptures and disappearances, for these clash with (unproven, yet strong) conceptions of human history as a (dialectical) progressive development in the sense of improvement.[13]

From a moderate materialistic perspective we can, likely we must, work at the improvement of society. Even changing society itself is allowed. What is not permissible is to challenge it—to imagine, and work toward, its disappearance. The specter of the return of barbarism in all its forms is waved before the sinners. Anarchy, death,[14] violence, and free sex are thrown in the face of opposers as if they were evils and, funnily, as if they did not exist in the world as we know it.

The assumption behind the moderate position is that what we have is working, after all: to chase off revolution, moderatism endorses the present. In so doing, it cuts itself off from the natural, falling into the intellectual trap we have been describing in the present volume and that is not an obscure, abstract concept, but a sad, actual fact.

It is interesting to consider the forms taken by moderate thought; but before, we should emphasize the coincidence between moderate materialistic approaches and the bases of capitalist intellectuality. Given the nonsubversive character of moderate materialism, such coincidence is almost complete (except for some bits that lead back to the empty rhetoric of propaganda: take Gramsci's conception of change). Moderate materialisms are just one more of the many iterations of capitalist intellectuality.

While the logical explanation of such a sad fact is in the theory proposed so far, the historical evidence is somehow polluted by the remaining bits of the useless diatribes internal to capitalism as we know it. Perfect instances of moderate materialism, such as dialectical Marxism in general or the Bolshevik Revolution and the USSR, are still discussed as if they were attempted breaks with the routines of capitalism. This is understandable, because it is precisely what conservatives will want to discuss and moderates (progressives) will want to contend to conservatives.

This misleading discussion between pseudoconservatives and pseudoreactionaries covers up for a true, inner tendency of capitalism. Both sides of the controversy have in the back of their minds, as discussed throughout this book, something different from capitalism and communism: they have "actual" instances of those two impossible models they are unable to even conceive in abstract. Like Hayek for the free marketeers and Lenin or Gramsci for the "socialist" camp, what they have in mind is a reformed capitalism with communitarian features.

The rule of law, which one is supposed to believe rather than just obey, the sense of community, the national character (this can be ethnical, multiethnical, commercial, military, geographical, and any of the other hybrid categories capitalism as we know it has kept from noncapitalistic periods and cultures), the management of the economy that depends both from the fact that true markets do not exist and that the "community" has a national character and international relations are made of trade and war, the need for a government that grants an orderly functioning of all the above items, the need to give a justification to all this together in the name of the ideal categories of capitalism (which, therefore, include noncapitalist categories such as nation/nationalism), all point to what we have seen to be the fascist character of the actual management of capitalism as we know it. This character embodies the barbarism that lurks at capitalism from the dark, as well as the solution to it.

Whatever its name, this undeniable phenomenon is present in all the countries that we consider as capitalistically developed. It is a further, institutionally enforced, actual set of material limits imposed upon the already limited and limiting intellectuality of capitalism. What would we call it? We cannot any longer say culture, like we have been doing occasionally for the sake of making the argument understandable. Capitalist (as we know it) intellectuality, limited and limiting, brings about further intellectual, emotional, and even bodily limitations by favoring all those practical devices listed earlier. It is not a culture: it is an anticulture.

Both conservative supporters and progressive reformers, as long as they share in the moderate frame of mind, contribute to this fascist feature of capitalism as we know it; its anticultural character.

REVOLUTION[15]

The possibilities to break out of capitalism as we know it amount to moderatism unless we leave the dominant logic and pose ourselves in a different intellectual world. The main point is, as might be predicted by now, to reconstitute direct, sensual links with nature—reality as a whole—without mixing that up with institutional organization. This is revolution.

We still are a long distance away, however, from being able to work out this idea satisfactorily. We lack a number of arguments: a taxonomy and genealogy of the present, the full definition of emancipation, the definition and use of naturalism, and the difficult discussion of detachment. These topics are better left to a next volume.

Here we can only discuss what so far has been called, and still is called, revolution (the capitalist definition). We can also start defining "our" revolution as rupture with oblivion. In fact, this is its main aspect, as we shall see, the rest belonging rather to the realm of how to do it.

Let us have a look in the first place at "actually existing revolutions": these span a historical time that goes from the preparation of capitalism to our days. Some are directly political (hence military, and whatever else politics is made of), while others are technological before taking political features. Of this last type only one is unequivocal and unanimously recognized: the so-called set of complex phenomena known as the Industrial Revolution.

Among the revolutions of the first kind we find the English Revolution, the American Revolution (this is contested by those who claim it to be an independence war; even in this reduced role, however, still it contributed to a systematic change in capitalism), the French Revolution, and the Bolshevik Revolution. There also are minor types, whose status is challenged and controversial, and whose features are incomplete when compared to the others (e.g., the Chinese Revolution).

This simple taxonomy conveys an unmistakable message: what has been called "revolution" is in fact a sudden, violent movement within the general progression toward the present form of capitalism. We are witnessing events that, despite their disruptive power and in many cases (take the Bolsheviks) their profession of anticapitalist faith and their conspicuous "human losses," amount to iterations of capitalist functioning of the type described in chapters 4 and 5.

Anticapitalist revolutions originated in perfectly capitalistic reasonings made of moral arguments (the plea of the toiling masses, for instance); philosophical, logical arguments should be pursued instead. Class struggle, that Marx had shown to be a typical, dialectical characteristic of the functioning of capitalism, becomes whenever "revolution" in the capitalist sense looks at hand, a moral argument to rally the toiling masses as well as the nontoiling minorities who feel sympathetic to the masses' plea.

But if class struggle is one of the main and typical mechanisms of the dialectical functioning of capitalism, how can it be used toward its destruction? Working dialectically to win a class struggle is no more and no less than what capitalism is about: proletarians do it to protect themselves, and capitalists do it to continue exploiting the proletarians.[16] Without it, capitalism would not exist.

I invite everybody to consider what else could be done within the framework of capitalist anticulture. In fact, the solutions at hand today, when the very concept of proletariat is becoming obsolete, are the same as a hundred years ago. Class struggle is a situation imposed by capitalism, in which we are compelled to participate to protect ourselves from exploitation or, in the worst case, from becoming ontologically noncapitalist (i.e., dead), and that is all.

The moderate approaches that continue to churn out these types of revolutions are, therefore, intrinsically cruel. I wonder how its proposers can conjugate them with their brotherhood with the toiling masses. Coming instead to the capitalist revolutions, say, the English and French ones, we find ourselves in a different set of troubles. These revolutions have contributed remarkably to make capitalism arrive where it is now. But what it is now is not, as argued in the preceding chapters, what it seemed it could become. We can now explain past revolutions.

In this empty dialectical confrontation that must find a mediated solution, some contradictions must exist. While in normal circumstances such contradictions are resolved on political and economic grounds, in "revolutionary" times a showdown is required (tautologically, this being the main requirement to call a time "revolutionary").

For the sake of the intrinsic "moderation" of the system and the dialectical resolution of the conflict, the mediation that produces a result that resembles both initial terms must take place. Destruction cannot take place, for it would bring about ruptures and oblivion: real oppositions rather than dialectical contradictions. The conflict must be resolved without losses for capitalism as we know it. The opportunity offered by proselytism is too perfect not to be exploited.

The wretched of the Earth, or more likely some categories of the many that compose this wide set of human beings, are then launched into action. With them go scores of upper-class heroes who sincerely care for the injustices of the world that have made them a privileged minority. Usually, many die, and many more are maimed bodily, psychologically, or economically.

All of these persons do not exit the capitalist game. In the worst case, they just lose their individual ontological consubstantiality with it (they die). This peculiar type of iteration has been consumed. The time has come to resume the appraisal of itself that the capitalist maieutics constantly operates.

The ontological disappearances of the individual victims of revolution, replaced in the capitalist (as we know it) "investigation about words" with their count, sets in motion the various institutional consequences that allow the economic and political turmoil to settle. I know of no revolution that has strayed from this general pattern.

It is important to say, in this respect, that even those who are disappointed by revolution and see its capitalistic outcome can be misled by the pattern described. The case of Trotzky and of the "state capitalism" criticism of the USSR is a most important instance: Trotzky's and the Trotzkyists's analyses of Bolshevism are right, and yet they miss the main point.

The difference and conflict between individuals and masses, the debasing of the latter when they become a mob, and of politeias when mobs storm them, is clear. As a consequence, the main problem is the negation of individuality. Revolutionary issues are important only in that they are misused by the capitalist intellectuality, which transforms them into issues of political philosophy, anthropology, psychology, and the like, as well as by the agitators who want to ride them. In practice the question boils down to how to whip up or cool down the revertible individual-mob transformation.

We should not be misled in our analysis by the fact that revolutions use typically bourgeois ideals (say, nation, justice, new institutions, market and anti-market rhetoric, and similar). Nor should we be misled by the use of noncapitalist ideals (communism, solidarity, brotherhood, peace, and love): the meaning of all these concepts, being impenetrable to capitalist intellectuality, is misunderstood and distorted by the maieutics we have learned to identify.

In summary, the intellectuality of capitalism as we know it conceives of revolution as derring-do: those *leaps* that Rees (1998) explains and praises as the outcome of dialectics.

Being constituted of identifiable categories, revolution in that sense is a typical topic for action by capitalist intellectuality. Categories can be disembodied from the whole: the "good" (the acceptably moderate-dialectical-discursive) can be isolated and used in normal capitalist polities by that unidentifiable ghost named "civil society" as well as by political parties of all kinds. Wherever we turn in capitalism, we are back to boredom.

Historical revolutions entail those "human losses" we have repeatedly referred to. These, in turn, with their frightening toll (the count), are an incentive to go back to "normal" boredom. Iterations that breed iterations at the cost of the individuals involved—can anybody imagine anything worse? Can anybody put an end to this endless chain of suffering?

Revolution to us here means instead to get ourselves out of capitalism. This entails two fundamental consequences: one is the complete destruction of capitalism itself, that would crumble down in its intellectual nature dragging also much, or preferably and more likely all, of its material consequences. This destruction with the entailed *tabula rasa* does not have to be a violent undertaking, for it lacks the moderate characteristics of bourgeois revolutions.

The second consequence is the fact that, capitalism being held together by a shared and enforced intellectuality that erodes the fundamental prerogatives of individuals, revolution is first of all an individual emancipative task. Saying it this way is bound to make those intellectuals giggle who have been frowning so far at what is being explained in this book. It looks, to their capitalistic mental syllogisms, impossible.

They would say it is an eschatological, idealistic, religious endeavor, meaning that it would take too much endurance and likely it would lose (look unfeasible, in capitalist political parlance). It might well lose: that is correct, but so what? This is normality in nature: every day we leave our homes in the morning and start observing the persons of the sex we desire in order to discover the highest intellectual and bodily beauty we can seek sexual liaison with, and almost every day we are defeated. We go back home alone or having settled for less.[17] Victory as achievement is a capitalist concept that is useless and meaningless in nature. In it, risk is a true thing and trying does not mean obtaining.

Human bonds are as yet an unknown in our story, for capitalism has been limiting them. How do we conjugate, our frowning/giggling intellectuals would ask, individual emancipation with its necessarily choral practice (by this they mean the will of the majority)? For the time being, our "provisional" answer can only go back to the basics explained in chapter 2.

In (1973) Colletti claims, justly, that Marx had a clear idea of the natural character of work as a relationship with nature itself, especially in the 1844 *Manuscripts* (1968b) and the *German Ideology* (1985), and of the naturality of human relationships.[18] Work as a necessary part of man's life (a different thing from capitalist pointless work, the hurrying around and waste of human and natural resources entailed by the so-called market in practice)[19] therefore is necessarily a collective enterprise.

In (1975) Colletti points out how in capitalism individuals live together, on the contrary, precisely "because they are separated from each other" by the complex of relations between them (see also Micocci 2002a). Alienation and contradiction are the same theory. Any type of work, in fact any type of human endeavor that directly relates to nature, is necessarily a collective endeavor, if only because of the sheer supremacy nature has vi-à-vis the human species's attempts to bend it. Capitalism has transcended this natural fact, transforming the collective character of human activities into the artificial, moralistic, intellectual bubble we have been explaining. This has produced alienation of the single workers from each other.

Alienation concerns workers as well as idlers; for the pervasiveness of the institutions of capitalism allows no exit. Work and idleness, and this is no news to those who made it reading this book to this point, are subsumed under capitalism and subtracted from nature: individuals are atomized, hence homogenized.

The consequence of all this is that individual intellectual emancipation, restoring relationship with nature (reality as a whole) is necessarily a collective task. It needs, therefore, no proselytism, no enforcement, and no convincing. All it takes is to get to that breaking point and pass it. The breaking point with capitalism is far from being elusive: we all can reach it, our own way, without reading this book.

The problem, the "impossibility" that our ideal giggling yet frowning intellectuals would point to, is emotional. The individual of capitalism, tamed by a life of limited and limiting intellectuality and trained by the consequences of revolution as derring-do—as iteration—can only see the choice between the boredom of fascistic "capitalism as we know it" and the blind, majoritarian violence of mob revolution.

We are trapped in a tautology: there is no emancipation without seeing what emancipation is about, but capitalism supplies an emotional blinker and a powerful security: its routines are everywhere and capillarily in charge.

There is no emancipation without an individual act of detachment, but individual emancipation is necessarily collective. The point is not the choice between action and nonaction. The point is understanding what ruptures and oblivion are about and what detachment is (or can be).

Let us, however, admit the evident. This whole discussion with its quasi-tautological character is a way to revolve around the true central point: natural drives in individual men. Whatever has been discussed above can only take place, and will inevitably take place, if man has a natural self. This natural endowment we do not fully know, but given the infinite potentiality of nature we can hypothesize it as potentially infinite.[20] Here we are faced by a terrifying problem: if man is infinite in potency, he can only explode in capitalism. If he is not, then it is that sad, tamed animal fit for capitalist life that mainstream theories describe. It is time we knew the truth about it.

So, what is the solution to this only apparent aporia? What is it that can spark revolution in the sense proposed, without having to condition our fellow human beings to act in the "right" direction?

If the whole argument of the book is to be followed to its inevitable consequence, all we can, and must, do to have revolution is to put our fellow human beings before the naturality of destruction. If we can express that as the liberation of an unknown potential that might well be infinite, we will have achieved that individual-collective bond we need—that natural bond capitalism has severed.[21]

At this point of the development of our argument we can only glimpse at the hypothetical *tabula rasa* after destruction. The expression *tabula rasa* identifies, when used in politics and in biology, a bare place where no settlement human, vegetable, and animal is possible. In our case it rather indicates a place that is "silent" in the sense hinted at in chapter 5 and here: the lonely endeavor of materialism.

It is a place in which univocal logics meant to reassure do not find believers and therefore which has no need for religion or for the fear of the supernatural that accompanies the "scientific" achievements of capitalism as we know it. In such conditions, what counts, and matters, is a detached view of reality as such, the materialist attitude that pushes us to accept the material reality around us, in the hope to understand.

Yet understanding does not mean "systemation" according to one or another of the dominant logics (which in capitalism, we proved, are all alike). Rather, a series of provisional taxonomies and genealogies could be produced,[22] subject to intersect each other, likely to be different from each other (individuals should be different), and in a word subject to endless scrapping, correction, and reworking.

I should like to emphasize the scrapping. Unlike capitalism, human endeavors would hopefully resemble natural ones, like the wolf who sets out to hunt and does not know whether it is going to be successful (each time! It might starve to death if it gets a whole row of failures, and yet it does not look scared of such normality), or the potential human lover who sets out with renewed eagerness every minute: the elimination of items, from ideas to material objects and creatures, would be accepted, its normality acknowledged.

This is, obviously, not much of a difference with capitalism in material terms. Capitalism is tied to nature's laws, and ruptures and oblivion take place despite the bubble's self-imposed isolation. The difference lies in the individual's capacity to take reality as it is, without living vicariously by means of the dominant culture and all that is entailed. This, importantly, is far from saying that the individual can understand the reality he can now see directly.

We cannot even tell whether he/she would fully see it. That is part of the excitement of being there: the feeling, open to all of us, that every day might bring you to unknown shores.[23] The bareness of the *tabula rasa* would grant the richness of our lives.

Last but not least, lest our intellectuals who have passed from frowning to giggling start shivering in terror, the postrevolutionary scenario would be the outcome of a collective, individually motivated, action. Actually, that would be no action at all, given the absence of proselytism and of mass uprisings. Human bonds of a natural kind would be there to tie us to each other in a way we can imprecisely anticipate as "sentimentally and sensually."

I think that it would be premature to say any more than this. The intellectual reader be warned: I am not proposing "ineffable" outcomes. I am only saying we do not have yet the means to describe the material, even the banal, things that would take place in a postrevolutionary world.

There is no denying, however, that physical destruction should take place. All the wasteful aspects of capitalism that are usually swept under the carpet of market functioning should also go for good, economizing the world resources and allowing men not to be continuously bothered by economic problems. Indeed, precisely this aspect of the absurdity of capitalism (its celebration of man's slavery to the market as liberty) should be the first to go, with its plethora of production plants and activities and the ensuing waste and the set of phenomena varied in intensity that can be put together under the generic label of consumerism.

Shall we then see debris, like in known capitalist revolutions? I should hope so, personally, but this is not the point.

Perhaps the image we can use to convey the whole thing is that of a world where everything human is "economical" (I use this word on purpose). Poles would be stinging the earth only for practical purposes and not to sign borders and delimit properties. This is not to say, however, that the management of planet Earth would be ecologically viable. It might well be worse than at present. But this is the point: let history take its course, nature supremacy, and let men express their qualities as well as their foolishness.

INDIVIDUALITY

Throughout this book we have been looking at the cruel absurdity of capitalism by means of the criticism of famous thinkers. We have been arguing that their thoughts present some basic flaws that make them amenable to signify the corresponding thought of capitalist times. This, capitalism being a hybrid rather than a pure (in the sense of fully achieved) mode of production, is valid for precapitalist thinkers as well: we have been studying in this chapter Francis Bacon and Giambattista Vico.

Also, the ideas that have helped us through our path through the debunking of capitalist intellectuality (Feuerbach's hypostatization, Marx's criticism of Hegelian dialectics, Colletti's settlement of the dialectics/antidialectics dispute) have been taken from other respectable thinkers without endorsing the whole of their thought. They are offered here as felicitous intuitions within the varied trajectory of some important philosopher or social scientist. This is not to mean that we should feel superior and look down upon these people who are justly admired by all of us. We should only, like Leonardo da Vinci warned in his aphorisms, strive to go beyond what our masters have been teaching us.

What we have been arguing is not the inadequacy of some famous thinker, but the homogenous influence, in logical terms, of an intellectual pattern we can call the anticulture of capitalism. This is what I have been seeking to do here, with no pretence to replace a set of established cultural topics and thinkers I cherish, respect, and work to preserve for everybody to respectfully study.

No matter how strong you are, as an individual your integrity is in constant jeopardy under capitalism. In the first place, individual integrity itself is rather unknown and unknowable, hence hard to use. Secondly, various arguments can be put forward, and not only from the materialistic perspective, that show the limited and limiting nature of capitalism: even if individuality were what the capitalist vulgata says, it would be limited.

As a consequence, in seeking emancipation we should not be awed by the power of thought itself, be that of the great thinkers or our own. The "philosophical" revolution that is entailed by the present argument is not a purely intellectual task. It is precisely by trusting to a purely intellectual treatment the consideration of economic and political institutions, habits, and traditions that the conservative (and atavistic, hence anticapitalist) forces hosted by the incompleteness of capitalism take primacy. We have collectively named that the fascist tendency of capitalism as we know it.

The materialistic option is not just worth considering: also, the only way to consider it is by pursuing it to the full. Let us conclude this chapter exploring the basics of what individuality is, if capitalism is its denial and repression.

In capitalism individuals are atomized in the sense that they are a homogeneous fraction carved out of the mass. They join up again en masse in those occasions when a mob is required to achieve an evolutionary leap, to use a straight dialectical concept. But matters are not as simple as this. The whole thing is polluted by a series of intermediate concepts and umbrella terms that serve to cover up for the logical faults of the theory and of the practice.

One could be led to hypothesize, like mainstream and Marxist social scientists often do, that the individual-mob dynamics could and should (take Gramsci, Lenin, and from an opposite perspective Hayek, who all aim at order or, as they say now, "governance") be used to keep institutions in place. Some even go so far as hypothesizing nothing else, inscribing within it all the other items of capitalism as we know it: take Fukuyama and Huntington.

Their end-of-history scenario is far from unjustified. If the alternatives to capitalism are what orthodox Marxists, communitarians, and self-appointed liberals have to offer, history is finished. We are condemned to a continuously shifting set of "capitalisms as we know them" that replace each other in turn and that will never reach the end goal of a pure market community at the world level. That in fact would signal the end of the various changes and "revolutions" that are suggested, even in our days and even by radicals and pseudorevolutionaries, as the movement of history.

Fukuyama (1992) and Huntington (1968, 2000), who are the last epigones of what used to be called "modernization theory" in the USA, are interesting also because of their acceptance of the cruel face of capitalism. Huntington in particular, with his "clash of civilizations" pornography, is a perfect example of the poor syllogisms capitalism as we know it keeps producing. His hypothesis about the inevitable conflict that his supposed civilizations will undergo is also telling of the intrinsically cruel consequences of a limited and limiting moderate thought.

In capitalism as we know it violence is inevitable (Weber's "monopoly" is a most telling rendition) and is not individual. (How can it be, if the individual is repressed and even impossible to formally acknowledge?) It takes constantly the form of organized, collective violence inflicted by the majority onto occasional minorities.

In fact capitalism can only conceive of occasional disturbances that must be repressed for the sake of governance. A global challenge is not even expressable with the language of the dominant intellectuality.

Revolutionary mobs, armies, police forces, the enforcers of economic policies exert all the time a set of violences onto the weak, because that is the essence of violence (the same actions from the weak to the strong are classified as foolishness, and among equals as a duel or a challenge). We should also notice that the minorities on whom violence is inflicted need not be numerical minorities.

Minority means in fact "weak" (wrong, backward, incompatible, riotous, and the like), in all its possible interpretations, for the elementary maieutics of capitalist intellectuality. Minority also means "other," in the case of Huntington and of many others like him, but that is just a different way to say weak. The point is not to identify possible enemies on whom to enforce violence. If the argument so far unfolded holds, enemies and disturbances to the bubble are infinite and always there: anything could jeopardize an intellectually kept monster.

We should rather concentrate on the collective aspect of the inevitable violence. While in fact it is intuitively easy to see that in an individual-repressing environment the instances of collectivization are the normality, and are necessary, it is important to see the similarity of the mechanisms used to enforce them. The mobs that storm the Bastille are not different from those who defend them, nor are they different, in terms of what binds them, from the disciplined armies and police forces that make up so much of recent history. The difference lies in the degree of formal organization, not in the motives and mechanisms that bind them together.

It is sufficient to look at the determination with which the police charges any demonstrator whosoever, regardless of ideology, social class, and motivation. What counts is to smash the protesters, who are treated by the police like nonhumans who should be beaten to obedience. It goes without saying that this sado-maso dynamic takes place at all levels: at the micro level, between each organized violence enforcer and his/her fellows and leaders, and at the macro level between the beater and the beaten (or murderer and murdered).

There is no denying also that this is not limited to the particular cases relative to institutional or revolutionary violence enforcement. It applies to work relationships, religious relationships, and even family relationships: to all institutionalized relationships involving limitation.

There is no need to be a Reichian to see that this is nothing but the absurd pleasure of sexual abstinence in various degrees that those who belong to a collective/community experience in repressing, sublimating, enhancing, and altering their natural sexual drives. It takes some masters to do it to a good effect in terms of collective discipline, though. "Sexual perverts" find a perfect job for their "abnormalities" in armies, governments, churches, and the like. The shame they feel for their own "perverted" desires is put to good use, and the more shame is felt the more disciplined the outcome is, like Adorno (1989) says in various occasions in the form of aphorisms.

In a world where minoritarian sexual mores were no shame, this would not take place: but the presence, signaled several times through the discussion of the whole book, of moralistic arguments whenever radical arguments should be needed, makes of this relationship between sex and capitalist discipline a vicious circle that cannot be broken. This also goes to reinforce the fascist features of capitalism in practice that we introduced and discussed in the past two chapters.

The usual reply to this kind of argument is not that it is not politically correct, although in the end it is, for it argues for perfect sexual freedom without shame. It is rather that it appears to lead to hypothesizing man as a "rutting pig" (see McCann 2005, Tassone 1999). I see no problem in being a rutting pig, but this is not the point. Behind such arguments is the accusation that one wants to give importance to instincts. This, it is implicated, is a form of "libertinism," a call for immorality.

Once again all is reduced to a count: you want to "do it" too often, and in inappropriate situations. The answer to this is I just want to avoid shame and self-repression and sado-maso outcomes at the economic, political, and social level. Pigs are not ashamed, so the analogy is fair.

Perhaps, for the purposes of this chapter, the best way to represent individuality would be to emphasize what it is not. No straightforward definition can be obtained from the discussion, which leads us to the second point: individuality, given the circumstances, can only be hypothesized as "observation." To understand this we must try to figure out a life without the protective apparatus of capitalist intellectuality as a means to interpret reality.

If we share the same nature as the rest of the concrete, we should not be afraid to participate in the flow of the material itself. That amounts to living to the full, and not by the proxy of our "capitalist" achievements (money, success, morality, agreement, or opposition, capacity to produce syllogisms of complicated and even creative nature, and the like). It is what I call "observation." The idea is that observation and participation, if nature is set free to act on us, are the same thing. Action and observation are also the same thing. Nothing would any longer, therefore, look eternal, or even long-lived. Everything could suddenly disappear, and even be forgotten.

This in relationship to capitalism as we know it would mean that it would be impossible to buy its dominant intellectuality as well as its single outcomes. The Hayek and Von Mises, as well as the Gramsci and Lenin, that have been taken here to signify and represent the banality of the ideas of capitalism and their being shared even by eminent intellectuals at the time of participating in social and economic life, would not fool anybody with their incoherencies and straightforward cruelties. A whole world of new intellectual productions would be open to us.

The presence of what here we can, for the sake of simplicity, call sensual perceptions and sensual drives, would pose the problem of expression. The simplified syntax and grammar of capitalist intercourses in fact is unable to convey the complexity of the results of the action of sensual perception and drives.

The tragic practical problem we face of the trade-off between survival and freedom, that drives our everyday actions and tortures our consciences, is at once an expression of our individuality and of capitalist intellectuality. Here we must be very careful not to go astray, for every direction we take other than materialism is likely to take us back to capitalism, or similar forms of sociality.

We have the inevitable constraints of life that the capillarity of capitalism at all level makes unavoidable. We all have to submit to them until capitalism is destroyed as a whole. But we should not make the mistake of starting from them in planning our emancipation. Here the Marxist vulgata is helpful: in the dialectical madness of capitalism as we know it, behaving dialectically is the only way to survive. But our cries for freedom and emancipation are a different thing from our cries for freedom from wants and emancipation from institutional repression.

The trade-off between survival and freedom is a matter of degrees of the two within the general logic of capitalism as we know it. It is nothing to do with individuality, except in the narrow capitalist sense. Escapist solutions such as those sought by pseudoartists and pseudohippies that pretend to live in splendid isolation are just, in fact, the apotheosis of capitalist mentality.

What we have been saying so far was already quite clear, despite the fundamental historical differences (once again, capitalism's historical incompleteness helps us see mainly the continuities), in the arguments of the Epicureans and of the Stoics in ancient Rome. Their almost suicidal solutions were just a splenetic answer to the tensions I have been referring to and that were partly present in those times as well.

These kinds of solutions keep coming back. Witness Turgenev's *Fathers and Sons* or Dostoyevsky's *The Devils* and Zola's *Germinal*. Terrorism is one hybrid, present-day practical instance. As long as they produce these (theoretical and practical) splenetic results they are bound to be ineffective in the first place, and nonemancipative in the second. They communicate with capitalism on the one hand and end up being ontologically other (hence bound to be recuperated and used through the count) on the other, when they produce death.

A last question must be considered that has been posed since the beginning of the present book: from the point of view of individuality, can economics be reformed, or should it be abandoned? The complete answer to this problem cannot be given here, for it requires some highly technical discussions (e.g., on mathematics) and the development of the taxonomy and genealogy argument.

For the time being, a "Marxist" answer suffices: political economy cannot exist without the study of history, indeed the two are one and the same thing. The point, however, is not the search for an elusive "equilibrium" (the transformation problem is a significant example of this typically bourgeois mistake we shall see next chapter). Reality is fluid and in constant flux despite the capitalist bubble. We cannot crystallize it into a priori formulas of productive departments and of prices deriving from the encroachment of "economic variables" reduced to a mathematical set of behaviors.

The fact that reality has been this way for quite a while is no proof that it is bound to be so forever. We have already shown the reason why the pseudo-mathematical reasonings of economics apply. The point is to give reality a chance not to be amenable to that application any longer.

The role of economics/political economy is to register the continued presence of that applicability: that is why economic theories as we know them should not be forgotten. They serve to explain capitalism, a mode of production that in itself is the archeology of itself. A new political economy should therefore be a set of communicating taxonomies and genealogies of the actual, while waiting for the new to come. But the details of this belong to a next volume.

A question related to this discussion that would greatly interest our imaginary frowning intellectuals would be whether we will need economic theories in anarchic communism, the postrevolutionary scenario. Insofar as that enticing situation is silent in the sense proposed in this book, the answer is an obvious no. There would be no economy and society to speak of. Yet the problem of production for survival would remain, as well as that of distribution. Is that an economic problem?

That would be, in present-day parlance, rather an engineering problem. That would make it, however, a serious difficulty in a world that is open to the possibility of ruptures and oblivion. Engineering is the application of some univocal logics to practical problems: we can calculate the width of a beam, or the amount of N, K, and P needed to grow so many potatoes. How would this incoherence act on a world that has rejected univocal explanations?

Answering this question with the inevitable "I do not know" gives me the chance to show the materialistic attitude in action, with its leaving the material open to supply a solution. The question is the same that anguished Hegel and Marx: take Marx's *First Manuscript* (1968b), especially page 75 and following, where Marx notices the inversion that takes place in the worker, who feels like an animal when he is working and human only when he is indulging in bodily needs and pleasures or in the best hypothesis when he can dress himself or has a home to live in.

The question that requires an answer that cannot be given here, and that nonetheless proves that we must proceed along the materialistic path, is whether man can be compared, and likened, to animals in his bodily activities and needs. Is planting potatoes the same as making honey for a bee or having a symbiosis with *Rhizobium leguminosarum* for a bean plant?

The "silent" argument might point to that solution. But the question remains that man might look, when compared to other animals, ill-equipped for life in the wilderness (this is also hard to satisfactorily prove, but let us accept it for the sake of argument).

Thirdly, and as likely, it might simply be the case that we are overemphasizing the difference between man's and animal's labor, mistakenly prompted by the fact that man's language has produced a huge rhetoric about man's doings and, worse, man's achievements in work.

A fourth, nonresolutive point has also been made earlier on when stating that even in anarchist communism man might make a mess of planet Earth. Although I can see no problem entailed by this question that could simply be wrongly posed, I'd like to finish this section leaving it hanging in the air.

CONCLUSIONS

With this chapter we have elucidated a few important consequences and nuances of the general argument of this book. The materialism produced here is of a naturalistic kind. It means individual emancipation. This last is a lonely endeavor in which we are all involved and that we must pursue on our own.

The whole argument of the book has been, I hope, clarified by the discussion of "revolution." This has at last specified the tremendous difference in terms of sheer communication between what is being proposed here and what the market of anticapitalist culture supplies us with.

A glimpse into a possible alternative to capitalism should both raise the right issues and entice us to go on by exciting our fantasy and whetting our appetite for the unknown. This last is the condition to go on with this work, and it is very painful to have to say this. When one feels he has to stimulate the desire for the unknown, times are hard.

The argument of this chapter is a final criticism of all those who have been passing themselves off as the defenders of capitalist and anticapitalist utopias. It takes more than social order to have capitalism, and more than organized mobs to tear it down. Above all, it takes more than tolerating these two attitudes to call oneself a defender or an opposer of capitalism.

NOTES

1. See Micocci (2000a, 2002a).

2. I doubt that Spinoza would approve of what Althusser, Negri, and their followers make of his philosophy. But considering that the exegesis of his work has always produced incoherent results, perhaps he would not mind that much.

3. The thrifty capitalist is far from being a myth. We meet them everywhere, in their luxury cars and yachts that are never as luxurious as they could be. Plus, the amount of work they have to perform to stay rich simply prevents them from having the time to enjoy what their wealth can afford them.

4. One might object that all good scholarship requires you to continuously select what is good. This would be true: but then comes the mediation/moderation character of dialectical forms of thinking that does not let you throw anything away and greatly limits your efforts to keep to what is best.

5. I should make clear here that the repeated appeal to senses made throughout the present book is not an Epicurean call for pure sensism. A method and a connection with science is needed but must be predicated on the theory and practice of detachment.

6. I interpret this way the very difficult expression *"aequalitate substantiae spiritus humani."*

7. Vico is concentrating on Bacon's *Cogitata et Visa De Interpretatione Naturae* (2004, 186).

8. There are much imprecision and sweeping generalizations in these statements. We shall see this fault to be systematic in Vico.

9. As usual Vico justifies his argument with unlikely etymologies. To our purposes, one cannot help seeing the analogy with fascist pure action, so important in Gramsci.

10. Very willingly I concede to Croce that here too Vico was prescient: his table looks remarkably like those useless tables and charts that are inflicted on us by PowerPoint in lectures and conferences.

11. Quoted on the back cover of the Paolo Rossi edition of *Vico's La Scienza Nuova* (2004) that I have used here.

12. "There seems no reason to doubt that nearly all the chief pioneers of progress have been Aryans" (278). On page 247 (chapter 8 on "Industrial Organization"), he praises Eugenics.

13. Such a position holds, and deems acceptable, tremendously different and even incompatible opinions on basic issues. For instance, evolutionists and creationists live together and tolerate "third" incompatible options (e.g., the extraterrestrial origin of man).

14. I fail to understand why religious people fear so much disappearance (death), given that we all are mortal and that they enjoy the advantage of going to Heaven. I also fail to understand why nonreligious people fear death, on the Epicurean grounds

that once dead you will be nothing, and will not suffer. Considering the disregard of the natural intrinsic to moderate positions, it seems evident that both categories have made up intellectual fears because they lack the natural, immediate fear of death we are all endowed with.

15. I should thank, without involving them in any way, Nino Pardjanadze, Luciano Vasapollo, Massimiliano Biscuso, Paolo Quintili and Alessandro Mazzone for patient discussions on this topic. It is sad that I am not discussing this any longer with the old comrades who have survived the 1977 movement. I should also thank Fred Halliday and his course on revolutions in the international system I attended at the LSE. I do not know whether he ever continued teaching it.

16. Present-day capitalism has given birth to new varieties of exploitation: the indirect type ensuing from layoffs, deregulation, and flexibility. The working logic and the result are the same.

17. Sometimes we win, though.

18. See Micocci (2002a), ch. 3, and especially 3.2.1.

19. The market's iterativeness burns resources, human and natural, as a matter of routine. Here the Greens, were they able to strengthen their reasons, would be right.

20. In *Anti-Hegelian Reading* (2002a) I conceptualized this argument by means of the category of the "unbound individual."

21. This is not a religious argument, nor is it idealistic. Like sex, its working out, and the time it takes is unpredictable, and it might not happen at all.

22. I put this remark in a footnote because it is obvious to me. I am delineating as a first approximation what individuals would be like vis-à-vis reality (nature). Some might misunderstand it, and so here is the disclaimer: I am not talking about a new science.

23. Here the need for a communist life is evident, for it would help the freedom here hinted at by depriving each of us of material properties, endowing us with the means to live without involving us in "politics."

Chapter Seven

Like Cut Flowers

The role of a final chapter is that of drawing the argument to a conclusion while summarizing it and showing the coherence of the whole. We shall do all of these things here, with a difference. I shall in fact summarize and complete the argument of this volume by going to the core of the process of valorization, so often referred to in the preceding pages as the center of everything we have been describing.

In preceding ages that were not endowed with an exclusive (dialectical) mediation/separation of man from nature, the idea of a value for the product of human labor was nonsensical, or when present it depended on so many, and so different, variables that it was aleatory and unruly.[1] It could not be explained by general rules, and therefore could not be linked to any hypostatized historical trend, or to that typical capitalist artifact known as human nature.

With capitalism what used to be absurd has become possible: economic explanations make sense because human reality is poor and predictable in its general behavior (not in the single results), and human beings are tied to the "iron cage" of their separation from nature. This consists in, as said, their having to perform natural activities only through the presence of a dominant, elementary, and univocal type of intellectual mediation.

Value in this framework can be imagined as existing and must be assigned according to the said univocal logic of mediation between man and nature, man and man, man and his labor. It exists as such for the first time, unleashing avarice and thrifty, accumulating behavior. Regularities are imposed, and value can be ascertained in monetary terms, for money has gained its modern role.

This basic regularity, with all its social consequences, allows, and even seems to prove, the whole set of dialectical relationships that we have been

describing in this book. That is why economists can (indeed, they must) start
their reasonings from the "Robinsonades" we have seen in chapters 2 and 3,
and that is why they attribute to "capitalism" a dynamism that is precisely the
opposite of the iterative reality of capitalism as we know it.

The processes of capitalist circulation can thus take place even when the
rest of reality, as repeatedly argued, has not been able to update itself to the
capitalist canons. Value can be attributed with the apparent equanimity of a
social law that keeps the game going. It is time to look at the subtleties of this
complex matter in order to see with the needed clarity the complete picture of
capitalism as we know it.

THE SO-CALLED TRANSFORMATION PROBLEM

The present section is the outcome of three published papers (2005c, 2006b,
2006c) I produced at the invitation of Luciano Vasapollo and of Micocci
(2007e, 2008d). To Vasapollo go my thanks while I lift from him any responsibility for what I say here.

The natural starting point to explain in detail the functioning of the process
of valorization is obviously Adam Smith (1999). Adam Smith's world presented him with the unprecedented set of potentialities that have been referred
to ever since as the invisible hand. That is meant to indicate the transfer of
economic initiative from various kinds of primitive dealings to the potentially
explosive power of free private initiative. But this meant a number of incoherencies hard to reconcile with each other and with the general framework.

In the first place, as we have noticed already, it meant the acceptance of,
and identification with, the nation-state.[2] That in Smith meant the acknowledgement of the role of the state institutions as managers of the two basic
tools of international affairs: war and trade. As a consequence of this old (Medieval) pattern of state-to-state relationships made of war/invasion and trade
(or, alternatively, beggar-thy-neighbor, protectionism, isolation, self-sufficiency, import substitution growth, etc.), economic theory has been viewing
international trade with the same spectacles as the behavior of individuals.
"States" trade—they regulate their "openness" to foreign goods according to
patterns of wealth accumulation determined by the manipulation of "comparative advantages."

Although as discussed earlier the general meaning of the comparative advantages argument points to the absolute convenience to trade, the theory
hosts its own negation in its theoretical core. The presence of states in the first
place, and the potentially endless number of exceptions (from infant industry
to the Leontief paradox, to underdevelopment, to the presence of multina-

tional corporations, just to mention a few banal instances), return international trade to the iterative, unevolutionary pattern of all the rest under capitalism we have been seeing in this book.

Imperialism, which we have treated in chapter 5, follows suit. So does state-led management of the economy, be it favorable to oligopolies—liberal, socialist, or neoliberal. Transactions are taken to signify increases, or alternatively decreases, of monetarily defined wealth: economic transactions are what a state's economic activity is about. The economy becomes, without distorting in any way Adam Smith's argument, a set of processes you can render by means of the measurement of Gross National Product (GNP)/Gross Domestic Product (GDP)[3]

This observation lands us upon the second main set of problems Adam Smith, and all of his mainstream and Marxist epigones, present: a profound, and unsettling, difference between material and nonmaterial wealth. To Smith, and to the Marxists, wealth/opulence (Smith freely exchanges these two terms, to signify the accomplished identity between the wealth of the individual and the opulence of the nation) should be linked to a material base on which economic operators supposedly work. Economic activities should primarily be labor activities of transformation of material items into exchangeable (if and when needed) goods.

Yet, if everything so far said is true, there is a nonmaterial type of wealth. Adam Smith, seeking a coherence between his belief in the material nature of opulence and his acceptance of the state and the sovereign and of the entailed war-trade alternative at the international level, linked it to the presence of trade. Throughout Smith (1999) is desperate to point out[4] that the basis for a nation's opulence is in the production of material goods. Yet, he must acknowledge that trade, which we can identify here with money-based (value) rather than goods-based dealings, can be a much more powerful aid to GNP growth than material production.

He has to acknowledge (Vol. 1, 1999, 515–16) that "the commerce and manufacture of cities, instead of being the effect, have been the cause and occasion of the improvement and cultivation of the country." "The silent and insensible operation of foreign commerce and manufacture gradually brought about what the violence of the feudal institutions could never have effected" (512).[5]

Such order, however, is "contrary to the natural course of things" (516). Despite his opposition to thinking economic wealth in money/gold terms (take his praising the Tartars vis-à-vis the Spaniards, Vol. 2, 6), he has to acknowledge their dynamic power: "Money is neither a material to work upon, nor a tool to work with, [but] . . . real revenue consists, not in the money, but in the money's worth" (Vol. 1, 1999, 392).

Neoclassical economics' utility theory of value, which has set the foundations for the mainstream approach by transferring the basis of economics to transactions rather than production, does not contribute to solve the problem. It just helps to see the relevance of using GDP/GNP to measure economic activity in capitalism as we know it. The fact that economics can measure, and act upon, what it deals with, as has been proved in the course of this volume and in Micocci (2002a), is precisely the proof of its epistemic impotence.

The question, however, is purely empirical—that is, actual: material and virtual wealth are not the same thing. Worse, the latter has power over the former.

Both forms of wealth operate at once, with material wealth tied to the limits of its material nature and virtual wealth free to define its own bounds. In fact money is not, in our times of financialization of the economies (see e.g., Glyn 2006; Vasapollo 2007), nor was it ever Adam Smith's money's worth. It is, and was, Marx's tool of self-defined multiplicability, whose links to the material items are, if at all present, hazy and formal. Virtual wealth (as long as it is defined, i.e., operated, in money/gold terms) is not only the bearer of the mechanism whereby capitalist relationships are acknowledged and practiced. Virtual wealth, once defined and given a value, sets its own infinite multiplicability by leaving behind its supposed ties to material wealth.

The limits to the multiplication of virtual wealth are determined by two sets of circumstances. The first is the war and trade alternative at the international level. The second is the market, in a paradox that is only apparent. If in fact we had the free market of capitalism—what is opportunely relegated to the theory (the capitalist impossible)—the expansion of virtual, and secondarily of material wealth, would be bound by the coming of "Walrasian" equilibria, to which a static state corresponds. This needs some elaboration.

That Walrasian equilibria are static is a long-recognized truth on which there is no need to dwell. Reflecting on why, despite this, the dominant approach in mainstream economics is based on general equilibrium would be very enlightening, but is also beside the point here.

What matters instead is the fact that while the classical economists, at least with Mill (1998), were worried by the possibility of a "stationary state" as the final outcome of economic activity, neoclassical economists have successfully worked at eliminating this kind of preoccupation. On the one hand capitalism is attributed by definition with a dynamic nature, especially, but not only, to do with technology. On the other, attempts to supply general equilibrium with dynamism are rejected and/or ignored, sweeping the problem under the carpet.

Yet there is no denying that after Walras's ripples in the mountain lake, or Schumpeter's *kreislauf*, there is a static situation waiting for a savior. In plain words, if we had a market working like it should—if we had the free market—we would soon end up in a sort of stationary state both at the domestic and at the international level. Profit enhancement and differentiation would disappear or be confined to windfall situations that, if the free market worked unfettered in practice, would be only and exclusively theoretical.

Fortunately for our hypocritical free-market supporters, we do not have any of that, nor are we progressing a single inch in that direction. The war and trade alternative, the presence of the nation-state, the obsolete political institutions that capitalism has so carefully preserved, the unresolved virtual-material wealth dilemma, by imposing the dialectical mystifying intellectuality they come from, have evoked those monsters (imperialism, protectionism/neoliberism, fascism, socialism) we have been seeing in action in this volume and of course in reality. Like free trade, the idea of equilibrium has gone in practice, thus ensuring its solid presence in theory: not just in economic theory, but in the general logic (intellectuality) of capitalism as we know it.

The compulsory production and exchange of goods that has followed "once the division of labor has been thoroughly established" (Smith, Vol. 1, 1999, 127) has transformed man into a "merchant" (a euphemism that indicates the necessity to trade everything for a living, and the consequent obligation to sell one's labor power, oneself), society into a "commercial society" (127), and "all countries" have been united in this game of domestic and international commerce by "giving preference" to money/precious metals for the exchanges (127).

This is, centuries after Adam Smith first stated it, the incoherent core of the capitalist (as we know it) economy and polity. Economic theories have a practical use under it: they share in the same nature and the same basic incoherencies, with the ensuing omissions. We are quickly approaching the nature of value.

Thus, the value of any commodity

> to the person who possesses it and who means not to use it or consume it for himself, but to exchange it for other commodities, is equal to the quantity of labor which it enables him to purchase or command. Labor, therefore, is the real measure of the exchangeable value of all commodities. (Vol. 1, 1999, 133)

But the man who intends to exchange a product he does not use or consume himself is not the capitalist man. He is man before turning into a compulsory merchant in a commercial society by means of the division of labor.

Only with the division of labor and the coming of commercial society we have mass production. Hence, in Smith's and Marx's times we have the war and trade alternative, plus a proletariat practicing class struggle (just to mention a few salient characteristics); in our days outsourcing, financialization, an impoverished mass, class struggle (performed more often by the capitalists than by the oppressed classes), war, and trade. The dynamism of the economies is granted, or more precisely replaced, by noneconomic variables.

Institutional interventions, war, class struggle, the fictitious technological and commercial revolutions we have seen, are among the factors that allow the economies to grow and have their crises, pursuing the self-fulfilling prophecy of economic cycles.

Hence,

1. "Though labor be the real measure of the exchangeable value [of] commodities, it is not that by which it is commonly estimated" (Smith, Vol. 1, 1999, 134).
2. Therefore, "some allowance is commonly made" (134) not by "accurate measure" but by the bargaining of the market (everything nonmarket that actually replaces the market is here comprised), at a level of precision sufficient for "carrying on the business of common life" (134).
3. In other words, commodities are "more frequently exchanged for, and thereby compared with, other commodities than labor" (134).
4. "Every particular commodity is more frequently exchanged for money" (135). The conclusion is inevitable as it is clear: although "labor alone is the ultimate and real standard, or real price, money is the nominal price" (136).

But although labor "from century to century" is the only "universal . . . measure of value" (136), it is the nominal or money price of the goods that governs economic intercourses (141): common life. There is a hiatus between man and the capitalist man, defined by the lack of determination of the value of exchangeable goods, which corresponds to the hiatus sought for in economic theory in the solution of the transformation (of values into prices) problem. Under capitalism as we know it the market, that does not exist, determines in practice the value and price of things (of everything, potentially, another fundamental difference from precapitalist times) independently from their relationship to their material origin.[6] The metaphysics in its glory is at work. Value is given only empirically.

We have reached the core of the logic of capitalism as we know it. Let us translate it into a rigorous language, not contaminated by the faulty logic of the social sciences.

The attribution of value to tradeable objects in capitalism as we know it is determined by the reality of economic and political intercourses and by the institutional necessity to communicate it, making it explicit through a money price. Money has the role of Jesus Christ of commodities discussed in the preceding chapters, which ensures the mutual recognizability of the participants in the exchange, and of the exchange itself. That is why all this, when acted out in practice, is referred to, when formally talked of (i.e., always, even when operated in apparent silence) and described (this rarely happens), the laws of the market that economic theory, mainstream and mainstream Marxist, are about, despite the actual place where the transaction has taken place not even resembling such laws.

The implicit or explicit references to the laws of economic theory are compulsory and inevitable. The deal in fact is valid only in that it is practiced as a reference to a general logic. Otherwise, it would be dangerous to go back to a primitive form of exchange, without capitalist features. The presence of money is not sufficient, for in extreme cases it could even be thought of in the precapitalist terms of pieces of metal and paper meant to facilitate trade, for instance, by their transportability/circulability.

In these conditions it appears evident that economic intercourses are what GDP/GNP are about. Transactions with a nominal money price are what is needed. The problems that afflict Adam Smith's *Wealth of Nations* and contemporary economic theories—the set of phenomena summarizable as war and trade and the different role of material and virtual wealth—can blur to the point of becoming invisible. They are downgraded to the category of economic transactions and consigned both to economic theory and to actual capitalist practice.

The question of the material/virtual nature of wealth/opulence is very interesting to our purposes. This difference should have struck the classical political economists as important to spot the tendencies of capitalism once the momentum of the Industrial Revolution was gone. This has not happened, although we must exclude in part Marx from this mistake, for he clearly saw the potentially autonomous power of capital (although this only led to Hilferding, Luxembourg, and Lenin's imperialism).

In the world we have just described virtual capital is by far the most economically dynamic thing we can think of. Given its metaphysical endowments that make it simultaneously a repository of value and a guarantee of reciprocal capitalist homogeneity between the persons and the institutions, and its virtual nature, it can ride the electromagnetic waves: the means of communication. Its last speculative links to material production such as its employment in speculations concerning the price of commodities, have become a secondary, obsolete feature. Now it works on its own, using itself for its own multiplication. You still need the firm form often and the war and trade international environment, but capitalism is well on its way to liberating all of its autonomous metaphysical potentialities.

Vasapollo and collaborators (2004) and Sylos Labini (2004) are just two of an endless list of authors dealing in various ways with this phenomenon (see

Glyn 2006 as well) that looks new despite being as old as capitalism as we know it. It is worth quoting what Kropotkin was writing in 1879:

> Capital . . . accumulated in the hands of a few escapes . . . agriculture and in-
> dustry [because] there are more advantageous employments! It . . . will feed
> wars . . . or one day it will serve to create a shareholding company, that will not
> deal with production of anything, but will be simply directed to shamefully fail
> in two years [and] it will be used in building useless railroads . . . but above all
> . . . the Stock Exchange is big game. The capitalist will speculate on the ficti-
> tious oscillations . . . in politics, on value increases produced by some rumour
> of reform . . . Agiotage killing industry, that is what we should call the intelli-
> gent administration of businesses. (no year, 37–38, translation mine)[7]

Things are only worse in our days (Blackburn 2008, 91):

> A well-regulated stock exchange is a phenomenal source of information for all
> market participants. . . . The analytic feats of the financial economists were
> themselves based on such data. Yet the advent of structured finance generated a
> gigantic volume of direct trades between institutions whose details were only
> known to the participants. These over-the-counter transactions exceeded stock-
> exchange transactions . . . and led the exchanges to skimp on procedure in order
> to remain competitive. Here we have both the cause of the credit crunch and the
> ultimate irony of the western crusade to marketize the globe. . . . It succeeded in
> submerging the world's main capital markets in a deluge of non-performing and
> unpriced securities. The fog of grey capital descended on the financial districts,
> shrouding the great banks and clouding the view of investors and regulators
> alike.

There is an evident logic in all this. In a self-contained world that bases itself on a faulty intellectuality that shields it from the variability of nature and
of man's intellect, financial deals are the most consistent form of activity. But
financial economic activities present capitalism as we know it with the "problem" of its own fragility. This can potentially unleash all of the phenomena
typical of capitalist intellectuality we have seen.

That is why we should not underestimate material production. In its unim-
portance in terms of enhancement of individual and social wealth/opulence,
it is necessary to the whole. It serves to remind everybody that the material
can be dominated—dealt with economically and politically—and yet it can
inflict pain (unemployment, hunger, natural disasters, excuses for war). Also,
it is there to prove what technology can achieve, and we are back to square
one in the useless mainstream economic terms.

What about the transformation problem that has aroused so much rage for
so long and that despite being declared dead several times resurfaces every

now and then, to go back to oblivion again? We can exclude, to start with, the mainstream utility solution. We have seen that it skips the issue, nesting it in a theory that is useful in practice because it is worthless in theory. The utility theory of value is one of the many useful fictions of mainstream theory, like the marginalistic approach and its mathematical derivatives justly derided by Sylos Labini (2004). Like everything in mainstream theory, it is there to be dispensed with in practice.[8]

We can also discard the Marxist approaches to the question, for they base themselves upon various forms of *tableau economique* that require one type or another of equilibrium.[9] The transformation, we have been showing so far, simply consists in the actual practice of capitalism as we know it. While it has a theoretical explanation, which we have sketched above, and an actual functioning going on, it has no solution. Actual processes, taking place in the metaphysics of capitalism as we know it, affect the material. The question is rather why Marxists have been bothered so much by it.

What scares mainstream Marxists is not the lack of solution to the problem, which has proved to be no difficulty in practice. What terrifies them is that their full immersion, by means of their understanding of class struggle as the path to socialism, in the metaphysics of capitalism, is jeopardized. They cannot get a neat and uncontroversial theoretical rate of exploitation, for instance (a labor theory of value is not proved unless you solve the transformation problem, in their view). This is, I am afraid, just part of the "inculcation of the right values" that Arthur (see chapter 3) so impertinently talks about.

As a matter of fact not only everybody sees the existence of exploitation under capitalism as we know it. Nobody with ears, eyes, and a heart, however steeped in the subtleties of the dominant mentality, would be able to deny it. It is there. So are the effects of the varying organic composition of capital (e.g., outsourcing). So are the absurdities of the existence of private property, states, wars, nationalisms, and so on.

The working of the metaphysics of capitalism defuses the rupture and oblivion consequences when describing reality and acting upon it. Take a worker, or a middle-class person in any country, and ask them: they can list the injustices of capitalism and their indignation at them. Take any Marxist work, and everything is there: even the indignation. And yet no reformist or revolutionary action has ever eliminated any of the capitalist faults. What their discourses lack is consequence. Their way of putting things, however precise their rendition, is impotent.

The "appropriate values" that are supposedly in need of inculcation are as impotent. They can only express themselves as interventions on the system, thus playing the dialectical game and consigning themselves to the moderate, nonrevolutionary intellectual routines of capitalism as we know it. This is no problem in itself. But it is the endless source of that blind, collective violence that has marked capitalist history: in order to make dialectical means change reality, you have only dialectical means. Evil is a flawed logic for the understanding of, and intervention upon, reality.

INTELLECTUAL DRIFT

The sketch of what capitalism is about and that we have been developing in this book is now complete. We can draw some conclusions of a general nature. The first and foremost is the fact that there is no room for the individual. Single persons exist only in that they can, instead of living their life, practice it according to an all-encompassing maieutics dictated by a general intellectuality—let me say it once more—that is, limited and limiting.

Nobody is free to leave this self-enforced bubble because nobody is allowed to work out solutions in terms of ruptures with oblivion. Whatever alternative is envisaged to the present, ahistorical, hypostatized state of things can only be dialectical: this is not to say that it is impossible to admit in one's thought of the presence of ruptures and oblivions. It means that there is a thorough incommunicability and incompatibility between these two visions. The moderate inner logic of the whole is the only one operating in practice. It does so not by omitting the needed clash of ideas. It simply rules out, by declaring it a priori impossible, all extreme ideas implying ruptures and oblivion.

A univocal intellectual logic is almost impossible to challenge in the first place. Secondly, there is the glamour and comfortableness of evil. A limited and limiting understanding of, and action upon, reality as a whole is evil. There are innumerable instances of this in reality (the last and most astonishing being Bush Jr.'s handling of Afghanistan and Iraq), but as usual we shall stick to theory.

What are Weber's monopoly of violence, or Hayek's view of the working of the market, or Lenin's dialectical ramblings, but erudite versions of evil? Why should a cop or a money-value-price relationship or a member of a revolutionary party have a right to kill or maim and feel excused and justified? The answer is simple: the moderate pattern of thought of capitalism as we know it is a way to justify its violence and simultaneously soothe, with the same arguments, both its perpetrators and its victims.

Plus, there is the lure of violence to consider. In these conditions in fact violence is the closest thing to natural emotions the capitalist man has at hand. Exceeding with it always happens within the limits of the general logic (that is why it can be punished), and yet it has the glamour of the "beastly outburst" it cannot be.

Lombroso (1994), whom we take here for his being representative of the capitalist age and for his concern for the stability of the institutions, put it beautifully.[10] What distinguishes revolutionaries from terrorists for him is not just altruism and a peculiarly beautiful mind and body (all translations are mine):

> More than that it is the lack of that "misoneismo" [fear of the new] that is in all men, and above all in men of little culture like some of them are. (87)

In fact,

> anarchists and Fenians, regicides have a complete criminal type. . . . while the true revolutionaries . . . present an absolutely normal type, even more handsome than average (23). These offenders because of pure passion are, for their honesty, the opposite, the antithesis of born-criminals. (53)

Very interestingly, to Lombroso, in order to prevent the presence of anarchists and revolutionaries due to the

> general "discrasia" . . . [we must change] first of all the basis of our practical education, which in the admiration of beauty, and even more of violence without a practical aim, leads us directly to rebellion. (103)

A classical education, with its grand ideals of beauty and morality, is an impending danger for capitalism as we know it. Fortunately for Lombroso, who was sympathetic to it, "socialism, despite being believed by incapable politicians . . . a trusty ally of anarchism, is instead its greatest enemy and the best preventive remedy" (106).

> Socialism, in sum, confutes anarchist theories before those very social groups that are more seduced by it, with the conclusion we formed experimentally . . .: it shows, that is, that no new political or economic form arrives if it is not prepared most slowly—only a slow, ordered change in the capitalist system [will bring economic justice, eliminating revolutionary ideals]. (107)

The intellectual activity of individuals must be relieved of all those items and ideas that predispose to abstract thinking. But the solution is not, despite Lombroso, in eliminating the great ideals of classical authors from education. Individuals do not need to be educated to great ideals to be able to conceive of nonmoderate ideas. The very exhaustion caused by the boredom of the continuous iteration prevents individuals from listening to their inner compulsions (which hopefully are many more than the altruism Lombroso feared so much). This too would not be enough, however.

What destroys independence in individuals is the fact that not only are you surrounded by a homogeneously limited and limiting environment but also that the market of the theory does not exist and therefore nobody is expelled and destroyed. Some are actually killed or maimed, but that, we saw, poses them ontologically out of the reach of capitalism as we know it.

Thus what happens is that this intellectual monster keeps moving, grinding its way to no outcome—to its own survival as such—disguised as change, revolution, or at least a constant danger of change and revolution.

The intellectual nature of capitalism as we know it can, and indeed must, entertain relationships with its own incommunicable and incompatible enemies; for instance, revolution as anarchism-nihilism-communism. It is precisely this failed relationship that supplies it with that degree of actual movement that transforms its intellectual *motore immobile* into a vague, hardly perceptible intellectual drift. Such drift, whose manifestations are various and depend upon the phases of the capitalist cycle, is the closest concession capitalism as we know it can make to historical evolution.[11]

The intellectual drift of capitalism is yet another *motore immobile* whose outcome usually boils down to pseudorevolutions with the ensuing true repressions, Negri's and Hardt's indignations of the multitude. Putting down such phenomena with violence is justified from the institutional and from the general, intellectual point of view: it is, as we have proposed in this chapter, evil. It is not a sudden outburst of violence on either side, which could be thought of as innocent and natural, but a premeditated and accepted bowing to a faulty logic and to the organized violence ensuing.

All this leads us to the need to say a few final words about the role of economics, the social sciences, and philosophy.

A first and important conclusion is that economics and the social sciences can only be pursued by returning them to a wider and rigorous logical frame that only philosophy can supply. This is different from multidisciplinarity. Economics and the social sciences need a logical base that comprises all the logical possibilities supplied by nature's evolution: by the material. Only this way can they hope to grasp the actual, the material.

The great problem that a materialistic stance in philosophy poses to us is not that of accepting the presence of ruptures and oblivions, frightening as it might look to those used to dialectical patterns of thought. It is not the discovery of the stunted development of capitalism and the evil ensuing. It is not the possible end of the social sciences, either.

Materialism, by identifying the sources of our own limitations, poses us before the issue of the natural, which is independent from us and from our logic: words do not capture it, let alone convey it. Lombroso identified this with the altruism of the revolutionary, reducing it to the poverty of a capitalist category. I have been tempted to call it instinct, in polemic with the natural sciences that attribute to instincts in animals great importance but are unable to tell us what they are and how they work.

At this stage of the discussion, however, and given the nature of the present volume, we should call them the inner compulsions of individuals. This permits us to individuate them by means of recognizable phenomena. Take, to mention only what has repeatedly been dealt with, the psychological repression capitalism as we know it enforces on us, the boredom deriving from its working, the hiatus between amorous rapture (sex) and any other kind of rapture we are allowed by economic and social reality, and the ambivalent feelings generated by the victims of capitalism (their ontological disappearance satisfies us only on certain occasions).

The number of things out there that we do not even take notice of, which capitalism as we know it denies and which materialism infinitely can push us back to. There is in all of us the excitement of the unknown. It either draws us to, or pushes us away from, this as yet undescribable infinity of possibilities. It is time we started to at least acknowledge its presence in us, if it were only to admit a lack of courage to pursue it.

But if that is so, then Lombroso, and the high priests of capitalism as we know it, will not get what they want by pulling us away from Plutarch and the classics of ancient and modern philosophy. The philosophical drive toward and against the unknown and its infinite possibilities is in us; *misoneismo* is in the dominant culture of capitalism only.

Pursuing the philosophical drive is the only way to break with the compulsory dialogue that we have with capitalism as we know it. Such pursuit is endless and will hopefully lead far from evil as above defined, for it leads away from capitalism as we know it and from pursuing the useful and the practical.

There is nothing original in this conclusion. In a divulgative work, the *Convivio* (1980), which Dante Alighieri claimed to have written in order to entice readers to undertake "philosophy" in the ancient sense of "rigorous knowledge," we read,

> "Nè si dee chiamare vero filosofo colui che è amico di sapienza per utilitade, sì come sono li legisti, [li] medici e quasi tutti li religiosi, che non per sapere studiano ma per acquistare moneta e dignitade; e chi desse loro quello che acquistare intendono, non sovrastarebbero allo studio." (XI, Trattato Terzo, 187) (We should not call a true philosopher he who is a friend of knowledge for reasons of utility, such as legal experts, medical doctors, and most of the religious scholars, who study not in order to learn but to gain money and positions; if we gave them what they want, they would not be studying. Translation mine)

The need for communism in an anarchist sense stems from this as immediate. The pursuit of knowledge (i.e., philosophy) is independent from worldly positions and properties and from useful practical sciences; only through the elimination of positions and property can we pursue it. The pursuit itself is a way to break with capitalism as we know it and to achieve anarchist communism. This is revolution in practice, without evil. It is up to each of us, and its practice needs no tool and no propaganda. There is no "historically ripe" moment to start it and achieve it: it is free from practically minded thinkers.

Lastly, it is imperative to notice that this means that with a materialistic philosophy we are, at least potentially, challenging science too, at a methodological level. It might well be that the natural sciences will come out identical from a materialistic scrutiny. But we do not know yet, and that is enough to whet our appetites.

WITHERED INDIVIDUALITY

The work we have done in this volume—the exploration in the name of a rigorous materialism of what we have called capitalism as we know it—is at once banal and different from anything that has been written about this topic. One difference worth discussing briefly here is that which separates it from the many theories that claim that we are assigned a role to play by the economic, political, and institutional setup. From Weber to Debord to writers of literature (for instance Pirandello, Musil, P. K. Dick), many have argued that capitalism allots a role to play for each of us. This volume has proved that this is not true.

The various roles we are playing in capitalism as we know it are the jagged tips of the iceberg of the dominant mentality. They offer only a formal, external variety that is negligible when compared to what cannot be seen of the iceberg. Plus, simply and more importantly, ice is what an iceberg is, its tips as well as its massive body below water. There is only one role we are allotted by capitalism as we know it. It is given by the reciprocal, mutual recognition determined by the process of valorization and is expressed in the same form in all its apparently multiform manifestations. Each of us could perform equally well in any role, or equally bad, for that matter.

It is worth going back to the miserable, sedulous fools we mentioned in the introduction, who refuse to get their hands dirty at raising broilers but willingly help Microsoft vex its customers. These unfortunates take, evidently, some pride in their contributing to technology and to the economic and social evolution ensuing from "technological" improvement. Broiler breeding feeds people but does not directly help innovation, especially of "frontline" technology.

There is one basic principle in technology, however, that makes one feel pity for it: it must be usable and repairable, or it must not be at all. Anybody can therefore handle it, with a bit of application. Thus Joseph Conrad can trust the engine of the boat that leads to the discovery of Kurtz in *Heart of Darkness* to

> the savage who was fireman. He was an improved specimen; he could fire a vertical boiler. . . . To look at him was as edifying as seeing a dog in a parody of breeches and a feather hat, walking on his hind-legs. A few months of training had done for that really fine chap. . . . He ought to have been clapping his hands and stamping his feet on the bank, instead of which he was at work, a thrall to a strange witchcraft, full of improving knowledge. (1989, 140)

Nobody is saved from the pervasive power of capitalism as we know it. A few months, and savages who can only stamp their feet on the bank of the river at the passage of a motorboat are engineers blowing the engine's whistle with justified pride. Even for free, such is the satisfaction. Or at the risk of their lives. No wonder one can hardly get a thing done on a computer without problems and interruptions. Individuals, despite the waste of physical and mental effort at tasks that are supposed to make capitalism progress, are sterile even in relation to their capitalist tasks.

Like cut flowers in a vase they live a withered, bland, and useless life. They are allowed to continue with their physiological activities for as long as the life breath that is in their bodies can operate, feeding on the water they are given. They blossom, their flowers open their petals and protrude sexual organs that can even have a perfunctory, bland, and joyless attempt at sex. But even in the unlikely case of seeds being produced, these would fall on a table's surface, or a floor, and reach only as far as the rubbish bin. Like the rest, they are perfunctory, bland, weak, and withered, and contain no life.

The flowers themselves, vice versa, can continue their physical presence indefinitely. The more thoroughly and homogeneously they get withered, the more durable they get. They pass to perform a much more appreciated role: that of simulacra, a still life. Such simulacra have the great capitalist (as we know it) capacity to spare those who relate to them the pain of witnessing their decay from formerly live, colored living beings, for they have a role rather than a life.

Some flowers may never reach this beautifully withered stage, for they lose their petals and purpose in the process, which puts them ontologically out of the system and down the rubbish bin, unless technology, by means of pressing them between the pages of a book, does not upgrade them with their unlucky similes.

But the most important thing is that despite the sterility of the withered, bland functions these plants have, there is an endless supply of them out there. The vases in our flats can endlessly host the sad process we have just described because out of the flats themselves are two huge reservoirs of flowers to cut: wilderness and cultivated fields. We can break and maim wild plants, or grow and harvest domesticated species, and make our homes gay with cut flowers to remind us that life means death, in a one-way process where time does not count.

Capitalism as we know it relies, like the housekeepers who fill our homes with cut flowers, on the natural, be it wild or domesticated. That moment of naturalness it allows out of it is the source of survival for its artificial, deadly, and above all sterile, iterative, and boring mechanism. Homes can get gay and colored because flowers are gay by definition; little matter that those flowers we have so carelessly spread are bland and lifeless and condemned to a perfunctory set of limited and limiting fake life acts.

Whether we accept a domesticated or a wild naturalness, the question is that every time we indulge in a natural act, bodily or intellectual, we supply capitalism with another withered item to consign to its sterile, iterative sadness. We are not serving capitalism by participating in it, for this is as sterile as it is unavoidable. We are serving capitalism as we know it by continuing operating natural acts as episodes.

Intellectual and bodily emancipation is, naturally enough, impossible to define in its full import at this stage. What we have are those bits and pieces that are actually possible every now and then because we have the time to practice them, occasionally. The question, the core of the present argument, is that we must subtract ourselves from the working of capitalism as we know it. There is only one way to do so: pursuing naturalness to the full by abdicating the intellectual mediating (moderate) attitude toward things. That means practicing philosophy. This is what materialism is about, intellectually and bodily. This is what revolution is about.

EPILOGUE

Hypothetical readers who have gone as far as this point of the book might want a proof of their having understood the argument. Here it is.

By discussing the general determining characteristics of capitalism as we know it rather than the empty category of capitalism, I have sought to show the basic features and consequences of a materialistic approach to the study of reality. This has allowed me, or so I hope, to show the emancipative power of a materialistic philosophical stance, which could lead us to break ourselves free as individuals from capitalism as we know it. The reader who thinks, and feels, that I have painted a gloomy picture has not understood the argument. Reality is neither good nor bad: reality is reality. The succession of feelings we get by dealing with it is just part of reality itself.

NOTES

1. Plus, the drive to hoard and the thrifty (capitalist) attitude was considered a sign of mental and moral weakness and perversion in the ancient ages; witness, for instance, the lyrics of Solon and Teognides, the legend of Midas, and the story of the Gracchi's mother. Money interest was considered usury in the Middle Ages.

2. Nation-states, it is worth repeating, can be multinational.

3. This is not to mean that GDP and GNP are faultless indicators. For alternatives see Vasapollo (2007).

4. See chapters 2 and 3 and Micocci (2008b, 2008c).

5. I would like everybody to notice the "gradually" in this quotation, a most succinct way to render the working of the dialectical, intrinsic moderation of capitalism.

6. That is why a price can now be given to "goods" such as human labor, or human damage.

7. Quoted also in Micocci (2005a).

8. I teach economic theory in an English language university, and have to make do with present-day textbooks that explain the concepts of marginalism without derivatives. See Micocci (2008f).

9. See Micocci (2007e).

10. Lombroso is one of those characters whom everyone loves to loath. We are neither endorsing nor discussing his silly theories here. We propose his book because it addresses precisely the question we are dealing with and is representative of an age, and a mentality, that are still with us, and fully fit capitalism as we know it. Many would happily recognize themselves in his words, if they did not know who is writing.

11. This is conceived, let me remind the reader, as separated and even independent from natural evolution.

Bibliography

Aa.Vv. *Omaggio a Vico*. Naples: Morano, 1968.

Adorno, Theodor. *Minima Moralia: Reflections on a Damaged Life*. London: Verso, 1989.

Adorno, Theodor, Horkheimer, Max. *Dialectic of Enlightenment*. London: Verso, 1979.

Alighieri, Dante. *Convivio*. Milan: Garzanti, 1980.

Allen, R. G. D. *Mathematical Analysis for Economists*. London: MacMillan, 1960.

Althusser, Louis. *On Feuerbach*. Milan: Mimesis, 2003.

Amin, Samir. "Geopolitique de l'Imperialisme Contemporain." *International Review of Sociology* 15, 1 (2005): 5–34.

———. *Unequal Development*. New York: Monthly Review Press, 1976.

Antomarini, Brunella. *Pensare con l'Errore*. Turin: Codice Edizioni, 2007.

Aristotle. *The Politics*. London: Penguin Books, 1981.

———. *The History of Animals*. R. Cresswell, trans. London: Henry G. Bohn, 1864.

Arrighi, Giovanni. "Hegemony Unravelling: I." *New Left Review* 32 (2005): 23–80.

Arriola, Joaquin, and L. Vasapollo. *La Dolce Maschera dell'Europa*. Milan: Jaca Book, 2004.

Arthur, Chris. "Reply to Critics." *Historical Materialism* 13:2 (2005): 189–221.

———. *The New Dialectic and Marx's Capital*. Leiden: Brill, 2003.

Aston, T. H., and C. H. Philpin. (eds.) *Il Dibattito Brenner*. Turin: Einaudi, 1985.

Bacon, Francis. *Dei Principi e delle Origini De Principiis atque Originibus*. Milan: Bompiani, 2005.

———. *La Grande Istaurazione Parte Seconda Nuovo Organo*. Milan: Bompiani, 2002.

Badaloni, Nicola. *Introduzione a Vico*. Milan: Feltrinelli, 1961.

Bakunin, Mikhail A. *Stato e Anarchia*. Milan: Feltrinelli, 2004.

Barkley Rosser, J. "Aspects of Dialectics and Non-Linear Dynamics." *Cambridge Journal of Economics* 24 (2000): 311–24.

——. "On the Complexities of Complex Economic Dynamics." *Journal of Economic Perspectives* 13, 4 (1999): 169–92.

——. *From Catastrophe to Chaos: A General Theory of Economic Discontinuities.* Nowell, MA: Kluwer Academic Publishers, 1991.

Begg, David, S. Fischer, and R. Dornbusch. *Economics*, 7th Edition. Boston: Mac-Graw Hill, 2003.

Bel, Germà. "The Coining of Privatization and Germany's National Socialist Party." *Journal of Economic Perspectives* 20, 3 (2006): 187–94.

Biscuso, Massimiliano. *Hegel, lo Scetticismo Antico e Sesto Empirico.* Naples: La Città del Sole, 2005.

——. "La Tradizione Come Problema. Progresso della Civiltà e Inventio della Verità in Lucrezio." *Atti del XXIII Congresso della Società Filosofica Italiana* II (1999): 105–10, Milan: Angeli.

Blackburn, Robin. "The Sub-Prime Crisis." *New Left Review* 50 (2008): 63–106.

Brenner, Robert. "The Economics of Global Turbulence." *New Left Review* 229 (1998): 1–225.

——. "The Origins of Capitalist Development: A Critique of Neo-Smithian Marxism." *New Left Review* 104 (1977): 25–89.

Brown, A. "A Materialist Development of Some Recent Contribution to the Labor Theory of Value." *Cambridge Journal of Economics* 32, 1 (2008): 125–46.

Callinicos, Alex T. *Social Theory: A Historical Introduction.* Cambridge: Polity Press, 2007.

——. "Against the New Dialectics." *Historical Materialism* 13:2 (2005): 41–59.

——. *Inequality.* Cambridge: Polity Press, 2001.

——. *Theories and Narratives: Reflections on the Philosophy of History.* Cambridge: Polity Press, 1997.

——. *An Anti-Capitalist Manifesto.* Cambridge: Polity Press, 2003.

Carchedi, Guglielmo. "Logiche Viziate e Risposte Mancate Una Replica a Micocci." *Proteo* (March 2006–January 2007): 116–18.

Casadio, Mauro, J. Petras, and L. Vasapollo. *Clash! Scontro tra Potenze.* Milan: Jaca Book, 2003.

Cassirer, Ernst. *Sulla Logica delle Scienze della Cultura.* Florence: La Nuova Italia, 1979.

——. *The Myth of the State.* Yale University Press: New Haven, 1961.

Chang, Ha-Joon. "Breaking the Mould: An Institutional Political Economy Alternative to the Neoliberal Theory of the Market and the State." *Cambridge Journal of Economics* 26, 5 (2002): 539–59.

Chiappori, Pierre Andrè, and S. D. Levitt. "An Examination of the Influence of Theory and Individual Theorists on Empirical Research in Microeconomics." *The American Economic Review* 93, 2. Papers and Proceedings of the 150th annual Meeting, Washington, D.C. (January 3–5, 2003): 151–55.

Cicero, M. T. *Sulla Natura degli Dei De Natura Deorum.* Milan: Oscar Mondadori, 1997a.

——. *De Senectute De Amicitia.* Milan: Oscar Mondadori, 1997b.

——. *Dello Stato De Re Publica.* Milan: Oscar Mondadori, 1992.

Colletti, Lucio. *Tra Marxismo e No*. Saggi Tascabili Laterza, 1979.
———. "Marxism and the Dialectics." *New Left Review* 93 (1975): 3–30.
———. "A Political and Philosophical Interview." *New Left Review* 86 (1974): 34–52.
———. *Marxism and Hegel*. London: New Left Books, 1973.
———. *From Rousseau to Lenin*. London: New Left Books, 1972.
———. *Ideologia e Società*. Bari: Laterza, 1969a.
———. *Il Marxismo e Hegel*. Bari-Rome: Laterza, 1969b.
Conrad, Joseph. *Heart of Darkness (Cuore di Tenebra)*. Milan: Rizzoli, 1989.
Croce, Benedetto. *La Filosofia di Giambattista Vico*. Bari: Laterza, 1911.
Debord, Guy. *Comments on the Society of the Spectacle*. London: Verso, 1989.
———. *The Society of the Spectacle*. Detroit: Black and Red, 1983.
Debray, Regis. "Socialism: A Life-Cycle." *New Left Review* 46 (2007): 5–28.
Della Volpe, Galvano. *Rousseau e Marx*. Rome: Editori Riuniti, 1997/1957.
———. *Logic as a Positive Science*. London: NLB, 1980.
———. *Rousseau and Marx*. London: Lawrence and Wishart, 1978.
———. *Critica dell'Ideologia Contemporanea*. Rome: Editori Riuniti, 1967.
———. *La Libertà Comunista, Sulla Dialettica*. Milan: Edizioni Avanti!, 1963.
———. *Per la teoria di un Umanesimo Positivo, Studi e Documenti sulla Dialettica Materialistica*. Bologna: C. Zuffi Editore, 1949.
———. *La Teoria Marxista dell'Emancipazione Umana. Saggio sulla Trasmutazione Marxista Dei Valori*. Messina, 1945.
Desai, Meghnad. *Marxian Economics*. Oxford: Blackwell, 1979.
Desiderius Erasmus. *The Praise of Folly*, 2nd Edition. C. H. Miller, trans. New Haven: Yale University Press, 2003.
"Dialectics." *Historical Materialism* 13, 1 (2004): 241–65
Diesing, Paul. *Hegel's Dialectical Political Economy*. Oxford: Westview Press, 1999.
Diogene Laerzio. *Vite dei Filosofi* 2. Bari-Rome: Laterza GLF, 2002.
Dobb, Maurice. *Welfare Economics and the Economics of Socialism*. Cambridge: Cambridge University Press, 1978.
Dumenil, Gerard, and D. Levy. "Neoliberal Income Trends." *New Left Review* 30 (2004): 105–133.
Dunne, Paul. (ed.) *Quantitative Marxism*. Oxford: Polity Press, 1990.
Einzig, Paul. *The Economic Foundations of Fascism*. London: MacMillan, 1933.
Ekelund, B. R., and R. F. Hebert. "The Origin of Neoclassical Microeconomics." *Journal of Economic Perspectives* 16, 3 (Summer 2002): 179–215.
Emmanuel, Arghiri. *Unequal Exchange*. New York: Monthly Review Press, 1972.
Epicuro. *Opere, Frammenti, Testimonianze*. Rome: Universale Laterza, 1994.
———. *Opere*. G. Arrighetti, ed. Turin: Einaudi, 1973.
Fedeli De Cecco, Marinella. *Rousseau ed il Marxismo Italiano nel Dopoguerra*. Bologna: Biblioteca Cappelli, 1982.
Feuerbach, Ludwig. *Spiritualismo e Materialismo*. Rome: Editori Laterza, 1993.
———. *Gesammelte Werke*. Berlin: Akademie Verlag, 1972.
———. *Principles of the Philosophy of the Future*, M. H. Vogel, trans. New York: The Bobbs-Merrill Company, 1966.
———. *Essence of Christianity*. T. M. Evans, trans. New York: Harper and Row, 1957.
Fineschi, Roberto. *Marx e Hegel Contributi a una Rilettura*. Rome: Carocci, 2006.

———. *Ripartire da Marx*. Naples: La Città del Sole, 2001.

Fischer, Stanley. "Globalization and Its Challenges." Ely Lecture. *American Economic Review* 93, 2 (2003): 1–30.

Foster, John Bellamy. *Marx's Ecology: Materialism and Nature*. New York: Monthly Review Press, 2000.

Fracchia, Joseph. "Beyond the Human Nature Debate." *Historical Materialism* 13.1 (2005): 33–61.

Fukuyama, Francis. *The End of History and the Last Man*. New York: The Free Press, 1992.

Garegnani, Pierangelo. *Marx e gli Economisti Classici*. Turin: Einaudi, 1981.

Georgescu-Roegen, Nicholas. *The Entropy Law and the Economic Process*. Cambridge, MA: Harvard University Press, 1981.

———. *Analytical Economics*. Cambridge, MA: Harvard University Press, 1966.

Giacché, Vladimiro. "La Democrazia in Ostaggio." *Lavoro contro Capitale*, Forum Internazionale della Rete dei Comunisti. Rome: Quaderni di Contropiano, 2005.

Glyn, Andrew. *Capitalism Unleashed: Finance, Globalization and Welfare*. Oxford: Oxford University Press, 2006.

Gordon, Robert J. "Does the 'New Economy' Measure Up to the Great Inventions of the Past?" *Journal of Economic Perspectives* 14, 4 (2000): 49–74.

Graziani, Augusto. *Teoria Economica Prezzi e Distribuzioni*. Naples: ESI, 1980.

Hayek, Friedrich A. *New Studies in Philosophy, Politics, Economics and the History of Ideas*. London: Routledge and Kegan Paul, 1978.

———. *The Constitution of Liberty*. London: Routledge, 1960.

———. *Individualism and Economic Order*. Chicago: The University of Chicago Press, 1948.

Hegel, Georg W. F. *Hegel's Logic*. W. Wallace, trans. Oxford: Oxford University Press, 1987.

Helman, Alfredo. "Peronismo e Sindacalismo." *Proteo* 2 (2005): 131–39.

Hobsbawm, Eric J. *I Ribelli: Forme Primitive di Rivolta Sociale*. Turin: Einaudi, 2002.

Hobson, John A. *Imperialism: A Study*. London: Allen and Unwin, 1968.

Holbach, Paul T. d'. *Il Buon Senso*. Milan: Garzanti, 1985.

Hong, Hoon. "Marx's Value Forms and Hayek's Rules: A Reinterpretation in the Light of the Dichotomy between Physis and Nomos." *Cambridge Journal of Economics* 26, 5 (2002): 613–35.

Hourani, Albert. *Storia dei Popoli Arabi*. Milan: Mondadori, 1998.

Huntington, Samuel P. *Lo Scontro di Civiltà e il Nuovo Ordine Mondiale*. Milan: Garzanti, 2000.

———. *Political Order in Changing Societies*. Yale: Yale University Press, 1968.

Hutchison, Terence. *Changing Aims in Economics*. Oxford: Blackwell, 1992.

Jones, Peter E. "Discourse and the Materialist Conception of History: Critical Comments on Critical Discourse Analysis." *Historical Materialism* 12, 1 (2004): 233–46.

Karatani, Kojin. *Transcritique: On Kant and Marx*. Cambridge, MA: MIT Press, 2003.

Keynes, John M. *Social Political and Literary Writings: The Collected Writings of John Maynard Keynes*. D. Moggridge, ed. Cambridge: Cambridge University Press for the Royal Economic Society, 1982a.

———. *Activities 1931–1939, World Crises and Policies in Britain and America. The Collected Writings of J. M. Keynes Vol. XXI*. Cambridge: Cambridge University Press, 1982b.

———. *The General Theory of Employment, Interest and Money*. London: MacMillan, 1973.

Khalil, Elias L. "An Anatomy of Authority: Adam Smith as a Political Theorist." *Cambridge Journal of Economics* 29, 1 (2005): 57–71.

Kliman, Andrew. *Reclaiming Marx's Capital*. Lanham: Lexington Books, 2007.

Knafo, Samuel. "Political Marxism and Value Theory: Bridging the Gap between Theory and History." *Historical Materialism* 15.2 (2007): 75–104.

Kropotkin, Piotr. *Parole di un Ribelle*. no place indicated: Edizioni Anarchiche, (no year).

Kuhn, Thomas. *La Struttura delle Rivoluzioni Scientifiche*. Turin: Einaudi, 1969.

Lambin, J. J. *Marketing Strategico e Operativo*. Milan: McGraw Hill, 2000.

Lawson, Tony. "The Nature of Heterodox Economics." *Cambridge Journal of Economics* 30, 4 (2006): 483–505.

———. *Reorienting Economics*. London: Routledge, 2003.

———. *Economics and Reality*. London: Routledge, 1998.

Lenin, Vladimir I. *Imperialism, the Highest Stage of Capitalism*. Peking: Foreign Language Press, 1972.

Lessig, Lawrence. "Do You Floss?" *London Review of Books* (August 18, 2005): 24–25.

Lewin, Moshe. *The Soviet Century*. London: Verso, 2005.

Lombroso, Cesare. *Gli Anarchici*. Milan: Claudio Gallone Editore, 1994.

Louça, Francisco. "Intriguing Pendula: Founding Metaphors in the Analysis of Economic Fluctuations." *Cambridge Journal of Economics* 25, 1 (January 2001): 25–56.

Löwy, Michel. *The Theory of Revolution in the Young Marx*. Leiden-Boston: Brill, 2003.

Lucrezio. *Sulla Natura delle Cose De Rerum Natura*. Milan: Oscar Mondadori, 1992.

Maddy, Penelope. "A Naturalistic Look at Logic." Romanell Lecture. *Proceedings and Addresses of the American Philosophical Association* 76, 2 (2002): 60–90.

Mandel, Ernest, and A. Freeman. (eds.) *Ricardo, Marx, Sraffa: The Langston Memorial Volume*. London: Verso, 1984.

Marcuse, Herbert. *L'Uomo a Una Dimensione*. Turin: Einaudi, 1967.

Marshall, Alfred. *Principles of Economics*. London: MacMillan, 1910.

Martov, Julij. *Bolscevismo Mondiale*. Turin: Einaudi, 1980.

Marx, Karl. *Grundrisse*. M. Nicolaus, trans. and foreword. London: Penguin Books, 1993.

———. *Capital* Vol. I, II, III. Moscow: Progress Publishers, 1978.

———. *Critique of the Gotha Programme*. Peking: Foreign Language Press, 1972.

——. *Critique of Hegel's Philosophy of Right*. J. O'Malley, ed. Cambridge: Cambridge University Press, 1970.

——. *Il Capitale* 1, 2, 3. Rome: Editori Riuniti, 1968a.

——. *Manoscritti Economici e Filosofici del 1844*. N. Bobbio, ed. Turin: Einaudi, 1968b.

Marx, Karl, and Friedrich Engels. *The German Ideology*. London: Lawrence & Wishart, 1985.

——. *Collected Works*. Moscow: Progress Publishers, 1975.

Mazzone, Alessandro. (ed.) *MEGA2: Marx Ritrovato*. Rome: Mediaprint Edizioni, 2002.

Menger, Carl. "Il Metodo della Scienza Economica." in G. Bottai and C. Arena (eds.) *Nuova Collana di Economisti Stranieri e Italiani*. Turin: UTET, 1937.

Micocci, Andrea. "Save the Theorist!" in *The Centrality of Theory for Class Struggle*. Rome: MediaPrint, 2008a.

——. "War and Trade Adam Smith Said," in L. M. Mollejas. *Italy and EU Globalization: Is There an Alternative to Free Trade?* Caracas: 2008b.

——. "War and Trade." Caracas: IIAESS, 2008c.

——. "Paradoxes of Marxism." *Revue de Philosophie Economique*. 2008d.

——. "A Discussion of Applied Economics." *Rethinking Marxism*. 2008e.

——. "On the Use of Mathematical Derivatives in Textbooks Economics." *Link International Economic Bulletin*. (2008f)

——. "The Perfidy of Moderatism." *International Review of Sociology* 17, 1 (2007a): 187–201.

——. "Lo Spettro." Appendix to *Trattato di Economia Applicata* by Luciano Vasapollo. Milan: Jaca Book, 2007b.

——. "Far Parlare le Mummie." *Il Cannocchiale Rivista di Studi Filosofici* 1 (2007c): 171–87.

——. "Organi, Macchine e Proiezione Infinita." in Antomarini, B., and S. Tagliagambe. (eds.) *La Tecnica e il Corpo*. Rome: Franco Angeli, 2007d.

——. "The Transformation Problem?" *International Journal of Applied Economics and Econometrics* (2007e).

——. "Discutendo l'Economia Applicata." *Proteo* 2 (2007f): 107–08.

——. "Economia Dominante e Marxista." *Nuestra America* 3 (2007g): 112 –13.

——. "Economia ed Agricoltura." in Torquati, B., and F. Valorosi. (eds.) *L'Economia Agraria e gli Scritti di Vito Saccomandi*. Bologna: Il Mulino, 2007h.

——. "Kant e Marx per Karatani." *Il Cannocchiale Rivista di Studi Filosofici* 2 (2006a): 173–80.

——. "Deorumque Nominibus Appellant Secretum Illud, Quod sola Reverentia Vident." *Proteo* (March 2006–January 2007, 2006b): 119–23.

——. "Il Mistero della Speculazione. Il Lavoro e l'Uso che se ne Fa sotto il Capitalismo." *Proteo* 2 (2006c): 106–12.

——. "Competizione Globale ed Imperialismo: Linee di Interpretazione." *Proteo* 1 (2005a): 110–15.

——. "Economia, Economia Applicata, Economia Agraria: Ma Quale Economia, Ma Quali Economisti." *Proteo* 1 (2005b): 139–44.

——. "La Presunta Varietà delle Idee Economiche." *Proteo* 2 (2005c): 176–84.

——. "Uncertainty in Market Economies." *International Review of Sociology* 1, 1 (2005d): 35–49.

——. "Review of Orati, Globalization Scientifically Unfounded." *Rethinking Marxism* 17, 4 (2005e): 647–50.

——. "Modigliani, Economics, Italy." *International Journal of Applied Economics and Econometrics*, Special Issue on Modigliani (March 2005f). Reprinted in Puttaswamaiah, K. *Franco Modigliani, Peerless Twentieth-Century Macroeconomist.* Bangalore: IJAEE, 2006.

——. "Critical Observations on Economics, Taxonomy and Dynamism." *Rethinking Marxism* vol. 16, no. 1 (2004a): 73–94.

——. "Vantaggi Comparati." *Il Ponte* 7–8 (2004b): 82–98.

——. "The Philosophy of Economics." *International Journal of Applied Economics and Econometrics* 12, 1 (2004c): 1–24.

——. "An Unchangeable Future? Lawson's Rescue of Mainstream Economics." *International Journal of Applied Economics and Econometrics* 12, 3 (2004d): 397–418, to be reprinted in V. A. Orati and K. Puttaswamaiah, eds. *The Future of Economic Science*, in preparation.

——. "Progresso e Razionalità: Il Materialismo Dialettico Secondo Tassone." *Il Cannocchiale Rivista di Studi Filosofici* 3 (2004e): 161–80.

——. "Filosofia Politica Classica, o il Potere Costituente di Negri." *Il Ponte* 12 (2004f): 85–100.

——. "A Theory of Economic Theory." *International Journal of Applied Economics and Econometrics* XI, 1 (2003a): 161–71.

——. "An Alternative, Materialistic Political Economy." Presented at the Economics for the Future Conference, Cambridge, UK (September 2003b): 17–19.

——. *Anti-Hegelian Reading of Economic Theory.* Lewiston: Mellen Press, 2002a.

——. "Le Basi Economiche del Fascismo: Una Vecchia Questione Tornata di Moda." *Il Ponte* 2 (2002b): 68–83.

——. "Sul Misticismo Dialettico dei Marxisti. Note sul Lavoro di John Rosenthal." *Il Cannocchiale Rivista di Studi Filosofici* 2 (2002c): 179–95.

——. "The Second Brenner Debate: A Survey." *Federico Caffè Centre Research Report* 2 (2002d).

——. "L'Ideologia dell'Economia." *Il Ponte* 4 (2001a): 51–61.

——. "Elefanti e Teoria Economica Dominante." *Il Ponte* 2 (2001b): 84–91.

——. "The Impossible Endeavour of Schumpeter the Neoclassical." in S. B. Dahiya and V. A. Orati (eds.) *Economic Theory in the Light of Schumpeter's Scientific Heritage.* Rhotak: Spellbound Press, 2001c.

——. "Althusser, Machiavelli e Noi." *Il Cannocchiale Rivista di Studi Filosofici* 3 (2000a): 215–22.

——. *Il Metodo delle Scienze Sociali.* Viterbo: TURMS I, 4 (2000b).

——. "Leopardi Antitaliano." *Il Cannocchiale Rivista di Studi Filosofici* 3 (2000c): 199–209.

——. "The Origins of Economic Efficiency Lie in Capitalism's Iterative Cultural Structure." *Il Cannocchiale Rivista di Studi Filosofici* 2 (1999a): 49–72.

———. "Reply to Tassone." *Il Cannocchiale Rivista di Studi Filosofici* 2 (1999b): 78–82.

Mill, John S. *Principles of Political Economy and Chapters on Socialism*. Oxford: Oxford University Press, 1998.

———. *On Liberty*. Hammondsworth: Penguin Books, 1974.

Mohun, Simon. "Ideology, Markets and Money." *Cambridge Journal of Economics* 27, 3 (2003): 401–418.

Montag, Le Tattiche dei Sensi. Rome: Manifestolibri, 2000.

Mood, Alexander M., F. A. Graybill, and D. C. Boes. *Introduction to the Theory of Statistics*. Singapore: McGraw Hill, 1974.

Montes, Leonidas. "Smith and Newton: Some Methodological Issues Concerning General Economic Equilibrium." *Cambridge Journal of Economics* 27, 5 (2003): 723–47.

McCann, Charles R. Jr. "A Philosophy of Anarchism." *International Review of Sociology* 15, 3 (2005): 584–93.

———. *Individualism and the Social Order: The Social Element in Liberal Thought*. New York: Routledge, 2004.

Napoleoni, Claudio. *Discorso sull'Economia Politica*. Turin: Boringhieri, 1985.

———. *Il Valore*. Milan: ISEDI, 1976.

Negri, Antonio. *Il Potere Costituente*. Rome: Manifestolibri, 2002.

Negri, Antonio, and M. Hardt. *Impero*. Milan: Rizzoli, 2001.

Orati, Vittorangelo. *Globalizzazione Scientificamente Infondata*. Editori Riuniti: Rome, 2003.

———. *Produzione di Merci a Mezzo Lavoro*. Naples: Liguori, 1984.

———. *Il Ciclo Monofase Saggio sugli Esiti Aporetici della Dinamica di J. A. Schumpeter*. Naples: Liguori, 1981.

Oxford Universal Dictionary Illustrated. 3rd ed. Oxford: Clarendon Press, 1974.

Panic, M. "Does Europe Need Neoliberal Reforms?" *Cambridge Journal of Economics* 31, 1 (2007): 145–69.

Pardjanadze, Nino, and Andrea Micocci. "I Nichilisti Russi." *Il Cannocchiale Rivista di Studi Filosofici* 2 (2000): 182–202.

Petras, James. "Il Significato della Guerra: Una Prospettiva Eterodossa." *Proteo* 2, (2005): 140–152.

Pietranera, Giulio. *Capitalismo ed Economia*. Turin: PBE Einaudi, 1966.

Polibio. *Storie* 3. Milan: Oscar Mondatori, 1979.

Rees, John. *The Algebra of Revolution*. London and New York: Routledge, 1998.

Reich, Wilhelm. *The Mass Psychology of Fascism*. New York: Farrar, Straus and Giroux, 2000.

Resnick, Stephen A., and R. D. Wolf. *Knowledge and Class*. Chicago: University of Chicago Press, 1987.

Rosenberg, Justin. *The Follies of Globalization Theory*. London: Verso, 2000.

Rosenthal, John. "Hegel's Decoder: A Reply to Smith's Reply." *Historical Materialism* 9 (Winter 2001): 111–51.

———. "The Escape from Hegel." *Science and Society* 63, 3 (1999): 283–309.

———. *The Myth of Dialectics*. London: MacMillan, 1998.

Samuelson, Paul M., and W. D. Nordhaus. *Economics*. London, New York: McGraw Hill, 2003.

Sayers, Sean. "Creative Activity and Alienation in Hegel and Marx." *Historical Materialism* 11, 1 (2003): 107–28.

Scarfoglio, Carlo. *Nella Russia di Stalin* (written 1932). Florence: Vallecchi, 1941.

Scarpari, Giancarlo. "Una Rivista Dimenticata: Il Diritto Razzista." *Il Ponte* 1 (2004): 112–45.

Schiller, Bradley R. *Essentials of Economics*. Boston: MacGraw Hill, 2002.

Schumpeter, Joseph A. *Sociologia dell'Imperialismo*. Bari: Laterza, 1972.

———. *Teoria dello Sviluppo Capitalistico*. Florence: Sansoni, 1971.

———. *Capitalism, Socialism and Democracy*. Hemel Hempstead: Unwin, 1987.

———. *Imperialism and Social Classes*. New York: Augustus M. Kelly, 1951.

———, *The Theory of Economic Development*, Cambridge: Harvard University Press, 1934

Science and Society 62, 3 (Fall 1998). Special issue on "Dialectics: The New Frontier."

Setterfield, Mark. "Keynes's Dialectic?" *Cambridge Journal of Economics* 27, 3 (2003): 359–76.

Shackle, George L. S. *Epistemics and Economics: A Critique of Economic Doctrines*. Cambridge: Cambridge University Press, 1972.

Smith, Adam. *The Wealth of Nations* 2. London: Penguin Books, 1999.

Smith, A. A. "Hegelianism and Marx: A Reply to Lucio Colletti." *Science and Society* L 2 (Summer 1986): 82–100.

Smith, Tony. "The Relevance of Systematic Dialectic to Marxian Thought: A Reply to Rosenthal." *Historical Materialism* 4 (Summer 1999): 215–40.

Stanley, John L. "Marx's Critique of Hegel's Philosophy of Nature." *Science and Society* 61, 4 (Winter 1997/98): 449–73.

Sweezy, Paul M. *The Theory of Capitalist Development*. New York: Monthly Review Press, 1970.

Sylos Labini, Paolo. *Torniamo ai Classici*. Turin: Laterza, 2004.

———. *Oligopolio e Progresso Tecnico*. Milan: Giuffrè, 1956.

———. (ed.) *Karl Marx: E' Tempo di un Bilancio*. Turin: Laterza, 1974.

———. *Le Forze dello Sviluppo e del Declino*. Bari: Laterza, 1984.

Tacito, Publio C. *Annali Libri ad Excesso Divi Augusti*. Milan: Rizzoli, 2007.

———. *Storie*. Milan: Garzanti, 2000.

Tassone, Giuseppe. *A Study on the Idea of Progress in Nietzsche, Heidegger and Critical Theory*. Lewiston: Mellen Press, 2002.

———. "An Objection to Andrea Micocci." *Il Cannocchiale Rivista di Studi Filosofici* 2 (1999): 73–77.

Terray, Emmanuel. "Law versus Politics." *New Left Review* 22 (2003): 71–79.

Thom, Rene. *Structural Stability and Morphogenesis: An Outline of a General Theory of Models*. Reading, MA: The Benjamin/Cummings Publishing Co., 1978.

Tinbergen, Jan. "Do Communist and Free Economies Show a Converging Pattern?" *Soviet Studies* (1961): 333–41.

Traversa, Guido. *La Metafisica degli Accidenti*. Rome: Manifestolibri, 2004.

Vasapollo, Luciano. *Trattato di Economia Applicata*. Milan: Jaca Book, 2007.

Vasapollo, Luciano, M. Casadio, J. Petras, H. Veltmeyer. *Competizione Globale*. Milan: Jaca Book, 2004.

——. (ed.) *Il Piano Inclinato del Capitale*. Milan: Jaca Book, 2003a.

——. (ed.) *Eurobang 1/2/3 An Inquiry into Labor and Capital*. Naples: Mediaprint, 2003b.

——. (ed.) *Un Vecchio Falso Problema/An Old Myth*. Rome: Mediaprint, 2002.

Vico, Giambattista. *La Scienza Nuova*. Milan: BUR, 2004.

——. *The New Science of Giambattista Vico*. T. Goddard Bergin and M. H. Fisch, trans. Ithaca: Cornell University Press, 1984.

——. *Le Opere*. Milan-Naples: Ricciardi, 1953.

Voltaire. *Candido*. Milan: Rizzoli, 2003.

Von Mises, Ludwig. *Human Action: A Treatise on Economics*. New Haven: Yale University Press, 1949.

Warren, Bill. *Imperialism: Pioneer of Capitalism*. London: Verso, 1980.

Weber, Max. *Essays in Economic Sociology*. Princeton, NJ: Princeton University Press, 1999.

Wikipedia, The Free Encyclopedia, *Marketing*.

Wilczynsky, Joseph. *L'economia dei Paesi Socialisti*. Bologna: Il Mulino, 1973.

Williams, Michael. "Mysticism, Method and Money in the Marx-Hegel Dialectic." *Cambridge Journal of Economics* 25, 4 (2001): 555–68.

Wood, Ellen Meiksins. *Empire of Capital*. London: Verso, 2005.

——. "The Non-History of Capitalism." *Historical Materialism* 1 (1997): 5–21.

——. "From Opportunity to Imperative: The History of the Market." *Monthly Review* 46, 3 (1994): 14–40.

——. *The Pristine Culture of Capitalism*. London: Verso, 1991.

Zamagni, Stefano. *Microeconomic Theory*. Oxford: Basil Blackwell, 1987.

Zanini, Adelino. *Un Capitalismo Incerto Incertezza e Normazione nel Pensiero di Keynes (1921–1939)*. Ancona: Quaderni di Ricerca, Dip. to di Economia, 2003.

Index

Perle, Richard, 170
peronismo, 156, 184
Petras, James, 133, 147, 178, 252
Pheidon, 61
Physiocrats, 93
Pietranera, Giulio, 43, 252
Pisarev, Dmitri I., 120
planning, 79–80, 83
Plantagenets, 60
Plato, 33, 202
Plekhanov, Georgij V., 38, 63n8
Plutarch, 239
polis, 1, 150
politeia, v, 7, 144, 149–50, 158, 163–64,
    179–81, 184–85, 192, 213
political economy, v, 8, 30, 35–36,
    39–41, 57, 63n4, 64n21, 67–68,
    74–75, 77–79, 84, 91–93, 131, 154,
    179, 184, 186, 223
Polybius, 51, 192
post-fordism, 137, 142, 159, 193
PowerPoint, 225n10
praxeology, 75, 209
Prebisch, Raul, 83
Preobrazhensky, Evgenij A., 106n15
prolepsis, 54–56, 58, 62, 64n26, 91–92,
    96–97, 111, 143, 198
proselytism, 8, 21, 31, 104, 185–86,
    213, 215, 217
Proudhon, Pierre Joseph, 35–37
Providence, 202–3, 205–7, 209

Quintili, Paolo, 226n15

Rawls, John, 15, 73, 188
Raz, Joseph, 15, 55
real opposition, 38–41, 63, 68, 92,
    99–101, 185, 213
Rees, John, 64n11, 213, 252
Reich, Wilhelm, 181, 189, 205, 252
revolution, 10, 12–13, 16, 20–22, 29,
    31, 38–39, 44, 49, 52, 79, 87, 96,
    100, 102, 104, 109, 113, 116, 119,
    125, 127, 136–38, 145n1, 154, 156,
    160, 165, 185, 187, 191–92, 209,

211–19, 224, 226n15, 232, 238, 240,
    242
Revolution, American, 211
Revolution, Bolshevik, 210–11
Revolution, Chinese, 211
Revolution, English, 211
Revolution, French, 102, 211
Revolution, Industrial, 96, 112, 114,
    116, 125, 144, 159, 211, 233
Ricardo, David, 72, 76, 84, 100, 168
Robbins, Lionel, 17
Rome, 1, 49, 97, 222
Roosevelt, Franklyn D., 183
Rosenthal, John, 41, 43–47, 57, 64n15,
    64n16, 64n18, 78, 94–95, 97, 106n6,
    158, 180, 252
Rossi, Paolo, 195, 203–4, 225n11
Rousseau, Jean Jacques, 15, 34, 56
routinization, 115, 121, 124, 134, –35
rupture(s) and/with oblivion, 19, 21, 24,
    57–58, 60, 85, 92, 112, 157, 185,
    208–9, 213, 215, 217, 223, 235–36,
    238
Russian nihilists, 120

Sakharov, Andrej, 106n16
Sandel, Michael, 15
Scarfoglio, Carlo, 106n15, 253
Scarfoglio, Carlo, Jr, ix
Scevola, Mucius, 164
Schumpeter, Joseph, A., 44, 87, 95–96,
    107n22, 113–16, 121–22, 124, 132,
    134, 156, 176, 230, 253
Science and Society, 41–43, 64n11, 253
Sekine, Satoshi, 42–43, 84
Sen, Amartya K., 73
Setterfield, Mark, 68, 253
sex, 7, 19, 53, 117, 145, 205, 209, 214,
    221, 226n21, 239, 241
Shackle, George, L. S., 70–71, 87,
    106n5, 253
silence, 6, 24, 27, 195, 233
Singer, Hans, 83
slippages, 122, 126, 146n16
Smith, A. A., 63n9, 253

About the Author

Andrea Micocci was born and lives in Rome. He teaches economic theory at the University of Malta Link Campus, Rome, and political philosophy at the Jean Monnet Faculty of Seconda Università di Napoli (SUN), San Leucio, Caserta. He got his first degree (Laurea) in agricultural economics and engineering in Perugia, Italy. He then moved on to postgraduate studies at LSE (international politics) and Sussex (M. Phil. Development Studies). He holds a D.Phil. in political philosophy of the University of York. He has taught in various institutions in Europe. He also performed professional activities in several countries comprising the USSR and with the FAO, and he participated in international EU research projects. He is the author of *Anti-Hegelian Reading of Economic Theory* (2002) and of many essays in international academic journals.